Women's Crusader

Women's Crusader

Catharine Beecher's Untold Story

R Lee Wilson

R. LEE WILSON

GLANDERSTON
HOUSE

Copyright © 2025 by R. Lee Wilson

All rights reserved.

No part of this book may be reproduced, or stored in a retrieval system, or transmitted in any form or by any means, electronic, mechanical, photocopying, recording, or otherwise, without express written permission of the publisher.

Published by Glanderston House, Sanibel, Florida
rleewilson.com

Edited and designed by Girl Friday Productions
www.girlfridayproductions.com

Design: Paul Barrett
Project management: Kristin Duran
Editorial production: Katherine Richards
Cover illustration: Charles Utting

ISBN (hardcover): 979-8-9914515-0-5
ISBN (paperback): 979-8-9914515-1-2
ISBN (ebook): 979-8-9914515-2-9

Library of Congress Control Number: 2024918802

First edition

*For my granddaughters,
Amelia, Abby, and Anne*

CONTENTS

Preface ix
Introduction: Untold Story xi

Part I: Principals

1 Kate 3
2 Alexander 23
3 Dispatched 41
4 Focused 54

Part II: Relationship

5 Second Chances 63
6 Courtship 76
7 Trouble 92
8 Romance 101

Part III: Metamorphosis

9 Tempest 117
10 Forlorn 138
11 Renewed 155

Part IV: Career

12 Crusader 175
13 Legacy 206

Epilogue 221

Acknowledgments 229
Appendix 231
Notes 239
Bibliography 271
Index 277
About the Author 287

PREFACE

Catharine (Kate) Beecher was a pioneer advocate for women's education. Based on her success as a popular author of advice books, she was also one of the most famous women in America during the first half of the nineteenth century. But her fame was eclipsed by that of her younger sister, Harriet Beecher Stowe. In the twenty-first century, Kate's name is barely recognized outside academic circles. I first learned about her in a history course I took at Columbia University twenty-three years ago. She had a notable career as a leading educator, a unique feminist thinker, and a bestselling author. She was an innovator who applied the latest science to advocate strikingly progressive ideas about improving the health of women and their families. She even believed that women exercised better while listening to music. She should have gotten a patent on that idea. But what I admire most about Kate is her selfless crusade to improve the lives of American women in the face of opposition from a misogynist male establishment. It is the inspiration for my book's title—*Women's Crusader*.

The purpose of this book is to raise awareness of Kate to help her achieve the greater recognition she deserves. My goal required a fresh approach to her story that could capture the imagination. I also wanted to keep it short enough to appeal to a wider audience. Ultimately, I decided to focus on Kate's romance with Alexander Fisher to meet my objectives. Three reasons made it a compelling choice. First, it is a touching love story. Kate was a smart young woman who overcame parental expectations about marriage to find love with a fellow musician, only to lose him in a tragic shipwreck before they could marry. Second, it's a powerful turning-point story. Dealing with the loss of her fiancé proved to be the catalyst for Kate's amazing career. And finally, this is an untold story. There is surprisingly little written about Kate's connections with Alexander and his family. Some of the tale was simply overlooked, but important evidence was also deliberately destroyed. Fortunately, persistence yielded enough critical threads to weave the tapestry of their romance. It became the core of my book and provided the subtitle—*Catharine Beecher's Untold Story.*

The challenge was to tell a nonfiction story where significant gaps remained. Some people suggested that I write this book as historical fiction. But I felt it would defeat my purpose if readers couldn't distinguish what parts were real, so this book is written as a biographical slice of Kate's life. Its value is that despite some missing details, it is both true and has never been told. Hopefully, its theme of fighting for women will inspire current and future generations.

INTRODUCTION

Untold Story

The historian's task is that of the detective.
—David Herbert Donald, Pulitzer Prize–winning historian

The untold story of Catharine (Kate) Beecher is actually wrapped within the larger forgotten story of her life. She was an intellectual who battled misogyny to help provide American women the education they deserved. Kate was the oldest daughter of Rev. Lyman Beecher, the fiery evangelist and patriarch of the nationally prominent Beecher family. Her siblings included the acclaimed author Harriet Beecher Stowe; the notable suffragette Isabella Beecher Hooker; the brilliant scholar Rev. Edward Beecher; and arguably the most famous man in America during his prime, Rev. Henry Ward Beecher. But Kate was once one of the best-known women in America in her own right. She was a pioneer advocate for women's education and a bestselling author. She charted a successful life as an independent woman during the nineteenth century, a period when society marginalized unmarried females. Although you can find a useful summary of Kate's career online, a general lack of name awareness renders her life story effectively unheard. And to make matters worse, the most widely circulated photos of Kate make her look like a crusty old maid rather than an accomplished female crusader.

Catharine (Kate) Beecher. Courtesy of Wikimedia Commons.

The Beecher family. Seated from the left: Isabella, Kate, Lyman, Mary, Harriet. Standing from the left: Thomas, William, Edward, Charles, Henry. Inset: James. Missing: George. Courtesy of the Litchfield Historical Society, Litchfield, CT.

Sometimes it's difficult to imagine that Kate was once a young romantic who was engaged to a brilliant Yale professor named Alexander Fisher. She was a talented, fun-loving extrovert. Kate used her natural intelligence to breeze through school with minimal effort. She preferred music, poetry, and drama to academic subjects. She became a popular young woman in Litchfield, Connecticut, with a wide circle of friends. Although she signed letters *Catharine*, she was known by her nickname, Kate. I have seen a few examples of people writing it as *Cate*. But I prefer spelling it with a *K* rather than a *C* because that was the letter she chose for her early poetry. Although she used her formal name, Catharine, during her career, *Kate* is used throughout

INTRODUCTION

this book for consistency. Her fiancé, Alexander Metcalf Fisher, was an introverted math prodigy with a warm heart and a gift for music. He achieved a meteoric rise in academic circles and became a Yale professor on his twenty-third birthday. He was a serious scholar with a penchant for propriety who was always known among his professional colleagues by his formal name, Alexander. The names *Kate* and *Alexander* capture the divergent yet complementary personalities of the couple.

The interesting question is, What caused a lighthearted romantic like Kate Beecher to become a pioneer advocate for women's education? Kate's life has been well studied in two celebrated biographies: *Catharine Beecher: A Study in American Domesticity* by Kathryn Kish Sklar and *The Beechers: An American Family in the Nineteenth Century* by Milton Rugoff. Both biographers included highlights of Kate and Alexander's engagement. But these books treat the courtship as a minor detour in her consequential life. Sklar dismissed the relationship as a "brush with dependency" and "perhaps an aberration beyond [Kate's] control."[1] She described it as a match favored by Kate's family and certainly not a romance. But both biographers described an event that hints at a more complicated reality. Near the end of her life, Kate retrieved Alexander's love letters, which she had curiously entrusted to his family for fifty years. In an eyewitness account, she sat by a fireplace, slowly reread them, and then burned his letters one by one. Rugoff described the scene as "poignant beyond words."[2] It didn't appear to fit the narrative that she was pressured into a loveless engagement. If she didn't love him, why did she save the letters in the first place? And why did she wait fifty years to burn them? There seemed to be something missing from Kate's story.

So how does one probe the cold trail of a two-hundred-year-old love story? It took years of tracing and reading unpublished letters and diaries. There were numerous chance discoveries, including a quote from one of Alexander's love letters. These revelations helped reconstruct Kate and Alexander's romance. What emerged was a relationship more intimate and influential than previously imagined. It provided a more complete understanding of how the playful Kate became a serious advocate for women's education.

Although the emphasis is on Kate's relationship with Alexander, this is *not* a typical love story. The voice is that of a biographer, not a romance novelist. This book examines the significance of their relationship and provides enough information about her career to inspire others. But this book is not intended to serve as a comprehensive biography. The focus is on a slice of Kate's life that was a key turning point. It is designed to supplement the excellent work that has already been published.

The book is divided into four parts (Principals, Relationship, Metamorphosis, and Career) to emphasize the trajectory of Kate's character development. The following overview provides a helpful guide to the relevance of the important discoveries.

Part I, "Principals" (chapters 1–4), introduces Kate and Alexander, the circumstances that shaped their characters, and the pertinent historical context. It explains why these two very different people were ripe for love. In 1819, Kate had a failed romance in Boston, which has been viewed by other biographers as a rite of passage. But new findings revealed the identity and conflicted motives of her clever matchmaker. Some of Kate's intimate correspondence with her best friend, Louisa Wait, was purposely destroyed to hide the full story. But enough survived to provide a reasonable account. The Boston affair is unmasked as Kate's rejection of a marriage proposed by her family. Her action demonstrated both independence and a commitment to romance. This casts Kate's subsequent relationship with Alexander in an entirely new light.

Part II, "Relationship" (chapters 5–8), explains why a serious, introverted workaholic like Alexander decided to pursue the hand of a fun-loving, extroverted romantic like Kate. It explores the influential roles of poetry and music in their relationship, the misunderstandings that nearly derailed their courtship, and the romance that ensued. Similar to her Boston relationship, some of the correspondence about Alexander appears to have been deliberately destroyed. But surviving intimate letters between Kate; her father, Lyman; and her friend Louisa allowed the story to be pieced together. No one could push Kate into an unwanted marriage. She was clearly in control of her emotions and destiny as she declared her love for Alexander and chose to marry him. Kate was heartbroken to part with him two months later when he embarked on a long-planned academic journey.

Part III, "Metamorphosis" (chapters 9–11), chronicles Alexander's tragic death in a shipwreck, the misogynist attacks on Kate during her bereavement, and the crucial relationship she developed with Alexander's mother. Three eyewitness accounts from survivors provide the details for a gripping account of Alexander's harrowing death in the shipwreck of the *Albion*. Kate was blissfully unaware of his demise until her father callously broke the news in a letter and used the occasion to launch a quest to save her soul. Yale's contempt for Kate during her bereavement is fully exposed based on a close reading of family correspondence. But the major revelation is how Kate bonded with Alexander's mother, Sally Fisher. The previously unreported relationship is revealed, and the role it played in defining Kate's new purpose in life is explained. It helps clarify why Kate left

Alexander's love letters in the possession of the Fisher family for fifty years.

Part IV, "Career" (chapters 12 and 13), provides a summary of Kate's amazing career, assesses her accomplishments, and examines how she attempted to position herself for posterity. It traces the evolution of Kate's character as she continuously battled the male establishment and sparred with rival feminist leaders. A sampling of Kate's published works provides insight into her evolution as a feminist thinker, as well as her spiritual journey. Kate didn't write about her relationship with Alexander in her memoir because she sought to establish her independent career legacy. But the inclusion of unnamed yet unmistakable tributes to both Alexander and his mother, Sally, indicates deep connections. Previously unexamined accounts of Kate's funeral offer intimate family perspectives on her relationship with Alexander.

The book concludes with an epilogue that separates fact from fiction about Kate burning Alexander's love letters and offers a salute to their romance. It validates much of the story but relocates the event based on a careful examination of property records. Never-seen photos show Sally Fisher's memorial box that apparently housed Kate's love letters from Alexander. A short and slightly dramatized account of Kate burning the letters is offered as a closing tribute to their love.

PART I

Principals

KEY BEECHER CHARACTERS—OCTOBER 1815

	Age	Connection	Location
Kate Beecher	15	Student at Litchfield Female Academy (LFA)	Litchfield, CT
Lyman Beecher	39	Minister at First Congregational Church, Kate's impulsive, affectionate father	Litchfield, CT
Roxana Beecher	40	Kate's reserved, intellectual mother	Litchfield, CT
Louisa Wait	22	Kate's roommate and LFA music teacher	Litchfield, CT
John P. Brace	22	LFA teacher and Kate's friend	Litchfield, CT
Lucy Porter	18	LFA schoolmate, boarded with Beechers	Litchfield, CT

1

Kate

> I "came out" & made my first appearance
> at a Commencement Ball.
> —Kate Beecher

October 1815–September 1817
Kate Beecher's emotions must have swirled as she anticipated the arrival of her gallant escort for the Annual Commencement Ball. She was a popular extrovert who was eager to attend the biggest social event of the season. It was October 1815, and she had just turned fifteen the prior month. Coming out was a major rite of passage for a young lady in Litchfield, Connecticut. It was a signal to the community that she was deemed ready to begin courtship. Like most of her friends, she had been carefully groomed for matrimony by her family. But now, her parents' marital expectations had to be reconciled with the hopes of her romantic heart. She was crossing an emotional threshold where men sought more than friendship. It was simultaneously scary and exciting. Her choices among suitors and the turn of events would determine

her future happiness. The stakes were high in the pursuit of marriage, and this was Kate's first big step.

The event that she was about to attend was likely cosponsored by the male students at Litchfield Law School (LLS). There were roughly fifty young gentlemen, mostly college graduates in their twenties, who studied at the prestigious institution each year. Their primary objective was a legal education that would launch a successful career in law, government, or business.[1] The nearby Litchfield Female Academy (LFA) was an academic and finishing school for girls. It was founded in 1792 by Miss Sarah Pierce. The school boasted between 60 and 120 teenage girls each year, plus a few local boys. About half the young ladies were ages fifteen and up, old enough to begin considering marriage in the early 1800s. Prosperous families from across the Northeast sent their daughters to LFA for a proper education and the possibility of making elite marital connections.[2] Male students at LLS were only too happy to accommodate their desires. The pursuit of feminine companionship was a sufficient incentive. But an added benefit was that advantageous matches could help advance a young man's career.[3] As a result, each fall, the men of LLS helped arrange a ball where dancing was viewed as an appealing way to meet eligible young females. The Annual Commencement Ball was the celebration of the granting of LFA diplomas in late October.[4]

Kate's escort arrived wearing formal attire, including expensive kid gloves. Although he was a bit large for his height, he was nevertheless handsome—and considering his attire, perhaps wealthy. Kate would have worn a modest gown consistent with her status as a minister's daughter. As the couple entered the ball, they found that the great hall at LFA had been transformed. Tables and chairs had been moved to the sides to create a sizable dance floor. The chamber was adorned with seasonal decorations, which, combined with the soft, flickering light of candles, gave the room a delightful, romantic ambiance. A sizable professional orchestra was seated at the far end of the hall. The presence of a large ensemble marked this as a memorable affair.

At the appointed hour, the musicians began to play a popular cotillion tune. The ball was opened when the most beautiful girl in the room was led to her place by her escort, perhaps the most stylish gentleman in attendance. Kate and her partner were honored to take the second place on the floor, and she was gratified to receive such notable attention. Then the other dancers fell into formation. Each group of four couples formed a square and promenaded to the music and the directions of the caller.[5] Kate switched partners for successive dances, and in this fashion, her acquaintances multiplied. During breaks, there was ample time for conversation with her escort, as well as newfound prospects. An extrovert like Kate would have thrived in this social environment. But during the final interlude, a young man approached Kate to engage in conversation. Unfortunately, he proceeded to contradict her repeatedly in a rather ungentlemanly fashion. He may have been solely at fault for the altercation, but Kate's temper could have played a role. She rarely backed down when challenged, which might have added fuel to the fire.[6] Regardless of blame, Kate's chivalrous escort defended her honor. Words of a duel ensued, but the two gentlemen were quickly separated by friends, which ended the ball in a civil but somewhat dispirited manner.[7]

With the sentiments of the evening still fresh in her head, Kate sat down to memorialize the ball with a poem. She often used poetry to capture the spirit of major occasions. Her verses established social leadership among her friends by determining everyone's proper place in the narrative. With a whimsical flair, she penned a humorous parody titled "The Bumble Bees Ball," where she attended an insect ball as Miss Katy Did, escorted by Colonel Bumble Bee. It marked her debut in the courtship mix, as expected by society. But she didn't meet the man of her dreams that evening. Perhaps Kate realized, for the first time, that romance was easier to find in books than in real life. So she ended her poem with a dramatic flair and without a beau:[8]

> This broke up the ball & next day a duel
> was fought in which the noble Colonel was
> slain leaving me in deep affliction
> 						Respectfully grieve
> 						"Katy Did"

Kate's invitation had arrived none too soon, coming only three days before the ball. Perhaps local gossip had telegraphed that the daughter of a Litchfield celebrity was still awkwardly available. Her father, the Reverend Lyman Beecher, was a nationally famous figure and the minister of the prestigious First Congregational Church in town. He had been recruited to this position on the strength of his reputation for fiery Calvinist sermons and a moral crusade—ironically, against dueling. His pulpit in Litchfield was consequential because of the town's unique role at the center of an extraordinary network of power and influence in America. LLS had trained over seven hundred highly successful men since it was founded by Tapping Reeve in 1784. At the federal level alone, its graduates included numerous congressmen, senators, and cabinet members connected through a significant web of relationships in Litchfield, Washington, New York, Boston, and other centers of power. The influence was amplified by the numerous links among the wealthy families of their LFA spouses.[9] This clout was a magnet that drew ambitious young men to LLS. Kate entered this rarefied community when her father received his call to the Litchfield position in 1810. She was privileged to attend LFA in return for the spiritual guidance provided to the school by her father. Given Lyman's prominence, someone was bound to invite Kate to the ball to spare her the humiliation of staying home alone when it was her moment to enter the stage.

Love and marriage in America were in transition in 1815. Before the American Revolution, most matches were arranged by families based on economic, social, and cultural considerations. But children typically had veto power over their parents' choice of a marriage partner. If a couple happened to fall in love, that was fine, but expectations for intimacy were not very high. Although socioeconomic factors remained prevalent, by 1800, many individuals began to select their own spouses based on compatibility and chemistry, which resulted in more affectionate relationships. During the first quarter of the nineteenth century, the Victorian concept of romance emerged. Rising middle-class women demanded more from marriage. They sought to build enduring emotional attachments. Couples shared secrets about their innermost thoughts to create lasting bonds. Love letters were a key part of this process and served as the personification of an absent lover. Evolving courtship practices from these three time periods overlapped, and each played a role in Kate's search for romance.[10]

The pursuit of passion was a finely tuned art among Litchfield students. As Kate reminisced decades later, "Every pleasant evening witnessed troops of young people passing through the broad and shaded street to and from the favorite Prospect Hill. Of course, the fashion extended to the law students, and thus romances in real life abounded on every side."[11] She knew exactly what transpired during those evening strolls. Although such a scene would have appeared charming to an observer, the competition in this matrimonial arena was formidable. The men were all smart, powerful, or both. Male students actively orchestrated moonlight walks and sleigh rides in hopes of amorous adventures with females. The women were mostly attractive or well connected. Young ladies behaved in ways designed to attract men's attention and flattery. The stakes were high, and the players were skilled. Gossip abounded in these deep waters, and Kate Beecher learned how to swim.

Kate was successful and popular at school, so she had ample reasons to be optimistic about finding a promising suitor. Since moving to Litchfield in 1810, she had gathered a strong circle of friends and had become a social leader among students. She was the oldest of the eight Beecher siblings and the undisputed head of merriment in a household that was as boisterous as it was fun. She was empathetic and outgoing, with a flair for humor and drama. These were all essential elements of her winsome personality. Kate was quite smart and was awarded the First Prize for scholarship at LFA in the spring of 1814. Her teacher, John P. Brace, recorded in his journal, "For a small girl [she] shows great fertility of genius & strength of memory."[12] Because of her natural intelligence, she breezed through academics at LFA without much effort. Sarah Pierce, the school's founder, wondered how and when she learned her lessons and deemed Kate "the busiest of all creatures in doing nothing."[13] The "nothings" that Kate preferred most were dramatic writing and acting.[14]

Despite her numerous strengths, Kate was realistic about her prospects for matrimony. She was a keen observer of male behavior. Although Kate was smart, a woman's intelligence was often not important to suitors and a negative for more than a few. She undoubtedly noticed that men seemed to value a female's physical appearance above other attributes. Kate was not deemed beautiful, but she was passably attractive. She looked more like her father, Lyman, than her more attractive mother, Roxana. Kate had brown eyes and wore gold-rimmed glasses, and her dark-brown hair was fashionably parted in the center and worn in ringlets. Combined with her modest dress, she projected a pleasant, studious appearance.[15]

Kate Beecher. Courtesy of Harriet Beecher Stowe Center, Hartford, CT.

Kate's views on desirable suitors were influenced significantly by her family as she approached courtship. Her father, Lyman Beecher, shaped her as one of the playmates he never had, growing up as an only child. To compensate for his lonely childhood, Lyman sought to create a lively Beecher family of his own. Later in life, Kate declared that she had a "decided genius for nothing but play and merriment," which she attributed to her father's influence.[16] Lyman was imaginative, impulsive, and averse to hard work, and he affectionately hugged his children.[17] Kate inherited or learned these behaviors from her adored father. As she approached the selection of a potential husband, she sought the passion and intimacy of someone like Lyman Beecher.

Roxana Foote Beecher. Courtesy of Harriet Beecher Stowe Center, Hartford, CT.

Rev. Lyman Beecher. Courtesy of Harriet Beecher Stowe Center, Hartford, CT.

Her mother, Roxana Foote Beecher, was the perfect complement to her husband. She was an attractive and intelligent woman, the product of a distinguished military family from Guilford, Connecticut. Roxana preferred intellectual pursuits as pastimes, often solving math riddles for amusement.[18] Her distinctive personality was captured vividly by her grandfather, Revolutionary War general Andrew Ward. He loved to contrast his three granddaughters with his favorite anecdote, "When the girls first came down in the morning, Harriet's voice would be heard briskly calling, Here! Take the broom; sweep up; make a fire; make haste. Betsey would say, I wonder what ribbon it's best to wear at that party? But Roxana would say, Which do you think was the greater general, Hannibal or Alexander?"[19] Roxana was calm, self-possessed, persistent, and benevolent like an angel, but she rarely embraced her children physically the way Lyman frequently did.[20] She was the prudent one who juggled her household duties, the children, and the family finances. She started a small school in their first home in East Hampton and later took in boarders at Litchfield to help make ends meet when her husband's meager salary proved insufficient. A man with her mother's personality might have been a nice, complementary match for Kate. But she aspired to someone with the warmth and affection of her father.

Roxana's younger sister, Mary Foote, was the warm, maternal influence who inspired Kate as a poet. Aunt Mary came to live with the Beechers at East Hampton shortly after Lyman and Roxana were married in 1799. She was fifteen at the time and a striking presence in their home. According to Lyman, "She was a beautiful creature, one of the most fascinating human beings I ever saw. Her smile no man could resist . . . Her mind was well cultivated . . . rich in all that pertains to belles-lettres and literature."[21] Kate remembered her aunt Mary as "the loveliest and most beautiful [woman] . . . with soft brown hair, dark blue eyes & graceful figure & movements."[22] Aunt Mary understood Kate's strengths and weaknesses. Praising Kate's intellect but concerned about her temperament, Mary admonished Lyman in a letter "to pay attention to her temper, so that we may love what we are compelled to admire."[23] The attentions of Aunt Mary were instrumental in developing Kate's romantic yearnings. Kate explained, "I remember my imagination being fired by hearing her [voice] . . . She was a beautiful reader, and the poetry of [Sir Walter] Scott and [Robert] Burns are embalmed in my memory in those charming tones . . . She was the poetry of my childhood."[24] It was Mary's sense of poetry and romance that compelled Kate to search for a special, warmhearted suitor. Unfortunately, Aunt Mary died of consumption when Kate was only thirteen.

Literature was also a powerful influence on Kate's concepts of love and courtship. She had unusual access to books through her mother's brother, Uncle Samuel Foote, who was a prosperous sea captain. Uncle Samuel brought the latest novels and poetry from London after each of his international voyages. Many of these volumes were recent works by romance writers like Sir Walter Scott and Robert Burns. These were the books Aunt Mary read to her. The Romantic movement at the time was characterized by its emphasis on emotion, individualism, and the idealization of nature.[25] As a result of her youthful exposure through Uncle Samuel and Aunt Mary, Kate was endowed with a romantic spirit.

Kate also would have had access to the latest courtship novels by Jane Austen, which were particularly applicable to her situation in 1815.[26] These works depicted the entrance of a young woman into adult society and her subsequent choices among suitors. There were important differences between England's landed gentry, as depicted in Austen's works, and America's upper-middle class, to which Kate belonged. But there was enough similarity that many of the issues posed in books like *Sense and Sensibility* (1811) and *Pride and Prejudice* (1813) were quite relevant to Kate.[27] Realistically, there were few good options for a young woman to maintain an independent life in New England in the early nineteenth century. She essentially had to choose marriage or become an old maid dependent on the generosity of her kinfolk. As a result, courtship was serious business. If a woman wanted to live a more comfortable style of life, she needed to marry someone with better economic prospects than those of her father. The trade-offs among her suitor's finances, personality, character, and physical appearance were quite consequential. An unmarried female much beyond twenty was considered a likely old maid. At some point, such a lady might have to settle for someone less handsome or personable, simply to achieve economic security. One can imagine romantic Kate's dismay when she read in *Pride and Prejudice* that Elizabeth Bennet's good friend Charlotte Lucas willingly pursued marriage with the pompous clergyman William Collins. Charlotte declared, "I am not romantic . . . I ask only a comfortable home; and considering Mr. Collins's character, connections and situation in life, I am convinced that my chance of happiness with him is as fair, as most people can boast on entering the marriage state."[28]

Kate would have carefully observed and pondered the courtship choices of her friends who lived with the Beechers, Louisa Wait and Lucy Porter. Louisa came to Litchfield as a music teacher at LFA in the summer of 1816. She was outgoing and described as having a "slight figure, pretty features, pleasant blue eyes and with an uncommon fresh blooming complexion. She was called very pretty."[29] While boarding with the Beechers, Louisa shared a room with Kate and became her confidant. Louisa had attended LFA as a student in 1805 but left school when her "father, Captain Thomas Wait of New London died and left his family poor."[30] Having studied at LFA at the age of twelve, she understood the limited romantic opportunities for an attractive but older girl of modest means in Litchfield. Louisa was twenty-three years old and a potential mentor in matters of the heart for Kate, who was only sixteen. Louisa had a penchant for smart men and strong emotional connections. This would have aligned nicely with the ideals of her young Beecher protégé.

Louisa was an accomplished pianist and delightful singer. She became Kate's music teacher at LFA. She made a strong addition to the musically talented Beecher household. Kate sang and played the piano. Her two younger brothers, William and Edward, played the flute. Lyman had learned the violin at Yale and enjoyed playing it regularly. So the family spent many pleasant evenings performing Rev. Beecher's favorite psalms and Scottish airs. Louisa loved Scottish tunes as well. The first one she taught Kate on the piano was "Auld Lang Syne" by Robert Burns. The sentimental song was a clue that she was a fellow romantic.[31] Music was an emotional bond that Kate shared with her family and something she someday wanted in a home of her own. It was the thread that connected her romantic dreams and her humble expectations for domestic life.

Lucy Porter became Kate's friend when she boarded with the Beechers while attending LFA in 1816. Lucy was nineteen years old, three years older than Kate. She was quite attractive, rich, and extraordinarily well connected.[32] Her father was a wealthy doctor in Portland, which was then part of Massachusetts before Maine became a state in 1820. Her uncle Rufus King had been a US senator from New York, held the position of minister to Great Britain twice, and was the Federalist presidential candidate in 1816. Lucy had been introduced to LFA by her cousins James (LLS 1810) and Edward King (LLS 1813–1815). Both married into other powerful political families through Litchfield school connections.[33] It was likely that Lucy Porter attended LFA to search for a similar political match. She certainly had the required looks and connections. Such an elite marriage was probably not of interest to Kate and certainly beyond her station. But her friendship with Lucy allowed her to experience the social benefits of such suitors vicariously.

Kate's likely path to matrimony was to find a successful, warmhearted LLS student who appreciated her personality and talents. But there was a notable chance to find someone who was raised in Litchfield. The obvious suspect was John Pierce Brace. He became a natural friend, mentor, and potential love interest for Kate when he returned to teach at LFA in 1814. He was seven years older than Kate, which was a reasonable age difference for couples in the nineteenth century. He was handsome, witty, and dedicated to providing the better education he believed women deserved. Brace grew up in Litchfield, where his father, who was married to Sarah Pierce's sister, was a writing instructor at LFA. "John P," as Kate called him, was not rich or powerful, but he was passionate like she was. He described his own character as "full of susceptibility, excitability, romance and imagination."[34] He had a torrid teenage romance with LFA student Eliza Johnston, whom he abandoned when he departed to attend Williams College in 1808. He ultimately returned to Litchfield in 1814 to help his aunt Sarah Pierce run LFA.[35] John P became Kate's closest male friend because of the LFA connection and their similar personalities. Brace was a Renaissance man. In addition to teaching and administration, he published original scientific research and was a poet like Kate. He wrote hundreds of poems that he presented to individual LFA students. He noted in his diary that during 1816, "My flirtations continued, but they were frequently merged with attachments."[36] A good-looking man with so many accomplishments must have been the object of numerous schoolgirl crushes. Although he would not have been rich enough for some LFA girls to marry, he would have been within the reach of a famous minister's talented daughter. Could a smart, passionate schoolteacher who appeared to play the field settle down with a girl like Kate who wanted a deep relationship? Only time would tell.

There was no explicit record of Kate's romantic activities during the 1815–1816 school year other than her attendance at the Annual Commencement Ball. Presumably, she took part in the courtship pursuits common among LFA girls her age. But what *is* certain is that she did not settle on a steady beau. With the help of her family and friends, she had begun to define the criteria for a desirable suitor. The young man would have to be smart and successful. Preferably, he would be a man who shared her interests in drama and music. Most importantly, he must have an affectionate heart to fulfill her dreams of romance. As the summer of 1816 drew to a close, she would have looked forward to the approaching fall courtship rites. A new school year would bring fresh faces to LLS. She and Louisa would enjoy speculating about the merits of each new arrival. Kate's journey was off to a reasonable start, and she had never been happier.

At the same time, in August 1816, her parents were suitably contented. Roxana Beecher was forty-one, and Lyman was forty. They had eight children, ranging from Kate, who was almost sixteen, to Charles, who was only ten months old. Their lives were hectic, but their children were a great joy. So it was a jolt to Lyman when, on their way home from visiting friends one evening, Roxana shivered and told him, "I do not think I shall be with you long." Lyman later told his family, "Your mother had consumptive symptoms for a year before her sickness, though we were ignorant of it."[37] Roxana undoubtedly recognized her ailment much earlier and had seen enough cases of consumption to know what to expect. *Consumption* was the nineteenth-century term for the highly infectious bacterial lung disease now known as *tuberculosis*.[38] That made it particularly dangerous for caregivers, who were typically women. Roxana may have been infected in 1813 while nursing her sister Mary, who died of the disease. But Roxana soldiered on and kept it hidden as long as she could. She didn't survive more than six weeks after her initial pronouncement to Lyman.[39]

During 1813, Kate had been sent to stay with relatives in Guilford, Connecticut, to spare her the trauma of witnessing Aunt Mary's death. But as the end neared for her mother, the eight Beecher children gathered in the room to provide comfort. Roxana was heavily sedated with laudanum and was conscious only part of the time. Kate and her siblings sat around their mother's bed, weeping pitifully. At one point, Roxana woke, and her breathing was quite labored. With great difficulty, she managed to speak to her children. She commended them to God's care and said they must trust him. She prayed that all her sons should become ministers. After several minutes, she lapsed into a deep slumber.[40]

About four hours before Roxana died, she had a lucid interval where she was able to converse with her husband. She told him about eagerly anticipating heaven. She remarked on all her blessings in life. She trusted that in time, God would provide him a companion to fill her place. According to Lyman, "Her state of mind was heavenly, and I have no doubt that her sorrow is turned into joy." Roxana Foote Beecher died September 24, 1816.[41] Lyman assured his children that she was safely in heaven.

After the funeral, the younger Beecher children were confused about what had actually happened. They were told that their mother had been laid to rest in the ground. But they were also told that she was with God in heaven. Young Henry Beecher, at the age of three, managed to conflate these two explanations. In a touching scene a few days later, Kate heard noise beneath her bedroom window. She looked out to see Henry vigorously digging in the yard. When she called down to ask what he was doing, he looked up and earnestly replied, "Why I'm going to heaven to find ma."[42]

The emotional impact of Roxana's death on Kate was concealed by the brave face she maintained. Losing her mother as she contemplated marriage herself must have been traumatic. They had spent countless hours together as Roxana prudently prepared Kate for matrimony, teaching her to read, write, draw, and sew. But unable or unwilling to express her deepest emotions, Kate set Roxana on a romantic pedestal and memorialized her with poetry. Her written sentiments, while heartfelt, lacked the simple tenderness of her brother Henry's feelings. However, her poem was effective in helping her family deal with their collective grief. The Beecher children all memorized Kate's verses and, over the years, ritually recited them, often in tears. The following are two of the ten stanzas:[43]

> Father in heaven, my mother's God,
> Oh grant before thy seat,
> Among the blessed sons of light,
> Parent and child may meet.

> There may I see her smiling face,
> And hear her gentle voice;
> And, gladden'd by thy gracious smile,
> Through endless years rejoice.

Caring for the large Beecher family in the absence of Roxana was a significant enterprise. Fortunately, Lyman's stepmother, Grandma Beecher, and his spinster half sister, Aunt Esther, lived in Litchfield. After the funeral, they stepped forward, as Kate remembered it, "to take charge of the family." The two of them moved into the Beecher home. Grandma Beecher positioned herself each day in the parlor next to the north entry of the house. With "her trim erect figure, black bright eyes and arched eyebrows," she sat quietly in a rocking chair in order to monitor the coming and going of each person. She kept the parlor neat and tidy, with everything, including the brass andirons, sparkling clean. Kate recalled that it was all calculated "to induce carefulness and quiet around the premises."[44] It was the antithesis of the happy yet hectic Beecher household of prior years.

Aunt Esther had never married and anxiously cared for her mother under a regime of extreme neatness for many years. The familiar, rigid lives of Esther and her mother were relinquished for a venture that attempted to impose order on a family better known for laughter and chaos. It was only natural that Kate, as the oldest daughter, would attempt to help fill her mother's place.[45] With Lyman's encouragement, she made a significant sacrifice when she withdrew from school. She allowed her sister Mary to take her place at LFA. Kate's participation in social and courtship activities in Litchfield came to an abrupt halt. She dedicated herself to supporting her aunt and grandmother. She recalled that Aunt Esther was "an accomplished cook . . . but with scissors and a needle she felt helpless."[46] So Kate took on the task of mending and making all the family's clothing, and Aunt Esther taught her how to cook.

What happened to all the Beecher boarders under these circumstances is unclear. The income from that enterprise was important to balance the family budget. But continuing the care for additional residents was a tall order. Lucy Porter apparently returned home to Massachusetts unengaged. Perhaps it was fallout from her uncle's resounding defeat in the 1816 presidential election.[47] Louisa Wait appears to have continued to live with the Beechers as Kate's roommate.

As fall turned into winter, the drudgery of Kate's new domestic routine was interrupted by vicarious romance. Two of her closest friends found sweethearts, which probably brightened her outlook during this difficult period of her life. Louisa fell in love with Uriel Holmes Jr. when he returned home to Litchfield after graduating from Yale in 1816. He was nineteen, and she was twenty-three. Uriel was a devout young man who planned to enter Andover Theological Seminary to pursue a career in the ministry. They probably became engaged before the end of the year. Louisa was undoubtedly one of the most attractive young women in town, and the chemistry between them must have been powerful. He chose to stay in Litchfield for the year and delayed his entry into seminary until the fall of 1817.[48] The two of them were known to be a couple, and it must have pleased Kate that her friend had found a beau. But Louisa and Uriel kept their engagement a secret, even from Kate.[49] Their reasons for hiding it were unknown but must have been significant because Kate could have been trusted not to reveal it.

The second affair was the engagement of her friend John P in January 1817. He always seemed to have a crush on someone, and this one progressed swiftly.[50] She was a young LFA student who was swept off her feet by John P's charm and poetry. Kate would have been pleased that her friend had found happiness. But she may have had mixed feelings about the engagement. It eliminated one of her best prospects for finding romance in Litchfield. But if she was disappointed, it didn't last long, for within a few months, the engagement was broken off. Brace blamed melancholy, his recurring personality trait, for alienating his fiancée and spoiling this "engagement with a talented and beautiful girl."[51] John P was interestingly back in the picture.

As the fall of 1817 arrived, Kate remained stuck in her housekeeping role. She had come out in promising fashion almost two years earlier, but her youthful excitement had been stilled by Roxana's untimely death. It was a devastating blow to Kate's heart when her prime romantic years were snatched away so cruelly at the age of sixteen. She had always expected to shed her innocence and take on the responsibilities of a mature woman, but not in this manner. She was a loyal daughter who sacrificed her own interests to help support the Beecher family. But bereft of her social activities at school, an extrovert like Kate was miserable. Her impulsive father also chafed under the strict supervision of Grandma Beecher and Aunt Esther. Kate later reminisced that "the experience of this year of our family history was similar to that of a landscape in sunshine suddenly overcast with heavy clouds."[52] The situation was not sustainable. Lyman needed to find a wife to rescue his family from their torment. But his age, income, and family situation didn't make him a particularly attractive suitor. All Kate could do was wait patiently and hope her father would make a wise choice.

KEY FISHER CHARACTERS—OCTOBER 1815

	Age	Connection	Location
Alexander Fisher	21	Yale tutor	New Haven, CT
Caleb Fisher	47	Farmer, Alexander's devout, hardworking father	Franklin, MA
Sally Fisher	44	Alexander's intellectual, musical mother	Franklin, MA
Denison Olmsted	24	Yale tutor and former Yale classmate	New Haven, CT
James Kingsley	37	Yale professor of ancient languages	New Haven, CT
Eleazar Fitch	23	Musical Andover Seminary friend	Andover, MA

2

Alexander

> I do not intend by any means, to give up hopes that I shall sooner or later gratify your wishes concerning me.
> —Alexander Metcalf Fisher

October 1815–September 1817
Alexander Metcalf Fisher was elated to return as a tutor to his alma mater, Yale. In the fall of 1815, at the age of twenty-one, he was launching his professional academic career. He wanted to become a professor, but his lofty intellectual ambition was to expand the realm of knowledge in his favorite subject . . . mathematics. Alexander possessed the requisite genius and work ethic to deliver on his bold aspirations. Yet this choice defined him at considerable cost to his personal life. It ended his father's dream for Alexander to become a Congregational minister. That increased parental pressure for him to seek religious conversion. He also deferred courtship to focus on his work. But as Alexander arrived in New Haven, he thanked God and dedicated the "intellectual attainments he has enabled me to make, to his glory."[1]

Yale College and the New Haven public square. Courtesy of Connecticut Museum of Culture and History, Hartford, CT.

As a graduate of Yale, Alexander was quite familiar with its system of education. The college had originally been founded to train Congregational ministers, and its religious mission continued. But by the early nineteenth century, the goal had expanded to providing a liberal education. Its objective became to lay the foundation of knowledge common to all professions. In 1815 Yale had fewer than three hundred students, who were guided by eight professors and six tutors. Professors supervised teaching within their respective academic disciplines, delivered lectures, and personally taught the senior class. The freshmen, sophomore, and junior classes were each separated into divisions of roughly twenty-five students. Each tutor took responsibility for a division and, under the direction of the professors, instructed his students in all subjects for three years. A tutor spent most waking hours with his charges, acting as both instructor and guardian to shape them intellectually and morally. The role was pivotal in the Yale educational scheme. Yet the position of tutor, which Alexander accepted, was considered a temporary bridge to becoming a professor or moving on to other pursuits.[2]

As Alexander pondered his prospects, the majestic public square adjacent to the college would have beckoned him to walk on a warm autumn day. He wore an affordable, oft-mended waistcoat that neither embarrassed nor distinguished him. His modest farm parents had invested well beyond their means to educate their brilliant son, and he willingly embraced their

Alexander Metcalf Fisher. *Courtesy of Yale University Art Gallery.*

frugality. Alexander was ambitious, yet his competitive nature was tempered by humility and an endearing, self-deprecatory sense of humor. He was introverted, although it was not because he was shy. He simply enjoyed solitary activities such as reading books more than social gatherings. Alexander was a serious individual, but those who knew him best appreciated his generosity and warm heart.[3] He was reasonably handsome, with wavy brown hair, brown eyes, a classic straight nose, and an angular jaw. His gold-rimmed glasses, thoughtful expression, and slight physique marked him as a scholar. Alexander's colleagues commissioned Samuel F. B. Morse to paint a somber posthumous portrait.

Alexander was a math prodigy.[4] His gift was recognized at an early age by his mother, Sally Fisher, who was a woman of uncommon mathematical ability.[5] The extent of his intellectual prowess became apparent at the age of eleven, when, disappointed with the math textbook at his disposal, he authored a more helpful and sophisticated version for his own use.[6] The sample pages from his book include the cover, table of contents, and two pages where he determined the proportionate dimensions of a ship with a smaller displacement and calculated a biquadrate root. While the substance of his volume was impressive, the sheer artistry of his penmanship was astonishing. He filled the otherwise open area at the bottom of pages with graceful artistic swirls. The fact that it was produced in ink by an eleven-year-old boy employing a blank, bound manuscript book, with no possibility of making corrections, gives a sense of his amazing concentration and talent. It marked him as a genius.

He loved mathematics because it was so elegantly logical. It provided the means to quantify and validate all the sciences. The nineteenth-century theoretical framework of mathematics

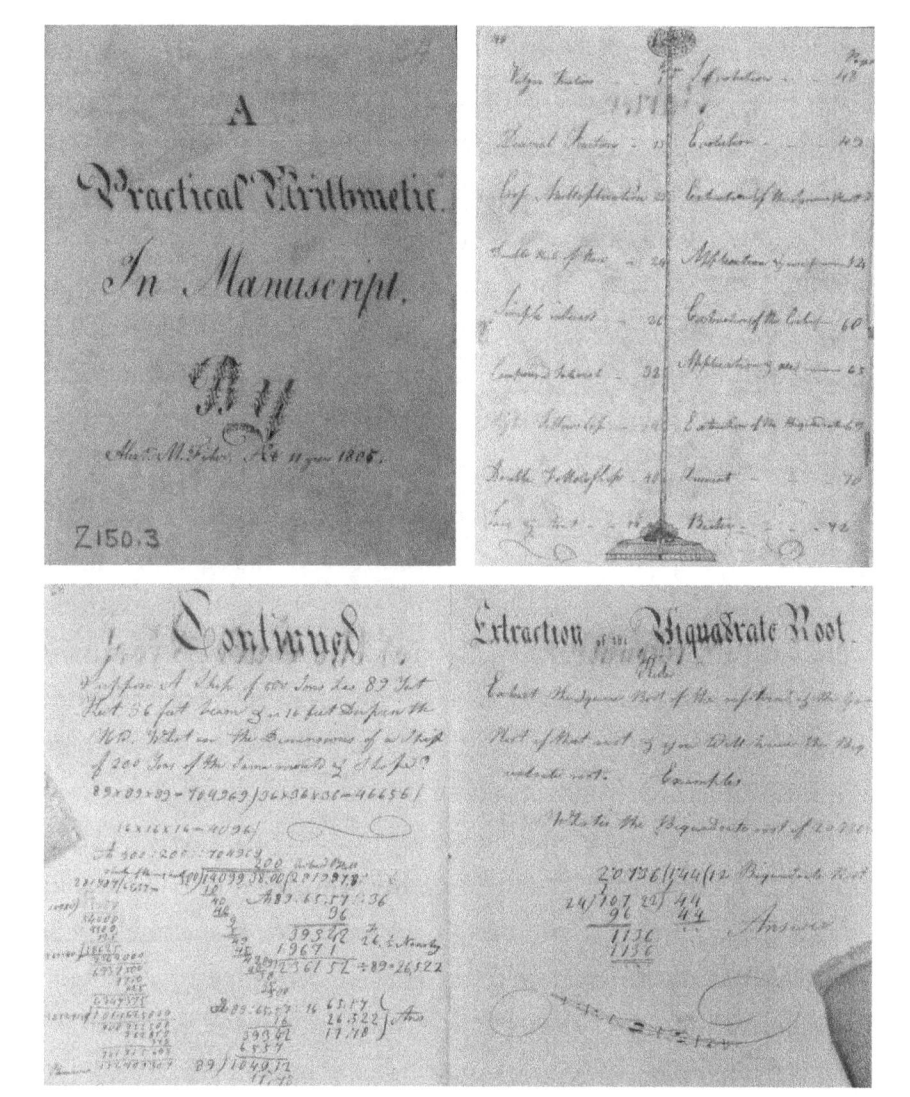

Alexander's math textbook. Courtesy of Beinecke Rare Book and Manuscript Library, Yale University.

was still a work in progress, which offered an opportunity for Alexander to extend its boundaries. France was where those frontiers were probed by the greatest mathematicians in the world. French scholars stood on the shoulders of intellectual giants like René Descartes and Blaise Pascal. Many of the cutting-edge academic papers were not yet published in English, so Alexander needed to become proficient in the French language to grasp the latest concepts. But his dream wouldn't be complete until he engaged the brightest minds in person.[7] The great Parisian universities were revered by the American elite as citadels of all forms of learning. During the first half of the nineteenth century, intellectuals were starting to make the "fashionable trip" by sailing to France to gather the latest wisdom.[8] Spending time in Paris could establish Alexander as a leading scholar and provide a platform to pursue his ultimate academic ambition. Becoming a tutor at Yale was merely the first step on his journey.

The Fisher family had sacrificed heavily to educate Alexander (b. 1794), in hopes that he would become a Congregational minister. It was the dream of Alexander's father, Caleb. The Fishers were a rural family with deep Calvinist religious roots. Ministry was a career of great significance in the small town of Franklin, Massachusetts, where they lived. A town minister was viewed by the faithful as God's direct representative on Earth and the only intermediary necessary for salvation. Caleb, a modest farmer, poured whatever cash he could gather into his son's education. Alexander's mother, Sally, managed to make household ends meet with a diminished budget. The education of his younger siblings—Willard (b. 1796), Eliza (b. 1803), and Nancy (b. 1806)—was put on hold while Alexander was prepared for college at Leicester Academy, one of the few coeducational schools in its day. He was admitted to Yale College in 1809 at the age of fifteen. He excelled as a student and graduated Phi Beta Kappa, second in the class of 1813.[9] His family was justly proud of him.

But Alexander's aspiration was a career in academics, not ministry. Although he continued to express doubts about his fitness to serve as a minister, he studied for a year with Rev. Nathanael Emmons, a noted theologian who was the

Congregational minister in Franklin. The fame of Dr. Emmons and his widely read sermons distinguished Franklin from other rural Massachusetts towns. Alexander subsequently agreed to enter Andover Theological Seminary in 1814.[10] Then he received an offer during the summer of 1815 to return to Yale as a tutor. He wrote his parents:

> I have been reflecting on this subject for some time, and am satisfied on the whole, that it is best for me to go... You have doubtless indulged considerable expectation that I should complete my term of study here, and become qualified for the profession of Theology. It is painful to me to take any course which will have a tendency to disappoint this expectation. But I must say that I do not consider myself as yet possessed of the most important qualification of the profession.[11]

The qualification Alexander lacked was a religious awakening called *conversion*. It would have a profound impact on his life and those he touched. The term had a distinct meaning in nineteenth-century Congregational doctrine. It was achieved when a person's soul woke to its sinful state, submitted fully to God, and received his saving grace. Conversion was an arduous process that typically required the maintenance of a detailed diary to reflect on religious resolutions and document sins. An individual's sinful state was carefully recorded in self-loathing detail to reinforce one's total depravity. Only by complete submission to the will of God could one receive his grace and obtain a renewed heart. The souls of those who were converted went to heaven, whereas those of the unconverted were eternally damned to hell. These were disturbing consequences for members of a church that believed in predestination. Because only the "elect" could achieve conversion, a lack of success was a strong indication that one was not among the chosen. It was considered beyond human comprehension why God chose some for damnation. One's fate was to be joyfully accepted as part of God's plan. Nathanael Emmons's bedrock test for religious fidelity in 1815 was a positive answer to the question, Would you be happy to be damned to hell for the greater glory of God?[12]

Despite Alexander's earnest efforts recorded in his religious diary, his own words documented his desire but inability to achieve conversion in the accepted manner:

> July 7, 1815—I find myself continually prone to lose sight of those relations which subsist between me and my Creator, and to forget that I am under the highest obligations to love and serve him with all my heart. That a sense of these obligations and relations shall be kept alive is infinitely important; for without it, there can be no sense of past guilt and no decided inclination to future obedience.[13]

Alexander had doubts about the validity of the process. Based on his study of the Bible during college and seminary, he was unable to reconcile the doctrine of conversion with either logic or scripture. As a college student, he believed a different approach, simple repentance, was the key to salvation.[14] But he blamed his own human frailty for lack of comprehension and continued to pursue the path of his father. Caleb Fisher did not give up hope for his son's salvation. In fact, Caleb had achieved conversion only in January 1809 at the age of forty. At that point, his wife, Sally, was thirty-eight and remained unconverted.[15] Alexander had thus far lived a good and moral life, but it might have been easier for someone with a checkered past to admit their sins and embrace God. It could be difficult for the children of those who were converted to follow in their parents' footsteps. Sometimes, a different approach than the one that inspired the older generation was required to move the hearts of the younger generation.[16] Caleb was crushed when Alexander abandoned the ministry to pursue an academic career, but he never gave up hope for Alexander's soul.

Alexander sought to make amends for his change of direction. Although he would not become a minister, he promised to continue to seek salvation through conversion. He wrote his parents, "In leaving this place, I do not intend by any means, to give up all hopes that I shall sooner or later gratify your wishes concerning me."[17] He drafted eight resolutions in his religious diary.[18] He also imposed two moral obligations on himself. First, he would repay his parents for his earlier schooling. Going forward, he would borrow any funds he needed from his father and pay interest. Second, Alexander promised himself to seek educational opportunities for his siblings, who had sacrificed their schooling for his.[19]

But the emotional trauma of his career choice took its toll on Alexander's mental health. Before he left Andover for Yale, he sank into a deep depression and sent for his father to retrieve him. Back home, his mood swung from depression to a manic state that alarmed his mother. His parents attempted to keep his strange mental circumstances a secret. They hid his shoes and physically restrained Alexander to keep him from leaving the house. Eventually, they sought medical care for him. He carefully documented each step of his euphoria, in which he believed he had received extraordinary powers from God to save the world.[20] His parents called it "derangement," but it was most likely what is termed *bipolar syndrome* in the twenty-first century.[21] Within a few weeks, his normal behavior returned, and he completed his preparations to return to Yale. Although he was excited about returning to academics, he would miss his family dearly.

Alexander had forged strong emotional bonds by living with three generations of Fishers. He was born July 22, 1794, in Franklin, Massachusetts. It was a small town perched on the south bank of the Charles River, equidistant (thirty miles) from Boston to the northeast and Providence, Rhode Island, to the south. He was raised in a humble farmhouse under the same roof as his grandparents Hezekiah and Dinah; his parents, Caleb and Sally; and his three siblings, Willard, Eliza, and Nancy. His grandfather Hezekiah died in 1809, just before Alexander went to college, and his grandmother Dinah died in 1812 while he was at Yale. Alexander's childhood was spent in the same community with four sets of uncles, aunts, and cousins.[22] The broader set of family members was relevant to Alexander's sense of identity. Life with his kinfolk was messy and sometimes illogical. But it was wonderfully alive with joy, sorrow, squabbles, and compassion. The rhythms of family life provided Alexander with a familiar sense of comfort.

The eventual happiness of a man like Alexander depended on starting a family of his own. Eliza Wheeler was the young woman whom people in Franklin probably expected Alexander to marry. Although Eliza and Alexander were well acquainted, they never officially courted. She lived in the adjacent village of Medway, Massachusetts, which was connected by a bridge, less than a tenth of a mile down the hill from the Fisher farm.[23]

Although the Fishers attended church in Franklin, they picked up their mail and purchased supplies at the store in Medway, which was much closer to home. When Alexander returned from Yale in 1813, he was nineteen, and Eliza Wheeler was sixteen. These were prime marriage ages in a rural community where potential spouses were often identified early through family and friends. Alexander and Eliza were a natural combination based on their geographic proximity and numerous family connections.[24] But like many talented men, Alexander was a captive of his intellectual ambitions. When he departed for Yale in 1815, he was still only twenty-one and chose to focus on academics rather than courtship.

Denison Olmsted. Courtesy of Yale University Art Gallery.

Colleagues became the academic family that filled Alexander's emotional space in New Haven. He was delighted to be joined in his new position by his fellow tutor Denison Olmsted, whom he described as "perfectly coincident as to the best mode of instruction."[25] Alexander had met Olmsted when they both entered Yale in 1809. Denison was the son of a modest farmer from East Hartford and three years older than Alexander. He was a superb scholar with a similar personality that soon made him Alexander's best friend.[26] Alexander also renewed his friendships with Professors Silliman and Kingsley at Yale. Both were married and significantly older than him. Benjamin Silliman, MD, was the professor of chemistry, pharmacy, mineralogy, and geology.[27] As a student, Alexander had always enjoyed his experiments and later found him to be an excellent scientific colleague. Silliman was a progressive educator who often invited young ladies from New Haven to attend his lectures even though women weren't allowed to enroll in the college.[28] James Kingsley was the professor of Hebrew, Greek, and Latin languages. During his first year at Yale, Alexander had mixed feelings about Professor Kingsley's language skills. But by the time he graduated, they had become good friends. Kingsley was likely an advocate for hiring Alexander and was the person who wrote the letter telling him of the job offer as a tutor.[29]

Alexander worked demanding sixteen-hour days during his first year as a tutor. Given his busy schedule, he needed to be quite organized. There was no time to spare, so every aspect of his life was subject to what he considered to be an optimal routine. Everything within this regimen was done in what he deemed to be the most efficient and practical manner. Alexander was like the humorous efficiency expert Frank Gilbreth in the popular 1950 film *Cheaper by the Dozen*.[30] Small details of life, such as his morning dressing routine, were subject to rules that he followed scrupulously. His friend Olmsted described it, saying that Alexander had a "reason for his opinions on common-place subjects, which most people take up without supposing them to be worth a reason."[31] Once Alexander created a plan, he stuck to it.

Music was Alexander's preferred form of relaxation during the few hours he could spare. He was raised in a tradition of sacred choral music and enjoyed singing at Andover and later upon his return to Yale. He had made a small keyboard out of wood and wire. When the keys were drummed, wires sounded the notes of his makeshift musical instrument. As he wrote to his father, "For amusement, I spend a little time almost every day when by myself in singing, and as no time is lost by it, I sometimes take out the set of keys which I made last fall, and drum the bass with my fingers while singing the tenor."[32] As a tutor, he was eventually able to obtain an organ for his room. Based on his musical talent, he could immediately perform pieces of moderate difficulty without any formal training. Gradually, his taste shifted from familiar church hymns to European classical composers such as Haydn and Beethoven.[33] Alexander was a talented musician. It was a gift he inherited from his mother. But he had the uncommon ability to read a complex musical score and hear all parts in his head as if he were actually listening to it being performed in a concert hall. At the end of the day, he might pick up a favorite score, such as Handel's *Messiah*. As he glanced at the pages, the joyous harmonies of the "Hallelujah Chorus" would fill his head, and he was at peace.[34]

Reading was his other favorite pastime. He was a sophisticated individual who waded through all the popular and scholarly journals to keep up on current events and the latest academic papers. But above all, he loved reading books. He believed that "to read Horace, was to unlock the great storehouse of all antiquity . . . To read Pope's Satires [of which he was very fond] was to investigate the spirit and manners of the age." His favorite writer was Jonathan Swift, author of *Gulliver's Travels*, whose wit and satire influenced Alexander's style.[35] In January 1816, he wrote to his parents, "It is now the middle of winter vacation. All the tutors except myself have taken an excursion into the country; but for my own part, I much prefer a warm fire and interesting books to the pleasures of sleigh riding."[36] Romantic winter sleigh rides with young ladies from New Haven would have been an appealing activity for most young men. But Alexander was socially awkward in such situations. Farm boys like him all knew about sex, but at the age of twenty-one, he had probably never kissed a girl.

During the fall term of 1816, Alexander felt comfortable adding additional studies on top of his tutoring responsibilities.[37] With his academic dream of sailing to Paris a bit closer, he wrote his parents in November 1816:

> I have been deeply engaged . . . in the study of French . . . I find it extremely easy, and now can translate it pretty fast, with the help of looking up a few words in the Dictionary. My principal object in this is to be able to read the French mathematical writers in the original, most of whom are not translated and who are thought superior to the English mathematicians.[38]

In January 1817, two events occurred that significantly advanced Alexander's career. The first was the completion of his major work "Essay on Musical Temperament." It was important to present scholarly papers to raise his profile among academics at other colleges. In an enormous flurry of activity, he completed the article and thousands of complex calculations in a mere two weeks. Alexander was a hard worker, but this may have been evidence of a second manic episode. He later wrote his parents, "Last winter I finished up a dissertation of 60 pages, containing scrolls of laborious calculations on the best adjustment of the musical scale, which I have presented to the Connecticut Academy of Sciences."[39] His friend Denison Olmsted wrote, "I always considered Mr. F's taste for music, and fondness for its scientific principles, as among the most remarkable qualities he possessed."[40]

Alexander's "Essay on Musical Temperament," which described a tuning system for pianos, was the perfect intersection of his musical and scientific interests. It was particularly relevant because pianos were becoming very popular among the middle class during the early nineteenth century. Many do not realize that it is mathematically impossible to tune a piano to create perfect harmonies across all key signatures.[41] Alexander's practical solution for tuning was an optimization approach to minimize the number and size of disharmonies with a single tuning. It was based on scientific observations of 1,800 pieces of music.[42] The equal tempering of twenty-first-century pianos is simple and effective but results in minor disharmonies. Some of the tonal richness of classical pieces is lost with current piano tuning.

The second major event in January 1817 was the death of Yale's president Timothy Dwight from cancer. Within months, this led to the election of Professor Jeremiah Day as his replacement. Yale's board needed to fill Day's vacated position of professor of mathematics and natural philosophy (science). New openings were rare and often went to one of the current tutors.[43] Alexander was a leading candidate, but he was young and had potential competition. His good friend Denison Olmsted was well qualified for the position and older than Alexander. However, Olmsted was simultaneously under consideration for a similar position of professor of mathematics and natural philosophy that had just become available at the University of North Carolina.[44] But the Yale job was the only one available to Alexander. The essence of academic hiring boiled down to connections and timing. Tutors tended to stay for only four or five years. This was likely Alexander's only opportunity to become a professor at Yale. It was an emotional pressure cooker as the two schools considered their candidates. Yale kept its choice a closely guarded secret until it was announced at its presidential inauguration in July. Olmsted later observed that Alexander guarded his sentiments "lest anyone should discover his emotions and impute them to weakness."[45] But what Olmsted interpreted as Alexander guarding his emotions also may have reflected his difficulty in sharing them.

In February 1817, while Alexander was being considered for the position of professor, he confronted his lack of progress toward religious conversion. During his first two years back at Yale, the frequency of Alexander's religious journal entries declined from weekly to monthly, and the tone became less contrite and more indifferent. He was dedicated to self-improvement and analyzed his lack of motivation more like a scientist than someone on a spiritual journey.[46] He traced his problem to the way he was reading the scriptures. His twice-daily Bible readings were being done in haste. He was glossing over things and not taking time to "judge" what he read. He resolved to read less but study it intently and "make a little my own." But three months later, in May, he lamented, "I have become more negligent for a fortnight past than I have been for 4 years before, in regard to reading the scriptures at all."[47]

During the period from February to June, as he waited to hear if he had been chosen as a new professor, he made a significant discovery that further distracted him. He learned that he could make considerable money as an academic writer. He wrote to his father, "I have written a Review which is to be published in the *Analectic Magazine* in Philadelphia ... It will make upwards of 20 pages of close print, and as they give 3 dollars a page for original pieces, it will bring me nearly 70 dollars."[48] That was almost 15 percent of his annual salary as a tutor for a single piece of work. Although it added to his already busy schedule, writing provided a powerful economic incentive. The catch was that journals were looking for authors employed by brand-name institutions. There would be plenty of opportunities as an author if he became a Yale professor. But if Olmsted got the job, the writing opportunities would eventually disappear unless Alexander found a similar position elsewhere.

By the time Yale's presidential inauguration was held in July 1817, Alexander was literally sick to his stomach from anxiety. It was coincidentally held on his birthday, July 22. He was physically unable to attend the morning ceremonies where the announcement was made. His friend Olmsted came to see him afterward and reported that Alexander had received the appointment as Day's replacement. Immediately, Alexander recovered his good spirits and was able to attend the afternoon activities.[49] So he became a professor on his twenty-third birthday. He jubilantly wrote his parents, "What would you think if I were to tell you that I am Professor of Mathematics & Natural Philosophy in Yale College?"[50] He wrote in his diary, "It gives me the prospect of a permanent settlement in life, but of one which is more honorable + lucrative than I deserve, or than I could ever have reason to believe would fall to my lot."[51] Denison Olmsted was subsequently chosen to become the new professor at the University of North Carolina.

The death of Yale's President Dwight reunited Alexander with a good friend, Eleazar Fitch, from his earlier studies at Andover Theological Seminary. Eleazar was three years older than Alexander. He was a rather shy man, the son of a military officer, who grew up in New Haven. He entered Yale in 1806 at the age of fifteen, and like Alexander, he was a distinguished scholar. Dwight had served as both Yale's president and its professor of theology. The board decided to split these positions and created a separate professor of theology. Alexander replaced Jeremiah Day as professor of natural philosophy, and Eleazar was elected as the new professor of theology.[52] It was a stroke of good luck that Alexander and his friend Eleazar were both elected Yale professors on the same day.

It was an appropriate moment for Alexander to reconsider his priorities. For two years, he had focused almost exclusively on academics, and his rise had been meteoric. Yet he made little progress toward conversion, and his faith had wavered. As he pondered his future, he was shocked by sad news in September 1817. A Yale classmate had apparently worked himself into the ground and died. After attending the funeral, Alexander wrote in his religious diary, "How great reason have I to fear that same fate . . . And how infinitely desirable is it, if my destiny, that I should possess that religion that carried him with resignation thru the dark valley!"[53] The potential consequences of Alexander's ambition stared him in the face. He needed to make space for faith and a personal life. It was a timely warning.

3

Dispatched

"Holding Out for a Hero"
—song recorded by Bonnie Tyler

October 1817–September 1819

Kate and her father, Lyman, knelt down to pray in his study. It was early in October 1817, and their hearts required heavenly guidance. Lyman had shared momentous news. He had gone to Boston on routine business and returned home barely a week later, surprisingly engaged to a woman he had just met. It had been only a year since the untimely death of Kate's mother, Roxana. Kate had forsaken her future to serve Lyman in his hour of need. She knew that eventually he would need a wife and mother for their family. But his sudden choice was so unexpected. This woman would become her mother and alter the intimate relationship between Kate and her father. She had no choice but to accept her father's impulsive decision. As the two of them knelt in prayer, asking God for his support, their sentiments swelled, and tears streamed down their faces.[1]

Lyman had traveled to Boston to preach at the ordination of

Sereno Dwight as the new pastor of the Park Street Church in September 1817.[2] After the sermon, he was invited to the home of Henry and Isabella Homes. That was where Lyman first met Isabella's younger sister Harriet. She was beautiful and sophisticated, the twenty-seven-year-old daughter of a prestigious Federalist family. They were engaged six days later. Kate was shocked. Harriet was only ten years older than Kate and fifteen years younger than her father.[3] She was young enough to be Kate's sister! The gossip in Litchfield was humiliating as girls speculated on the circumstances and giggled that Kate's father "had gone to Boston to buy him a wife."[4] The obvious question was how it had happened so quickly. The apparent answer was found in the torrid correspondence between Lyman and Harriet during their six-week engagement. Harriet belonged to the Congregational Church and had achieved conversion five years earlier. Apparently, after hearing Lyman's sermon, she concluded that it was God's mission for her to support him. Once Harriet decided that God had called her to marry him, she used her feminine charms to get the impetuous Lyman to propose. As a forty-two-year-old widower, Lyman was flattered to have the romantic attention of an attractive young woman. She impressed him with her piety as she admitted her "depravity" and pledged "obedience" in a manner Roxana had never displayed.[5] She offered to help convert his children to save their souls and sought his help to convert her parents.[6]

But perhaps the engagement was not quite as accidental as it appeared. Harriet had conveniently appeared out of nowhere and was seemingly the answer to Lyman's prayers. It may have been providence. But the troubling reality was that Harriet was the older sister of Kate's friend from Litchfield, Lucy Porter.[7] Lucy had lived with the Beechers and was in a position to know both Harriet and

Lyman's marital needs well in advance of their meeting. Everyone in Harriet's family was distressed by the betrothal except Lucy, who firmly supported it.[8] It seems likely that she played some role in the match, either before or soon after the couple met. Lucy was a politician like her Federalist relatives, and politicians always have interesting motives . . . It was deliciously complicated.

At Lyman's request, Kate wrote Harriet a letter of welcome on behalf of all the Beecher children. But its stilted language betrayed her bitterness and humiliation about the approaching marriage: "Dear Madame, the prospect of the connections to take place between my father and yourself, and the tender alliance so soon to subsist between you and this family, give me liberty and pleasure in addressing you."[9] The wedding took place on October 30, 1817, at the home of Harriet's parents in Portland, Massachusetts (now Maine).[10] When Lyman returned with his new bride, the younger children expressed joy, but Kate was overtaken with emotion and unable to join the initial introductions.[11]

It was difficult for Kate to accept Harriet as her new mother.[12] She sensed a threat to the emotional bond with her father. But there was nothing Kate could do to change things. So as a good actor, she put on a cheerful face and didn't ask too many questions. Beneath the surface, she resented her new stepmother, and their relations were mutually chilly at best. Harriet slyly disparaged Kate's looks, describing her as "not handsome but there is hardly anyone who appears better."[13] Harriet was unable or unwilling to provide the approval that Kate needed. Kate damned her with faint praise in her memoirs. She remarked that her stepmother's inability to show gratitude proved that "even the best of women have opportunities for improvement."[14] Kate wanted to stay with her family, but that was apparently not what Harriet had in mind.

Harriet lost no time in restructuring the Beecher household. Aunt Esther and Grandma Beecher were moved out with two weeks' notice. Gradually, Harriet waged a steady campaign to push the older children, including Kate, out of the nest. Harriet wrote to her sister Lucy in December that Edward "probably will be a great scholar. He and William are soon to be absent and never very much more under parental instruction."[15] Edward was to enter Yale in 1818, and William, who his father believed was not very smart, would be apprenticed as a clerk in a general store.[16] With Harriet's support, Lyman began pressing Kate, William, and Edward to seek religious conversion, but he had limited success. As the boys left home, he poured out his anguish about their unconverted state to William, lamenting that "my heart sinks within me at the thought that every one of my own dear children are without God in the world, and without Christ and without hope. I have no child prepared to die."[17]

Kate's closest friends in Litchfield became engaged or married in 1818. Although she was happy for them, it increased the pressure on Kate to consider her own prospects for matrimony. In February, her friends Betsy Burr and Stephen Mason, who boarded with the Beechers, were married by her father, Lyman, in the Beecher residence.[18] Kate was the maid of honor. She wrote a fanciful narrative poem about Roman gods to commemorate the event, in which she paired gods with goddesses as couples. Interestingly, she connected herself as Diana, goddess of the hunt, fertility, and the moon, with John P. Brace as Momus, the god of satire.[19] With a hint of her emotions about wedlock, Kate's verses noted ambivalently that "in the married state, some joys, but many crosses wait."[20] That summer, Louisa's secret fiancé, Uriel Holmes, tragically died of consumption. But by the end of the year, twenty-five-year-old Louisa was engaged to eighteen-year-old William Gould, son of Judge Gould, one of the proprietors of Litchfield Law School.[21]

John P. Brace. Courtesy of the Litchfield Historical Society, Litchfield, CT.

That left only Kate and John P. Brace unattached among her intimate social circle. At some point during 1818, Kate became a teacher at Litchfield Female Academy.[22] That put her in close daily contact with her best male friend. He was handsome, smart, and flirtatious. He seemed to prefer sizzling affairs, whereas Kate was looking for lasting romance. Perhaps they were just friends, but it's clear that they became unusually close colleagues. They shared gossip about romantic relationships in town. He was not bashful about using suggestive literary innuendos to make a point with Kate. John P had a pattern of falling quickly in love and then becoming depressed for fear his lover didn't completely return his sentiments. That's what happened when he broke off his engagement in 1817.[23] Kate was probably a welcoming shoulder he could cry on. But did their relationship ever cross over and become romance? It is a possibility.

Then, late in 1818, Lucy Porter came to live with the Beechers for the winter, apparently at the request of her sister Harriet, who probably wanted Lucy's help with her new son, Frederick Beecher. He had been born in September, just over ten months after her wedding to Lyman.[24] But Harriet also may have been trying to help Lucy, who had turned twenty-one and was still single and without a beau. Lucy needed to find a husband, and a winter in Litchfield might increase her chances. Her marital prospects had declined in tandem with the fortunes of the Federalist political party. Her uncle Rufus King had been the last Federalist presidential candidate in 1816, and the party was no longer a national factor.[25] As Lucy's proximity to power ebbed, many Litchfield Law School students were now beyond her reach. But the handsome and intelligent John P. Brace was squarely within her grasp. He was a charming lover but didn't have enough money to be a serious suitor for most of the wealthier women attending LFA. John P may have been the target of Lucy's affection from the beginning.

By spring, Lucy and John P were engaged. The nature of Kate's relationship with John P would have been critical to her feelings about what transpired. Was he ever Kate's beau or just an extremely close friend? Was Kate outmaneuvered by the clever and prettier Lucy? Or did Kate gracefully facilitate a relationship between Lucy and John P? Depending on Kate's true feelings for John P, she could have been depressed or satisfied. In April, Kate wrote her uncle Samuel about the engagement: "They will settle here which will be a great comfort to Mama & all of us."[26] If Kate had married John P, she would have stayed in Litchfield, and they might have lived with the Beechers like Lucy and John P subsequently did. That could have been a little too close for Harriet's comfort. With so many interests at work and no direct evidence, it is hard to be certain what happened.

One enigmatic clue is found in John P's diary entry years later, dated September 30, 1850. He described his serial love affairs, followed by depression and messy breakups, as a behavioral disorder. It may have been a mental state termed *limerence*. Some people with strong romantic attachments can become severely depressed. They fear their partner doesn't really love them, which can lead to destructive behavior. John P wrote, "I was cured of it, in the winter of 1819 by the efforts of Lucy Porter and Catharine Beecher."[27] Kate must have played a pivotal role, or he would have simply credited his wife, Lucy. Did his friend Kate talk him out of his depression so that he could marry Lucy? Or did Kate break off a romance in a manner that ended the behavioral cycle and paved the way for him to settle down with Lucy? It remains a complicated mystery.

Whatever the case, Kate was soon dispatched to Boston to consider a match proposed by her family. It was a marriage that would have permanently removed Kate from home. The suitor was smart, successful, witty, and interested in her. Kate was likely pleased to have a real chance at courtship, even if it was arranged.[28] She had no serious prospects in Litchfield. In an April letter to her uncle Samuel, she wrote, "I expect to spend this summer in visiting mama's friends in Boston & Portland in company with Mama's sister Lucy." Kate neglected to tell Uncle Samuel that she was resigning her teaching position at Litchfield Female Academy. Instead, she foreshadowed marriage: "This winter past I have been housekeeper & have learnt to do a great many things which I did not know before which every woman ought to know."[29] Lucy had played a suspicious matchmaking role for Lyman and Harriet. And she had multiple possible motives for Kate's match. It may have been simply a friendly act or a consolation prize for losing John P. It was certainly a convenient way to help her sister push Kate out of the nest. Was Lucy acting on Kate's behalf or as a double agent for Harriet? Situations like this appeared to be Lucy's specialty.

Kate took the coach for Boston in May 1819 and was soon joined by Lucy. Kate's next three months in Massachusetts were spent in the prosperous home of Harriet and Lucy's sister, Aunt Isabella Homes, and her husband, Henry, a prosperous merchant in Boston. Ironically, it was the same place where, two years earlier, Lyman Beecher had been introduced to Harriet Porter. Kate instantly adored her solicitous Boston relatives, whom she deemed attentive and generous.[30] She also wrote her friend Louisa a glowing report about a visit to her aunt Almira and uncle John Goddard's home outside Boston. Almira had created a country home with gardens of spectacular beauty. Uncle Homes arranged a coach to take Kate and Lucy the four and a half miles outside of Boston to visit one day. The intensity and impulsive nature of Kate's emotions regarding the visit provide a sense of her personality. Kate rhapsodized in a letter to Louisa:

> As we drove into her yard it seemed as if we were entering Eden . . . We wandered to the foot of the garden where was a large green & in the center among a multitude of trees were two large natural rocks & split open so curiously . . . Between the split rocks supported by two trees was a most romantic seat placed & all looked so beautiful & the air was so soft & perfumed with sweets & the landscape was so fine that if I may so speak I was mad with delight. Lucy & I climbed to the top of the rocks & shouted for joy . . . I was right glad there was no gentleman with us for

I should most assuredly have fallen in love in such a beautiful romantic spot.[31]

The power of such an attractive spot to call forth Kate's unabashed feelings was telling. Her notions of poetry and romance were clearly grounded in her love of Scottish literature. The romantic poems and novels of the period idealized the sentimental connection with beautiful places. But in this case, Kate suggested that a beautiful place could cause *her* to fall in love with a man.

As she sent letters from Boston, Kate demonstrated how her ego was still wrapped in Litchfield relationships. She begged Louisa for news about her friends.[32] The girlish manner in which Kate requested more information reminds one that she was still a teenager. She ended a letter to Louisa by asking, "Why did you not write by Mrs. Q—you naughty girl—You must answer speedily . . . I don't think our Litchfield friends have worn out mind or pens by their frequent communications."[33] One of the "pens" she lamented belonged to John P. Brace. He had remained in Litchfield while Lucy accompanied Kate to Boston. He planned to come to Boston to visit in the fall prior to their wedding in November.[34] He finally wrote to Kate—a three-page, closely spaced letter on long paper. It started with apologies for not writing sooner and was chock-full of the tidbits and gossip about people in Litchfield that Kate craved. He prefaced his remarks: "Do not be frustrated—it won't take you more than an hour to read it." It included everyday news as well as more suggestive comments about romances. "As for Dr. Catlin (shall I go on or shall I be silent) The Doctor is Dr. Sixpence yet to all intents & prospects—Helen Peck is one of the most beautiful girls I know."[35] This was a literary reference to "Sing a Song of Sixpence," which some believe was written about King Henry VIII's lust for Anne

Boleyn.[36] The fact that John P used a sexual innuendo as an inside joke underscored the intimate nature of his friendship with Kate despite his engagement to Lucy.

Boston stirred feelings of romance and longing for home. But courtship was the main purpose of Kate's trip, and she was ready to begin. Her objective was to consider Albert Hobart as a potential suitor. He was a prosperous merchant in Boston like his good friend Uncle Henry Homes.[37] Because Kate was staying with Uncle Henry and Aunt Isabella, it was natural that Hobart was introduced to her at their home. Her tantalizing tale of romance aroused the interest of her friend Louisa in a series of three letters between May and June. No context was provided by Kate at the first mention of Albert, and it was clear that none was needed. She and Louisa must have discussed him prior to her departure for Boston.[38] She recounted their promising first meeting:

> Night before last <u>Mr. [Albert] Hobart</u> spent the evening here—I was much pleased with him & became quite acquainted with him before he went away. Miss Gross spent the evening here also—she is one of the liveliest <u>funniest</u> girls I ever saw & as Lucy & I were in high spirits we had a truly sociable time. I am sure I never felt acquainted with two persons so <u>soon</u> in my life—It was a most beautiful moonlight evening & when they went home Lucy & I went out & walked the court with them some time.[39]

The presence of Miss Gross at Kate's meeting with Albert was not really required by the rules of propriety, since Lucy was the chaperone.[40] Its purpose was to provide sufficient social ambiguity to reduce the initial pressure on Kate and Albert. It was evidence of Lucy's experience as a matchmaker. But it was apparently unnecessary based on Kate's account of her moonlight walk with Albert. And Miss Gross, who supposedly became such a close friend, was never mentioned again in any further correspondence.

The relationship between Kate and Albert was reinforced the following day when Kate and Lucy stopped by Albert Hobart's shop. "Lucy & I went out shopping for Aunt Homes & we went to [Albert] Hobart's store . . . So after some very <u>witty</u> <u>remarks</u> from him we came home. Lucy seems to treat him like a brother & I feel quite at ease in his company."[41] The timing and nature of the encounter were intended to build on the "moonlight success" of the previous evening. Lucy Porter was a highly skilled operator.

The next rendezvous between Kate and Albert was set at the State House, and Mr. Willis replaced Miss Gross as the fourth person in the group. Kate related that they "had a charming time . . . Lucy & I seated ourselves in the speakers chair & [Albert] Hobart & Willis made speeches to us—quite in legislative style. The scene from the top of the cupola was superlatively grand. I never imagined any scene so beautiful."[42] Knowing the romantic effect of beautiful places on Kate, one can only imagine what came to pass. Later in May, Kate wrote to Louisa about a planned romantic moonlight walk with Hobart:

> This week we go to visit the glass house [greenhouse] as soon as the moon shines—for evening is the time to visit that—The above mentioned gentlemen are our prime beaux & almost the only gentlemen with whom I feel acquainted. Lucy is so well acquainted with them that she feels at liberty to call upon their services whenever she pleases just as I would with John P.[43]

In the same letter to Louisa, Kate related a curious incident. It involved a young woman named Miss Fay who spread gossip about Hobart. Kate leaped to his defense and angrily labeled Miss Fay a "scandalous liar." The passage reflected Kate's quick temper and fierce loyalty as she defended the honor of someone who had obviously become close to her.[44]

Kate concluded her letter by confiding in Louisa that "[Albert] Hobart is not at all the character I expected & looks no more like what I had conceived than 'I to Hercules' as Shakespeare and John Brace quaintly observe. However I like him very much so far."[45] The scholarly allusion to Hercules was a testament to Brace's influence and the quality of education at LFA. It was taken from one of Hamlet's famous soliloquies, which appears in act I, scene 2.[46] It must have been one of John Brace's favorite Shakespeare quotes for Kate to use it with Louisa without explanation.

A few weeks later, in an early-June letter to Louisa, the romance with Hobart was evident with the predictable impact of beautiful places on Kate's emotions. Litchfield had given her a sophisticated sense of emotional and physical relationships between young men and women. Kate was clearly aroused by her encounter with Hobart:

> We went with Willis & Hobart to see the New England Museum . . . After we left we went to walk in the Mall—It was calm & bright moonlight & I never had so delightful a walk. Oh that beautiful mall you can't imagine how sweetly it looks with its noble trees & the moon & the water & the buildings—Oh it is enough to make ones <u>Hair bristle</u> to see it.[47]

Louisa surely read between the lines. One can imagine Kate

and Albert holding hands and perhaps sharing a kiss or two. As was sometimes the custom with letters, Lucy filled the remaining empty space in Kate's letter to Louisa before it was sent. She added a few general comments and then penned the critical caution, "Louisa dear, now if you do let <u>any</u> <u>mortal</u> know what Catharine has written you, I will be mad—remember, It is for you and <u>you</u> <u>alone</u>."[48] Kate spent the rest of the summer and early fall in Boston and Portland before returning to Litchfield in October. There are no surviving letters from that period of her trip. It seems odd that she would suddenly stop writing to her friend. A reasonable assumption is that her correspondence was intentionally destroyed to erase conversations about Hobart.

Kate's family considered Hobart to be a promising suitor. From Kate's surviving letters early in her trip, a budding romance seemed likely to result in courtship. But the curious thing missing from these letters is any mention of music, which was so important to Kate. At some point, something happened, and Kate changed her mind. Perhaps she rebelled against the marital pressure of her family and friends. She later claimed that Hobart was not sufficiently affectionate.[49] By rejecting him as a suitor, she displayed an independent streak that became a hallmark of her character. But she equally demonstrated her commitment to romance. Kate Beecher could not be pushed into a loveless marriage. She was holding out for a hero.

4

Focused

> I never knew a man come to greatness or eminence
> who lay abed late in the morning.
> —Jonathan Swift

October 1817–September 1819

Alexander relished the challenge as he leaned into his career at Yale in October 1817. The newly appointed professor had been entrusted with an appealing array of academic and administrative tasks. Yet the intellectual stimulation of his expanded responsibilities siphoned emotional energy from his personal life. He had no extra time to spare for religion or romance. Alexander knew he needed to adjust his priorities, yet he was unwilling to compromise his professional standards. The consequences of continuing on the same path were loneliness and the potential loss of his soul. But the attraction of his academic pursuits drew him like a moth to a flame. On his first day as a professor, he faced a hundred pairs of inquiring eyes in the prestigious college hall. His relentless ambition focused his attention, and despite his fears, he dove into his lecture.

Delivering presentations was the only portion of Alexander's new role that troubled him. Although he was a gifted thinker and writer, he was not similarly endowed when it came to public speaking. He was a bit apprehensive and rarely used gestures, so the quality of his orations appeared to be below the caliber of their substance.[1] He was self-conscious about this defect and blamed it for being named salutatorian rather than valedictorian when he graduated from Yale in 1813.[2] As a new professor, he was asked to demonstrate science experiments as part of unscripted lectures. These were delivered to large gatherings that included juniors, seniors, medical students, and colleagues. He wrote his father in January 1818, "At first it seemed rather awkward to address a hundred present . . . especially as the nature of the lectures require me to extemporize; but I have now made it tolerably familiar."[3] In addition to the impromptu presentations, he was expected to work on a set of forty written science lectures to develop a new course of study. Each one required significant research and careful documentation in fields where he was not yet an expert. His boundless curiosity was aroused by topics that included astronomy, gravitation, motion, pneumatics, electricity, and optics.[4]

Alexander added two other significant responsibilities as an adjunct professor. He was asked to help his colleagues examine candidates for admission to determine their readiness for collegiate study. He also was charged with oversight of room and board for Yale's three hundred students.[5] But Yale expected him to perform these new functions in addition to continuing as a tutor for three more years. Although his salary was increased from $450 to $700 annually, he effectively had two jobs. Alexander was drawn to the challenge by his intellect and competitive nature. His mind was never at rest, which suited his personality. He had to reorganize his life to make sufficient time to focus on his academic career. His personal life had to subsist on whatever time and energy remained. When he finally found a moment to write his parents a month after school started, he apologized and blamed the delay on his heavy workload, which he termed "incessant engagement."[6]

Continuous self-improvement was Alexander's career maxim. He used his religious diary to reflect on his performance in his new appointment as a professor. He concluded that he could and must do better. Although his intellect had earned the respect of his students, he feared that his approach was too rigid. He aspired to "that deliberate, affectionate manner" of a mentor. He confessed in his diary that under the stimulation of work, he had "fallen asleep in regard to religious concerns." He questioned, "What less than a miracle of divine mercy will be hereafter able to rouse me from my slumber?" His neglect was a significant issue because religious devotion was an important element of education at Yale. A tutor was meant to be both an academic instructor and a moral guide. Could a man who had religious doubts play both roles? Strengthening his beliefs was a "necessity," given his new, broader "sphere of influence" as a professor.[7]

Alexander felt the strain of his work as the academic year progressed. By November 1817, he reflected in his diary that he had already lived a third of the normal seventy-year life span. It caused him to ponder "the shortness of a human life . . . [and the] necessity of laying up for myself treasures in heaven."[8] But he did not write in his religious diary again until prompted by his birthday in July 1818: "During this long interval that this manuscript has lain untouched, the subject of religion has been more nearly than ever banished from my thoughts." He also was troubled by his lack of progress as an instructor. In what may have been a bit of false modesty, he hoped he didn't "fall below mediocrity" in the eyes of his students.[9] Just two months later at commencement, he was gratified but again downplayed the compliment when his students "testified, by a splendid + significantly valuable present, that they have considered me as not wholly deficient in the discharge of my duties towards them."[10]

Alexander was too enthralled with academics to attend to his spiritual life. He continued to engage in public prayers, which were part of the Yale regimen. But he neglected his private prayers and religious diary. When he finally wrote in his diary on August 1, 1819, it had been eleven months since his previous entry:

> Another year has gone by + brought me to the commencement of my 26th year. In respect to performance of religious duties it has been a blank . . . On the whole I consider my neglect of the form of private devotion, to be reduced to an absolute certainty, unless almighty, unmerited and long abused mercy shall interpose for my rescue from final ruin.[11]

This was the final entry he made in his religious journal as he apparently abandoned the conversion process his parents had encouraged.

During his first two years as a professor, Alexander's heavy workload also caused him to neglect his personal life. All his friends had managed to make time for courtship despite their busy schedules. Alexander made light of his lack of romantic prospects. He observed to his father in a July 1817 letter that his new salary as a professor was plenty for a single man, "respecting which, by the way, there is no present prospect to the contrary."[12] Yet he reflected more seriously in November 1817 on his uncommon status as a bachelor. His friend Eleazar Fitch, at the age of twenty-six, was engaged to Elizabeth Wooster, a young woman he met in New Haven. Alexander wrote his parents that "our professor of Divinity, Mr. Fitch . . . is to be married soon, so that I shall be the only permanent officer here who has nothing to do with family concerns."[13] Alexander began boarding with Eleazar and his new bride in January 1818. "Mr. Fitch . . . gives universal satisfaction. His private character as a companion & friend is unusually excellent, and he is withal a great musician." Alexander loved singing and playing the organ with Eleazar. Making space for music in his life and living with the newlyweds awakened his desire to start his own family. He wrote to his father in January 1818, "Indeed I now feel very sensibly the evils of having been so long secluded from family."[14] His loneliness was reinforced when his good friend Denison Olmsted was married in June 1818 to a woman he had courted for years by correspondence.[15]

In the summer of 1818, Alexander began to consider his marital prospects more seriously. But where was a workaholic like Alexander to find a wife? It didn't appear likely in New Haven, where he tended to stay within the college walls. He had written his father, "I do not intend that intercourse with people in town shall ever employ any considerable portion of my time"— just enough to be respectable.[16] As he traveled home to Franklin to tutor his siblings that summer, his thoughts returned to Eliza Wheeler. Alexander would have seen Miss Wheeler at the post office in Medway and learned that she was going to attend Litchfield Female Academy.[17] The school was expensive, but Eliza's grandfather was a respected medical doctor in town with the means to help. He had served during the American Revolution as a surgeon on the staff of George Washington. His family was familiar with the Litchfield network and understood the benefits of sending her to LFA.[18] Eliza was approaching the age of twenty-one, where some might think she would never marry. She may have felt the pressure to find a suitor, and Alexander was a logical candidate. Perhaps she hoped to find a desirable match in Litchfield, or maybe her attendance was intended to attract Alexander's attention in nearby New Haven.

Alexander took a long journey during his September break in 1818. He wanted to visit scholars at two colleges: Hamilton and Williams. He then visited relatives in Vermont. He made it a point to stop to call on Eliza Wheeler as he started his trip. He wrote his parents that "we passed through Litchfield, where I saw Miss Wheeler, who is doing well."[19] The entry in his travel journal about the visit to Litchfield was a bit more revealing. "The only acquaintance whom I have found in town is Miss W. a young lady of the female school here, whose amiableness of character had interested me much in her behalf."[20] Alexander felt the peer pressure from his friends' weddings. Eliza was the logical choice his family expected him to pursue. The irony is that Alexander took his first tentative step toward courtship in Litchfield not with Kate Beecher but with her apparent rival Eliza Wheeler.[21]

But his intentions for courtship were soon set aside. When Alexander returned to New Haven in October, he dove back into work and became busier than ever writing for journals. In January he started contributing to a new periodical, the *Christian Spectator*, founded by Lyman Beecher and published in New Haven.[22] His career as a writer soared in 1819 when "Essay on Musical Temperament" was published by his friend Benjamin Silliman in the influential *American Journal of Science and Arts*. It provided Alexander immediate recognition, respect, and access to important academic circles in America and Europe.[23]

The appearance of the Great Comet of 1819 on July 1 captured Alexander's complete attention.[24] As a scientist, he was excited to study the unexpected celestial body. This was a major opportunity that could not be postponed. Meteorology was the perfect application of his mathematical skills to a natural phenomenon. Intense public interest stimulated demand for press accounts from experts like him. He wrote his father in August, "The comet has cost me a very laborious series of observations & calculations: you will see the results in the July No. of the Christian Spectator, & probably some of the newspapers."[25] The comet consumed all his free time and forced him to cancel his trip home for summer break. He was obliged to decline a request to deliver the prestigious annual Phi Beta Kappa oration at the commencement ceremony in September. It's not clear when the invitation was extended or what happened, but 1819 was the only year in which no oration was delivered.[26]

Alexander's interest in Eliza Wheeler was eclipsed by his academic endeavors in 1819. He did little to pursue his intentions toward her. Although Eliza and Alexander were a natural match, he unfortunately had a rival for her affections. When she returned home from Litchfield without a new beau that summer, a talented man named Sewall Harding was waiting. She was twenty-two, Sewall was twenty-six, and Alexander was twenty-five.[27] As smart as Alexander was about academics, he was not similarly gifted in matters of the heart . . . and the clock was ticking.

PART II

―

Relationship

5

Second Chances

> If music be the food of love, play on.
> —William Shakespeare, *Twelfth Night*

October 1819–March 1821

Kate returned home in October 1819 after she rejected the proposed match with Albert Hobart in Boston. Life was miserable. She had no probable suitors, her father pressed her to seek religious conversion, and her stepmother wanted her to move out on her own. Sunsets, music, and poetry were her primary sources of comfort. But she needed a source of permanent support. Her alternatives to marriage were to become a spinster housekeeper for some relative or get a job. Her brothers were too young to need a housekeeper, and returning to Boston seemed an unlikely prospect. Her position at Litchfield Female Academy had been filled. Yet her experience as a teacher could help Kate support herself at a school in a new town. And a fresh start might help her find romance. But there was no obvious place to go, and she would miss her family. Her life was at a crossroads.

As she contemplated her future, watching the lovely sunsets

that adorned the evening sky became one of Kate's favorite activities. The sun's rays passed obliquely through the atmosphere, creating intense red and yellow hues that danced upon the clouds. It was said in the Beecher family that "Litchfield sunsets were famous, perhaps because watched by more appreciative and intelligent eyes."[1] But for Kate, sunsets were also special because of the emotional connection. She sensed a romantic bond with her natural surroundings. These feelings were essential to her identity.[2] If she ever fell in love with a man, it would probably be while viewing beautiful sunsets together.

Romance and faith weighed on Kate's heart. She wanted to find true love with someone with a deep affection for her. But if that was not possible, she was willing to remain single. Her father wanted her to submit to God in order to save her soul. He pressed her to seriously seek conversion. But the traditional path to faith through conversion did not come naturally to someone with a sunny disposition like Kate. Although she didn't know it at the time, her mother, Roxana, had struggled in a similar fashion with conversion. Both of them saw life as good, inspired by a loving God.[3] One evening, Kate was deeply moved while watching the sun go down. The beauty evoked tender sentiments as usual. But as the light dimmed and the clouds dissipated, she was struck by the contrast as exquisite stars emerged in the darkening heavens. She saw it as a metaphor for the ephemeral nature of life and the enduring power of God. Inspired by her spiritual awakening, she sat down and penned these lines:[4]

The Evening Cloud

See yonder cloud along the west,
In gay fantastic splendor dress'd;
Fancy's bright visions charm the eye,

Sweet fairy bowers in prospect lie,
And blooming fields smile from the sky
Decked in the hues of Even!
But short its evanescent stay,
Its brilliant masses fade away,
The breeze floats off its visions gay,
And clears the face of heaven.

Thus to fond man does Life's fair scene
Delusive spread its cheerful green.
Before his path shine Pleasure's bowers,
Each smiling field seems dress'd in flowers,
Hope leads him on, and shows his hours
For Peace and Pleasure given—
But one by one his hopes decay,
Each flattering vision fades away,
Each cheering scene charms to betray,
And nought remains but Heaven.
                                    C. B.

Lyman Beecher was encouraged when he first read Kate's poem. He felt it demonstrated that she was making progress toward conversion. It was a promising step, which he rewarded by publishing her work in the February 1820 issue of the *Christian Spectator*. Her identity as the poet was indicated only by her initials. Lyman hoped it would inspire deeper expressions of her faith. He never expected it to improve her prospects for marriage.

In theory, there was plenty of time for Kate to find a beau in Litchfield. She was a talented, warmhearted extrovert. She was fun-loving and smart. Her friends Louisa and Lucy were well positioned in the community to make appropriate introductions.

But as 1820 progressed, Kate remained without any prospects. It was difficult to find a man who could match her sense of romance and passion. And her father's fiery reputation was not helpful with potential suitors. Rev. Beecher had offended many people during his unsuccessful fight against those who wished to disestablish the Congregational Church in Connecticut. Litchfield Law School student Horace Mann shared a common perception of Lyman in a letter to his sister, describing him as "a rigid, hidebound Calvinist, adding to the rigorous principles of his creed; the quarrelsomeness of old age & all the bigotry of Connecticut."[5] As time passed, Kate became less certain that she was meant to marry, and some in her family began to believe she would become an old maid.[6]

Given the pressure from her parents to move out, Kate chose to depart her beloved Litchfield to make her way in the world. A teaching position in New London, Connecticut, was arranged for her, starting in the spring of 1821. Music lessons would be an important part of her job. The piano was becoming a popular instrument, and cultured young ladies needed instruction. So Kate dedicated a significant portion of 1820 to mastering the portfolio of songs she had transcribed with her friend Louisa. But she also began to expand her repertoire by purchasing sheet music that was published in New York and Philadelphia. Her choices reflected a continuing preference for romance and love songs. Eventually, she selected twenty-five pieces, which were bound together in a leather folio. The cover had "Catharine E. Beecher No 2" embossed in gold letters.[7]

While Kate practiced piano in 1820, Alexander was enjoying his new celebrity status as a professor and author. When he had first visited Brown College in 1817 as a tutor, Alexander had been almost ignored.[8] He was not invited to dinner and had to sit with students rather than faculty during prayers. Since becoming a professor, he had been shown more attention as he visited most of the significant Northeast colleges during 1818 and 1819. The purpose of his visits was to establish professional connections and compare other institutions to Yale. Following the successful publication of "Essay on Musical Temperament," he was shown a flattering degree of respect during a visit to Princeton in May 1820. A week later when he visited Philadelphia, he was invited to dinner with gentlemen of distinction. As an introvert, he still favored solitary activities. Nevertheless, he was in great demand as an interesting conversationalist. He was even given a private tour of the US Mint by one of its directors.[9]

Alexander had built his reputation among scholars as a scientific writer. But in 1820, he demonstrated a creative flair in two articles published in the *Microscope*. He wrote a travel piece about his visit to Vermont and a fictional account of an interplanetary voyage by Captain Lemuel Gulliver, the hero from Jonathan Swift's novel *Gulliver's Travels*. The *Microscope* was a literary magazine that was published by twenty-five gentlemen in New Haven between March and September 1820. Alexander was both a subscriber and contributor. The magazine featured poetry, original stories, and essays. It favored the more serious poetry of John Milton, Alexander Pope, and John Dryden over the contemporary romantic works of Sir Walter Scott, Lord Byron, and Robert Burns.[10] The simple farm boy from Franklin had become the sophisticated Professor A. M. Fisher, a budding Renaissance man.

A series of events during 1820 combined to refocus Alexander on religion. In January, his mother, Sally Fisher, achieved conversion at the age of forty-eight. It was noteworthy because she was similar in many ways to her intellectual son. That summer, a major religious revival swept New Haven. Frequent meetings at the Congregational churches were heavily attended. Even the Episcopal Church was holding meetings two or three times a week, which, according to Alexander, was "an extraordinary thing for this denomination."[11] Alexander apparently had another bipolar episode, so he did not plan to return home during fall break. But a typhus epidemic swept New Haven and convinced him to escape town during September. In October, the day after he returned to Yale from vacation, a fire broke out at the head of the wharf in New Haven. Twenty-six stores were completely destroyed. He reflected to his parents in an early November letter, "This was a lesson on the uncertainty of the tenure by which we hold earthly possessions, which the most callous mind must have understood & felt."[12] By the end of the year, hundreds of new members had achieved conversion and were admitted to the two Congregational churches and the Yale College church.[13] Although Alexander's letters to his parents indicated a spiritual awakening, he didn't resume his religious diary. He needed to find his own spiritual path.

Recognition of his mortality also rekindled Alexander's desire to start a family. But news from home in Massachusetts was the psychological blow that dramatically altered his approach to courtship. Eliza Wheeler married Sewall Harding on November 3, 1820.[14] Alexander learned of their engagement while he was in Franklin during his fall break in September. It had been over two years since his friends Eleazar Fitch and Denison Olmsted had been married. Alexander had naive intentions to pursue Eliza, but he procrastinated until it was too late. His failure stared him in the face as that potential door to matrimony was permanently closed. Alexander decided it was time to find a wife. But the conventions of courtship were unfamiliar territory for him. He was uncharacteristically without a plan.

Alexander's thoughts were turned to Kate Beecher by chance one evening late in 1820. He was reading back issues in his stack of accumulated journals and picked up the *Christian Spectator* from February 1820. He had just finished an interesting travelogue on Montreal and was about to dive into a scholarly article that parsed the meaning of two Hebrew words in the Bible.[15] He noticed an interesting piece of poetry signed with her initials. He read it and recognized that the poet was clearly intelligent, sensitive, and spiritual. The poem touched his emerging religious faith. He must have enjoyed the imagery and artful selection of words. Best of all, it was concise and insightful. He liked it enough to ask his friend Eleazar Fitch, one of the *Spectator*'s editors, to identify the poet. Eleazar told him it was the work of Catharine "Kate" Beecher.

Alexander was acquainted with the energetic Lyman Beecher through various Yale connections. He had heard Lyman speak in New York at a Bible convention in May 1820. He noted candidly in his travel diary that "Dr. Beecher great, but too long."[16] Alexander was quite familiar with Edward Beecher, who was a junior at Yale. Edward was handsome, personable, and a brilliant scholar. If Kate Beecher was anything like her brother, Alexander was intrigued. Eleazar was one of Lyman Beecher's closest colleagues at Yale, so he was familiar with Kate's background.[17] He must have reported that she was talented, about twenty years old, and single. Most importantly to Alexander, she had no current suitors. In fact, her parents hoped that she might find a husband in New London, where she was headed to teach in the spring. Finding a smart woman was important to Alexander's plan. Based on his initial impression, he decided she was worthy of pursuit.

Although their characters were quite different, Kate and

Alexander were potentially a good match. They had complementary personalities that could benefit each other. She was an extroverted free spirit, and he was an introverted planner. She could help him embrace his emotions, and he could help focus her numerous interests. She was twenty, and he was twenty-six—common ages for couples to marry during the 1820s. Beyond the Yale connections, they had several things in common. Both were smart and preferred conversations with intelligent people. Both had been raised in Federalist, Congregational families, so their political and religious backgrounds were aligned. Both had struggled with conversion experiences and had been wounded by their unsuccessful attempts at romance. This was a second chance at courtship for both Kate and Alexander.[18]

The critical question was how Alexander could make the acquaintance of Kate when she lived in a different town. It was not like him to make a bold first move to meet a young woman, but that was precisely what he did. Beecher family lore, as told by family biographer Lyman Beecher Stowe, recalled that Alexander persuaded a "clergyman classmate who was to preach for Dr. Beecher" to take Alexander to Litchfield to meet Kate.[19] Alexander's friend Eleazar was the individual likely described by Stowe. Lyman was pleasantly surprised when Eleazar broached Alexander's interest in Kate. The ensuing conversation resulted in an invitation to bring Alexander to Litchfield when Eleazar visited to preach. How much of this plan was shared with Kate in advance is unknown. But she was likely aware and flattered by Alexander's interest.

One can imagine how Alexander and Eleazar traversed the muddy spring roads on horseback during March 1821.[20] They arrived in Litchfield on Saturday before the start of Sabbath. Alexander's voice would have been full of nervous anticipation.

A visiting clergyman like Eleazar typically boarded with the Beechers. But under the circumstances, the pair probably lodged at the public house where Alexander stayed when he had visited Eliza Wheeler in September 1818. Alexander would have been anxious as he prepared for his introduction to Kate. He had no idea what sort of man would be an appealing suitor for her. Kate would have risen that morning and wondered how their first encounter would unfold. True to form, her roommate Louisa would have teased Kate unmercifully about the prospects of courtship and romance with the young professor. It had all transpired so unexpectedly.

Kate smiled at everyone as she entered the church. She would have spotted Alexander immediately, the stranger who sat next to her father's clergy friend Eleazar. He was a bit serious, but the important thing to Kate was whether he had a warm heart. Everyone in Litchfield would have peered intently at the distinguished pair of visitors. Perhaps they perceived the purpose of Alexander's visit. Small-town gossip had a way of quickly discerning and communicating such affairs. Sitting in the pews, Kate and Alexander had ample opportunity to study each other during Eleazar's lengthy sermon. But they had to be careful to avoid drawing attention to themselves. Alexander would have followed the sermon intently and nodded in a scholarly manner as religious points were made.

After patiently enduring his friend's lengthy sermon and the pleasantries after the service, Alexander finally received his coveted introduction to Kate.[21] Eleazar and Alexander were invited for Sunday dinner, and Alexander gallantly escorted Kate the single block to her home. Once inside the Beecher home and out of the brisk March air, they likely warmed themselves by the fire in the parlor, away from inquiring eyes, until dinner was served.

There would have been a minimum of ten family members at the meal in the Beecher dining room: Lyman, Harriet, Kate, and five of her siblings, plus Lucy and John Brace. Combined with Eleazar and Alexander, there must have been a dozen people seated for dinner—a typical Beecher repast.[22]

The table buzzed with excitement and speculation at the sight of Kate seated advantageously next to the brilliant young professor from Yale. As usual, Alexander engaged those seated near him in polite and appropriate conversation. He always inquired about their interests and well-being. But he was particularly attentive and kind to Kate. It had been eighteen months since she had been treated that way by Albert Hobart in Boston. Alexander typically asked a new female acquaintance like Kate about her family and pursued whatever topics she preferred. Each sensed the natural intelligence of the other as smart people invariably do. Although his manners were polished, Alexander was socially awkward in dealing with a woman since he had no romantic experience. Yet he was a breath of fresh air compared to sophisticated Litchfield men. He was clearly a challenge, but sweet.

After dinner, the couple was allowed to retire to the relative privacy of the parlor, albeit with the doors open. Alexander asked Kate to recite some of her poetry for him. He was particularly interested in hearing the poem that had first turned his attention to her.[23] He wanted to understand her thoughts that had inspired it. The volumes she had available to read included her favorite romantic verses from Burns and Byron.[24] Alexander needed to broaden his tastes in poetry if he wanted to court this woman. According to family reports passed down to later generations of Beechers, Kate and Alexander recited many verses together that afternoon.

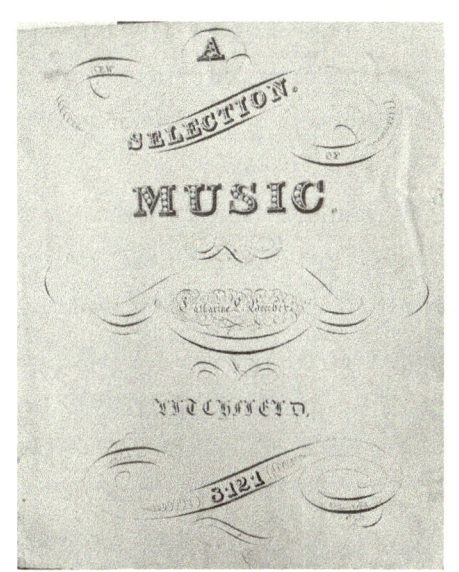

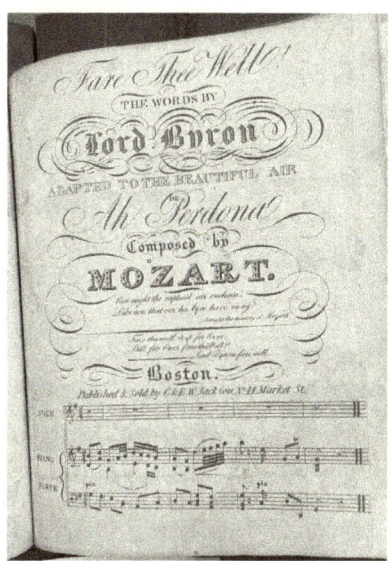

Kate's book of piano music. The lettering for the introduction of Kate's Music Book was done by her brother William. Note that he transposed the first two digits of the year 1821 as "8121," which is a clue that he may have been dyslexic. He was probably smarter and more capable than believed by his family, who didn't send him to college. Courtesy of Harriet Beecher Stowe Center, Hartford, CT.

One thing led to another, and at the piano in the parlor, they discovered their mutual talent for and love of music. It was an unexpected connection. Their acquaintance became more intimate when Alexander asked Kate to play the piano for him. He was totally enchanted and loved to watch her fingers as she played. This was the sort of attention Kate craved.[25] She must have been surprised when Alexander volunteered to play the piano. It was unusual for a man who was not a professional musician to play the piano. And he had enough talent to sight-read sheet music.[26] They learned to appreciate each other's singing voice as they explored Kate's songbooks. Most pieces were for a single voice, but there were four duets that they would have performed. Titles included "Love among the Roses," "Love's Young Dream," and "Blanche of Devan's Song" from a musical production of *Lady of the Lake* with lyrics by Sir Walter Scott.[27] The music connected Kate and Alexander at an emotional level that neither anticipated. Their afternoon together exposed Kate to the softer, emotional side of Alexander that his serious exterior often masked.

The first meeting between Kate and Alexander was a major success. Lyman and Harriet's prayers for her to find a suitor seemed to have been answered. Alexander was a promising young man, and if he married Kate, the couple would settle in New Haven. That was close enough to visit but far enough to remove her from the family payroll. Alexander was sold on Kate immediately. She was smart and delightful, and she could bring the music he adored to their family someday. He felt an immediate spark of affection for her. Kate was probably a bit surprised that they connected so well. It must have been the music. She had to endure Louisa's teasing that night about the charming young professor. He was an attractive match for most girls, but he was a bit reserved for an extrovert like Kate. She needed to learn more about him.

Alexander was clueless when it came to the protocols of wooing a young lady. He asked Lyman's permission the next day to start courting Kate. Although that was the ultimate purpose of meeting her, by 1821, men would have waited to become better acquainted with a woman first. They would have made sure she was similarly inclined before speaking to her father. Lyman's enthusiastic blessing gave Alexander little reason to believe he had done anything inappropriate. On the contrary, it bolstered his confidence that he was on the right track.[28] In hindsight, Lyman's impetuous response had been premature. He should have spoken to his daughter before providing a response. Kate was flattered by Alexander's interest, but they had just met. It was Kate's decision if she wanted Alexander as a suitor. It was an awkward situation.

Lyman was a strong advocate for courtship and made a determined effort to extricate himself from his predicament. He made a practical suggestion to get Kate and Alexander together for a long visit. She would be leaving soon for her new teaching job in New London. Lyman proposed that he would drive Kate to New Haven, and then Alexander could drive her the rest of the way to New London.[29] That would cut Lyman's trip in half. It would also give Kate and Alexander an excellent opportunity to become better acquainted in private. She could decide at the end of the trip if she wanted to pursue courtship. Although Lyman's suggestion was pragmatic, it was scandalous. It crossed the boundary of nineteenth-century propriety to allow Kate and Alexander to travel without a chaperone.[30] Kate had significant reservations. She had only met him once. One could imagine the gossip about a girl traveling alone with a man. Alexander also had strong concerns about the propriety of the plan. Regardless of Lyman's blessing, he would have to be extraordinarily careful about his behavior during such a journey.

This was a potential second chance at courtship for both of them. Serendipity and Alexander's uncharacteristically bold behavior had brought the young couple together. Music had connected them and was the food to nourish their relationship. Alexander was convinced that Kate was right for him. She was interested in Alexander, but she needed more time before proceeding. Traveling alone with Alexander was a major step. The ultimate decision was in Kate's hands.

6

Courtship

> He was exactly the man, who in disposition and talents, would best suit her.
>
> His understanding and temper, though unlike her own, would have answered her wishes.
>
> —Jane Austen, *Pride and Prejudice*

April 1821–August 1821

The temperature was brisk as Kate and Lyman set out at dawn for their nine-hour drive by carriage to New Haven. Their warm conversation reflected the strong bond between them. Yet something unspoken was different this time, a sentiment of sorrow often shared at such moments of separation between a parent and child. Kate was leaving for New London to start a new job. She had agreed to let Alexander drive her to New London without a chaperone. Lyman was taking her to meet him in New Haven. She was considering a potential courtship, as her father encouraged. But after the Boston affair, there was no way he could push her into an unwanted marriage. Yet Alexander was a most promising suitor. Romance was possible with a man who loved music and recited poetry. Perhaps there was a way for both Kate's and Lyman's dreams to come true. It all depended on a carriage ride with Alexander the following day.

Kate and Lyman arrived on schedule by midafternoon at the home of his good friend James Hillhouse, a former US senator and longtime treasurer of Yale.[1] After freshening up from the trip, Kate anticipated Alexander's imminent arrival. When he finally called for her, they took a leisurely walk, accompanied by her brother Edward, who was a junior at Yale. The conversation was lively, with Kate at the center, as usual. She would have been delighted to see the scholarly affinity between Alexander and Edward, imagining that one day they could be like brothers. Alexander was particularly attentive to Kate, which strengthened her attraction to him.[2] He noted the warm relationship between Kate and her brother Edward. It was the perfect opportunity to talk about the importance of family and his feelings for his brother and two sisters. He had been separated from his siblings for eight years, and it was primarily through holiday visits and letters that he maintained connections. Edward was particularly struck by Alexander's comments on the importance of kinship. In a letter to Kate the next day, he promised to establish a more regular correspondence with her. "I hope you remember what Mr. F. said during our walk & will act accordingly; we shall never regret that we acted like brothers and sisters."[3]

Kate and Alexander departed in his carriage for New London the morning after she arrived in New Haven with Lyman. The Post Road to New London was hilly as it traversed the rugged Connecticut coast. The terrain made it a longer drive than the fifty-four miles implied. They passed through Guilford, Saybrook, and Lyme, where they made stops as necessary. It was a scenic route, and the crests of ridges they crossed afforded magnificent vistas.[4] Flowering spring bushes and trees rendered the scene singularly beautiful, which would have put Kate in a romantic mood. A glance in any direction inspired conversation. True to form, Alexander discussed anything he thought was of interest to Kate. He was a walking encyclopedia and could converse on almost any topic.[5] He surely would have mentioned the landscape and towns and pointed out the original site of Yale as the "Collegiate School" in Saybrook.[6]

As their journey progressed, Alexander would have focused on the importance of his feelings for family, providing Kate with a sense of the life he hoped to create with her. This warm, affectionate side of his personality was sometimes hidden behind his scholarly facade. As usual, he inquired about Kate's family to discern her expectations for their future. They certainly discussed their mutual love of music and poetry. Perhaps they even sang a few songs they both knew. The hours together exposed Kate to Alexander's endearing wit and sense of humor and him to her kindness and delightful personality. She described the auspicious journey a few days later in a letter to her friend Louisa. "During my ride from New Haven conversation was intelligent, easy & agreeable."[7]

Alexander had agonized over how to handle his unorthodox excursion with Kate to New London. His parents had instilled strict adherence to the rules of propriety. A young man and woman were required to have a chaperone at all times when traveling together. Alexander hoped Lyman's blessing would shield them from too many questions when they arrived in New London. But he also needed to make certain that Kate had no cause to question his character. So he determined that the prudent course of action was to minimize physical contact with Kate if possible.[8] Little did he suspect that his parents' strong sense of propriety was rooted in shame from their own sexual conduct.

Alexander was born only eight months after his parents married, most likely conceived out of wedlock.[9] He would have been shocked by their behavior and the irony of what was to come.

Kate noted his awkward physical behavior during their journey.[10] Perhaps it was an accidental touch on her arm that he withdrew a bit too quickly. Or it might have included eyes averted when the moment called for them to linger. It was hard to miss for someone like Kate. His body language and difficulty expressing his emotions betrayed Alexander's lack of romantic experience. But there was perhaps an appealing sense of innocence about him. A mutual attraction developed, and before the end of their trip, they discussed courtship. Kate happily "consented to a friendly correspondence," which, by custom, she was at liberty to end whenever she pleased.[11] The romantic seed planted by their musical connection had begun to take root.

The enjoyment of their journey was interrupted upon their arrival at the home of Kate's new employer, Rev. Judd. He had neglected to make arrangements for her boarding. He apologized and offered that she could remain with his family until she found suitable accommodations. Unfortunately, there was no private space in the Judd home for her to entertain Alexander. Perhaps Alexander sensed the problem and, before departing, suggested they go for a ride to nearby Norwich on his next visit. This was a rather bold proposition. It was one thing for them to travel alone with Lyman's approval, but a second trip without a chaperone could put Kate's reputation seriously at risk. And yet, his invitation signaled a strong intent to pursue a more intimate connection. Such evidence of his desire must have appealed to her. She threw caution to the wind and said yes to his invitation.[12]

Courtship was not the only thing Lyman was pressing on Kate. Just before departing for New London, at his urging, she had drafted a set of religious resolutions "that during the approaching spring and summer I will seriously . . . seek the salvation of my soul as the first & most important object of all my pursuits. That I will allow no schemes of pleasure, no worldly plans or engage in amusement so to engross my mind as to banish the subject of religion."[13] In a letter, Lyman counseled her, "Read your own Resolutions should temptation or listlessness assail."[14] But she had clearly penned these objectives as a pious, dutiful daughter following the model for those seeking conversion. If Alexander's courtship qualified as a "scheme of pleasure," she could find herself with mutually exclusive objectives.

As Kate arose on her second morning in New London, she began to fathom the predicament she had gotten herself into by agreeing to teach at Rev. Judd's school for girls. It was more of a local finishing school for young ladies that Judd ran out of his parsonage. Judd apparently woke up "so sick with a swelled face that he could scarcely sit up." It may have been some sort of allergic reaction. Kate offered to take charge of the school until he recovered and wrote her sister Mary:

> I was an entire stranger & had never been in the school. Mr. Judd went down with me to introduce me there & I was soon seated in the great chair with a great desk before me, the presiding matron among about fifty young ladies of various ages. I felt it a great trial to begin in this manner . . . However I succeeded . . . kept the school in order & I believe gave relief & satisfaction to Mr. Judd.[15]

Kate was initially homesick in New London, but Lyman assured her that she would "recover from that as soon as the medicine of stated employment shall have time to operate."[16] Unfortunately, Kate detested teaching as much as her father did.[17] Her days were completely filled with work. Following academic subjects in the morning, she had to spend most afternoons providing individual instruction in either drawing or music. She fumed that Judd's piano was a terrible instrument, almost unplayable, and noted, "In addition to all these troubles my scholars in painting knew nothing at all... I felt discouraged & everything looked dreary."[18] Teaching in New London would be a challenge.

The lack of social activity in New London soon became unbearable for an extrovert like Kate. She reported to her sister Mary that "Mrs. Judd's youngest child was taken very sick... many people had called on me but no one could go out with me to return their calls & of course I was entirely without society of any kind."[19] The rules of nineteenth-century propriety deemed it inappropriate for Kate to go calling without an escort. She was eventually able to establish a pattern of social calls on Wednesdays and Saturdays. But ultimately, the combination of limited social interaction, the loneliness due to separation from home, plus the drudgery of teaching began to wear on Kate. She had no one in town to provide cheer and listen to her woes.

Shortly after his departure, Alexander sent Kate a nice letter about their journey. He was a good writer, and his practice was to include bits of news he believed would be of interest to the recipient, such as his safe travel home, surprises when he arrived, and his current health. For Kate, he would have provided intelligence about people of interest, such as how her brother Edward was doing at school. These were the sort of chatty letters that Kate enjoyed. And if she was looking for evidence of his attentiveness, she found it in his correspondence. Despite his hectic schedule, he was incredibly responsive. He answered the same day he received any letter she sent.[20] She was flattered but wondered if it was proper for a young lady to respond as quickly. She didn't want to appear too forward. It is unknown to what extent she shared her growing unhappiness about life in New London with Alexander. But his correspondence probably provided a consistent positive connection amid her misery.

Kate eagerly opened a joint letter from her good friends Louisa and Lucy in the middle of May. After expressing gladness that Kate was now settled, Louisa got right to the point:

> I think you must have enjoyed yourself much, while in New Haven & more going to N. London for such company as Mr. Fisher we can't meet every day. I dare say he rendered the journey peculiarly <u>interesting</u> . . . I have found out that he is the happy fellow to whom Lucy marries you in less [than] a year, so you need not despair for I don't believe you will die an old maid after all the sage prophesies of some of your relations.[21]

Louisa continued with the big news that one of the girls at school was engaged and remarked, "When one goes the rest will follow." After some family updates, she quipped, "I tease [Edward] most to death about Miss Gilbert. I shall have my hands full of teasing now Mr. F has come upon the carpet."[22] Louisa's good-natured humor as she eagerly welcomed Alexander into their intimate circle encouraged Kate. One can imagine the fun Louisa and Lucy had writing this joint letter and sharing their speculations that their friend Kate was potentially in love. While Louisa playfully pressed the case for marriage, Lucy used her page to advance Lyman's religious hopes for Kate. One can almost hear Lyman dictating the words to the accommodating facilitator, Lucy:

Dearest Kate . . . I have felt my dear sister that it was best for you to go from home & I hope you will feel so. I think you have in former days depended too much on human society & I feel a hope that you may after the first distressing loneliness of feeling is past be led to commune more with God . . . When I feel how holy & [heavenly] some have lived I feel a dread of all that is delightful & interesting.[23]

The emotional connections with Alexander were nurtured by his thoughtful letters. Her mood improved with the anticipation of his arrival later in May. He took advantage of Yale's summer break to visit Kate on his way home to Franklin. As promised, he took her for a horseback ride to Norwich, which was fifteen miles from New London.[24] It was a pleasant town with a thriving harbor where three rivers came together to form the Thames River, which flowed gently down to New London and Long Island Sound. It would have been a pleasure to escape the depressing routine in New London. Riding was an activity they both loved. Alexander believed it improved his health, and Kate adored the opportunity to commune with the beauty of nature. Riding on horseback along the lovely river road was a prime chance to share sentiments privately. He was very fond of Kate, and she began to feel more affection for him.

This was the fourth time Kate and Alexander had been together since they'd met two months earlier. They had enjoyed music in Litchfield, walked with her brother Edward in New Haven, and shared the long drive to New London. Conversation was likely warm and friendly, and yet at the end of the ride, Kate sensed something was amiss. She was an extrovert with a strong intuition about emotions. She had noticed his awkward behavior on the journey from New Haven but had not thought much of it at the time. But when he helped her down from the horse at the end of their ride, it appeared he was attempting to minimize physical contact. Helping a lady down from a horse was the perfect opportunity to hold her close to him, but he didn't. Kate was confused by his body language. She understood how courting worked in Litchfield. When a couple grew fond of each other, they began to express their sentiments in a physical manner. A simple touch that lingered a few extra moments was a sufficient signal. She was accustomed to the way Lyman shared personal affection for his family with hugs.[25] Something was not right. Perhaps it was just his inexperience, but the seeds of doubt were sown.

Back in the drudgery of New London, her imagination began to dwell on Alexander's lack of physical affection. She projected her fears onto his motivation. Within weeks, the doubts had become a contagion in Kate's mind. She read too much into the situation. Her friend John P had alienated several women because he feared they didn't love him sufficiently. Kate could not let go of her growing suspicions. But something else was missing. There was no private space for Kate and Alexander to share music. Alexander had difficulty expressing his feelings. He needed music to help animate his affections. The emotional nourishment they needed was missing.

The more Kate considered her relationship with Alexander, the more it bothered her. There were too many similarities to her failed experience in Boston. Albert Hobart and Alexander Fisher were both smart, witty, and interested in her. Both seemed to assume she would agree to their proposals, which her family and friends pressured her to accept. Neither man's emotional intensity met her expectations. But Alexander's physical behavior was different. It was odd.

In a letter to Louisa on May 31, she lamented her predicament: "As for the young gentlemen [in New London] they are polite but pretty shy, for from the ominous circumstances in which I came in town & my ride to Norwich it is pretty generally supposed I am engaged."[26] She continued in the same letter to share her secret concerns with Louisa:

> I shall confide some remarks on a delicate subject to your particular care, with the injunction that you share or repeat them to no one. As to your question shall I marry? I answer I know not any better than I ever did. If I think I can be happy and opportunity offers I shall . . . I am more pleased than I expected to be & more I doubt than I ought to be for I have not yet made up my mind whether it is best to be pleased at all. The truth is Louisa I feel more & more each day that talents, learning & good principals never could make me happy alone. I shall need a warm & affectionate heart & whether I can find it in this case I know not.[27]

Kate was profoundly unhappy with her life in New London. Her father was pressing too hard for her to seek conversion and marry Alexander. And she had no confidant in town to temper her rising sentiments. She dramatically projected her fears in her May 31 letter to Louisa in a manner that would have shocked Alexander:

> I never could give up such a father & such a home & such friends as mine for one who after the first novelty of wedded life had worn away would be so engrossed in science & study as to forget I existed . . . I could

never dispense with the little attentions & kindnesses ... which a cold hearted man never could bestow. The more I think of it the more I am sure that I ought to guard my heart from the fascination of genius & the flattery of attentions till I am sure that my happiness is not risked.[28]

With her negative emotions expressed, she concluded her letter to Louisa with a more positive view of Alexander but declared that she was still undecided and would not be pushed into marriage:

> The fact is he does write <u>confounded</u> pretty letters & has shown more good judgment & delicacy than I should have thought possible in such a kind of man as I used to think he was. What kind of man I think he is now I really don't know. One thing I am certain of, that I shall not be troubled by any <u>hard</u> <u>question</u> if I don't feel inclined to answer favorably.[29]

Kate had not confronted Alexander about her concerns but apparently felt quite comfortable posing them in a letter to her father. He was a strong advocate of the match, and perhaps she felt he could provide some context or comfort. But Lyman's cold, logical response touched a raw nerve and prompted an angry reply. Kate exploded in dramatic fashion in a June 5 letter to her father:

> As to the subject to which you write I do not need any exhortation to <u>think</u> <u>about</u> <u>it</u> or to think <u>seriously</u> about it ... It is true that intellect with me ought to

be a cardinal point, but I could in the trials & vicissitudes of domestic life better, far better dispense with it than I could with a social disposition & an affectionate heart.[30]

Once she had purged her pent-up emotions, Kate concluded her letter to Lyman in a more conciliatory manner. It was the same emotional-roller-coaster pattern that characterized her May 31 letter to Louisa. She reminded her father that lack of affection had doomed her earlier affair (with Albert Hobart in Boston) and said she hoped he was correct about his assurances regarding Alexander's affection.[31]

A letter to Louisa from Kate three weeks later, on June 28, was devoted predominantly to Louisa's own romantic turmoil. Louisa was considering a move to South Carolina with her fiancé William Gould as he established his legal practice. This had caused a major rift with Headmistress Sarah Pierce at Litchfield Female Academy. Louisa was the only music teacher at LFA, and without her presence, the school would have no one to teach piano. Louisa was caught in a test of loyalty between her fiancé and employer. Kate cautioned Louisa to "take Papa's advice before you take this step" and urged her to stay at least until the end of the school term to protect her reputation. Seemingly oblivious to the depths of her friend's dilemma, Kate hinted, "If you should leave L. do you suppose I should take your place next winter for at any rate I should wish to pass next winter at home."[32] Kate lacked a trusted advisor in New London to act as a sounding board. There was no filter between her thoughts and her pen.

Kate's own distress was signaled as she added an ominous postscript to her June 28 letter to Louisa: "There are some things said in this letter which would be sad enough to fall into any hands but yours. I wish therefore that you would burn this letter after you have answered it. Tell me when you do so that I may feel easy."[33] What remains of the letter shows a significant portion was torn off. It was the last surviving correspondence between Kate and Louisa in 1821. There was not a single reference to Alexander in the letter. The missing portion and subsequent letters were probably destroyed to hide discussions about him. It was ominously reminiscent of the end of her Boston letters in 1819. Fortunately, the earlier intimate letters survived, or this part of the story about Alexander would have been lost.

Kate continued her correspondence with Lyman about Alexander. He belatedly replied to her a month later, at the end of July. He was just about to set off on a journey with friends to visit Niagara Falls.[34] "Your letter too long unanswered remanded some surprises and pleasure." He then appeared to scold her about taking Alexander lightly. "Let no caprice or inconstancy on your part becloud a prospect so deservedly a subject of complacency to your friends & so full of promises of earthly good." Lyman concluded by counseling Kate against returning to Litchfield too soon:

> You speak of returning in the fall and passing the winter at home, however two things need to be consulted, 1 pleasure and 2 profit . . . both my opinion and advice is that you make us a good visit in your vacation & return to prolong your earnings thru the winter . . . You will need assistance my circumstances will not enable me to afford.[35]

The final admonition was an allusion to the money she would need for her wedding, which Lyman could not afford. There are no surviving late-summer letters between Kate and her family, so they were either lost or intentionally destroyed.

Meanwhile, Alexander was unaware of the extent of Kate's growing concerns about their courtship. He was busy in New Haven, turning his ultimate academic ambition to visit France into reality. During the summer of 1821, Yale agreed to sponsor his journey to France. He would travel as a college official to gather knowledge and materials for its library. His regular salary would be paid while he was abroad, and letters of recommendation from President Day would open doors for him at universities in Paris.[36] Alexander was charged with organizing and preparing for the trip to commence in April 1822. He changed his residence that summer to live in town with Monsieur Bonfils. Alexander spent one hour daily conversing in French with his host to improve his language skills. He wrote his parents, "I have now got to understand him almost as well as I do one who speaks English, and contrive (in a rather broken manner to be sure) to express most things that I wish to in the same language."[37] But despite his other preparations, Alexander had neglected to tell Kate about his voyage to France, which was rapidly approaching. It would send him to Europe for up to a year. Perhaps he feared a prolonged absence in France would hurt his prospects with Kate. Disclosure of his plans would have forced a discussion about engagement. It was difficult for a man who sometimes struggled to share his emotions. By procrastinating so long, Alexander had created an awkward situation for himself. He needed to find the right moment to discuss marriage with Kate.

Alexander was also preoccupied with the visit of his eighteen-year-old sister, Eliza, who spent the summer of 1821 in New Haven. She had attended Byfield Academy for one year, and Alexander was keen to help round out her education. Like

Benjamin Silliman, his fellow Yale professor, Alexander believed that women should have greater educational opportunities.[38] He was delighted to see her blossom, as he related in an August 6 letter to his fourteen-year-old sister Nancy:

> Eliza is getting to be something of a lady. She boards in a place where the people are well bred and visits in some of the genteelest families in town. I have now begun to give to her & some of her schoolmates a [set] of Lectures in Philosophy and intend to continue them one a week as long as she stays . . . she takes lessons on the piano; and can now play Bonaparte's March much as well as you could last spring.[39]

1821 COURTSHIP TIMELINE

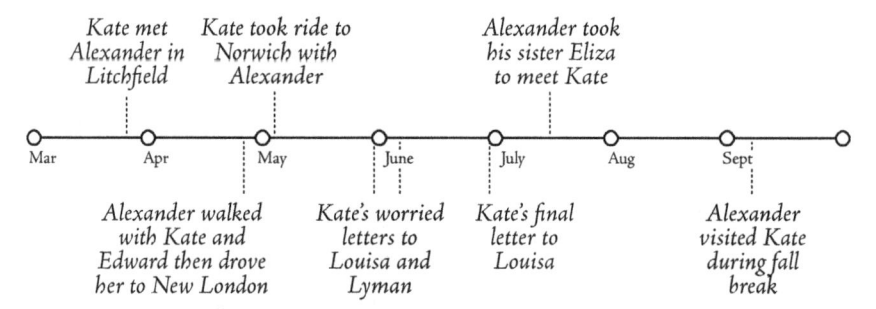

Kate met Alexander in Litchfield	Kate took ride to Norwich with Alexander			Alexander took his sister Eliza to meet Kate			
Mar	Apr	May	June	July	Aug	Sept	
		Alexander walked with Kate and Edward then drove her to New London	Kate's worried letters to Louisa and Lyman	Kate's final letter to Louisa		Alexander visited Kate during fall break	

Later that summer, Alexander took Eliza to meet Kate in New London. Introducing his sister was an important signal that Alexander was committed to Kate. There were no details recorded from that fateful visit other than it occurred and was pleasant.[40] Kate and Alexander may have taken a walk together with Eliza, like they had done with her brother Edward in the spring. Alexander wanted Kate and Eliza to become friends and someday feel like sisters. Kate apparently liked Eliza and presumably learned about Alexander's emotions by observing his behavior that day. But Kate was unable to discuss her concerns about Alexander's affection for her. Alexander could not discuss matrimony or propose with his sister present. Those discussions were deferred.

What and when Alexander told his parents about Kate is a bit of a mystery. He preferred to disclose such intimate feelings in person, and none of his letters mentioned her. Presumably, he had remained silent so far. But Eliza would have eagerly divulged the courtship to her parents when she returned home at the end of the summer. It was exciting news. So Alexander would have been compelled to speak about his intentions for Kate when he visited home during fall break. A man's parents are always the last to know about his romantic relationships.

It had been nearly six months since Kate met Alexander in Litchfield. In theory, he was a good match for her. But their courtship was dangerously off track. Kate was looking for romance with a warmhearted man. Those who knew Alexander best appreciated his kind heart. Yet his lack of romantic experience and extreme sense of propriety crippled his ability to share the tender physical affection Kate expected. Unfortunately, Alexander was not wired to understand the problem. She rationalized his odd behavior as that of a coldhearted scientist. Their joint failure to communicate let the issue fester. The more her father pushed, the more Kate rebelled against marriage. And there was no conducive place in New London for the one thing that could help . . . music.

Alexander planned to visit Kate on his way home to Franklin in September 1821.[41] Yet unless something changed, they could pass like two ships in the night. His approaching visit would be a pivotal, high-stakes encounter.

7

Trouble

> To err is human, to forgive, divine.
> —Alexander Pope

September 1821–December 1821

Kate wrote her father with troubling news and requested his help in late September 1821. She was at her wit's end with Alexander. During his recent visit, he had been charming but continued to minimize touching her and failed to discuss marriage. Nor had she voiced her concerns to him. In her mind, their courtship was at an impasse, and she put the matter firmly in Lyman's hands.[1] Kate asked her father to confront Alexander about his odd behavior and marital intentions. Pending a report from Lyman, she would suspend correspondence with Alexander. Kate's request may have been an attempt to force Alexander's hand. Or in frustration, she may have simply thrown her courtship back in the lap of its advocate. Lyman's actions could either get things back on track or end the courtship entirely. It was an approach fraught with risk. And Kate's request for intervention came at a particularly difficult moment for Lyman. He was beset by problems at home and was about to depart on a trip to Boston. He was also suffering from one of his periodic nervous collapses. Unfortunately for Kate, Lyman was out of time and energy.

Lyman's mental health in the fall of 1821 was a significant concern. He was traveling to Boston to consult with Dr. Jackson, a physician and professor at Harvard Medical School.[2] Lyman described his ailments as "nervous depression of spirits and lassitude debility."[3] The pressure of work and family issues tended to bring on these recurring episodes of depression, followed by bursts of manic energy. Milton Rugoff, a well-known Beecher family biographer, suggested that Lyman was bipolar.[4] Perhaps Kate saw a little bit of her father in Alexander.[5] There were several potential triggers for this bout of depression in 1821. Lyman's son Charlie had punctured his knee on a nail, and three months later, he still had a serious lingering infection. His wife, Harriet, was five months pregnant with a second child, having lost their first to scarlet fever the year before.[6] Neither Edward nor William had made discernible progress toward conversion, and both sons were pressing him for money that he didn't have.[7] Plus, his marital and religious plans for Kate were stalled. It was in this troubled state of mind that Lyman traveled to meet Alexander to discuss Kate's concerns.

Lyman summoned the emotional energy to put the delicate matter squarely on the table with Alexander when he stopped in New Haven on his way to Boston. He expressed frustration that Alexander didn't appear to understand the norms of courtship behavior. He accused the young man of trying to avoid physical contact. Lyman was a passionate extrovert like Kate and appreciated the benefit of tenderhearted physical affection. He elaborated on why Kate was put off by Alexander's odd behavior.[8] It was a strange situation—a father urging a young man to be more forward with his daughter.

Alexander was surprised at the nature and depth of Kate's sentiments about his physical behavior. He protested that his "unusual delicacy" was the result of his concerns about propriety. When he was with Kate, "he felt the awkwardness of the situation; felt that his attentions could not but attract notice."[9] Alexander feared that any public display of affection would draw attention and result in slanderous gossip. If he shared his emotions publicly, he had no plausible way to defend the decency of his behavior. And if he took liberties when they were alone, he worried that Kate would lose respect for his character. Alexander lived his life by a strict code of conduct, and those were the rules of decorum. Lyman must have shaken his head in bewilderment. After a lengthy discussion, Lyman sensed that Alexander's behavior was naive but not coldhearted. It was due to his unusually deep convictions and lack of experience with the opposite sex. Alexander may have been a math prodigy, but he was not a romantic genius.

Lyman forged ahead with his daughter's second complaint. Alexander had been courting Kate for six months and had never spoken to her about marriage. He had invited her to commence courtship, but that was a process, not the end of the discussion. A man could not expect a woman to say yes if he never asked the question. On this point, Alexander had no valid defense. He professed his love for Kate and blamed procrastination. Lyman dismissed Alexander's excuse. He accused Alexander of disregarding Kate and his own feelings on the matter. He challenged him to announce his plans "if he had any or discontinue his intentions wholly."[10]

Alexander finally appreciated Kate's concerns and the need to address them forthrightly if he wanted to win her heart. He proposed a private meeting with Kate where he could express his feelings and declare his intentions. He was loath to do so in New London, so Alexander invited Kate to visit in New Haven for a few days. She could stay with the Hillhouse family. There were places in town where they could be discreetly alone. Alexander trusted Lyman to deliver his invitation rather than writing directly to Kate.[11] Under normal circumstances, it was a reasonable approach, but Alexander didn't understand the distressed state of Lyman's mental health. At that moment, both Kate and Alexander had relinquished control of the critical next steps to Lyman, who was on the brink of a nervous collapse.

Kate expected to hear from Lyman immediately after his trip to New Haven. Unfortunately, he delayed reporting the results of his meeting with Alexander because of his nervous condition. She anxiously awaited Alexander's response, which would probably determine the course of her life. It must have been agonizing to sit in New London, teaching fifty young ladies while pondering the possible outcomes. She couldn't discern a plausible explanation for Alexander's behavior. Unable to bear the anguish any longer, she wrote to ask her father how the meeting had gone. But because of Lyman's travel, her letter did not reach him until October 10.[12]

Lyman's ongoing depression prevented him from writing a response until October 20.[13] In his letter, he scolded Kate for sending her letter to Boston rather than Portland. He blamed her, not himself, for the delay that had increased her apprehension. He reported fully on his meeting with Alexander. He lent credence to Alexander's propriety excuse for his lack of physical affection. But he agreed with Kate that Alexander must declare his intentions or bow out. He also extended Alexander's invitation for Kate to visit New Haven. This correspondence might have helped soothe Kate's nerves had it been received in a timely fashion. But Lyman planned to meet Kate and take her home. He delayed sending his letter until he could give proper instructions based on his travel arrangements. When he finally posted his letter to Kate, it was October 24. Lyman directed her to get to New Haven and stay with Mary Hillhouse until he arrived to take her to Litchfield.[14] It had now been a month since Lyman's meeting with Alexander in New Haven. Neither Kate nor Alexander had heard a word from him. It was their fault for putting him in control. They both wondered why Lyman had delayed his response. They understood the maxim that "Good news travels fast."

Lamentably, Lyman's letter never reached Kate in New London. She naturally assumed the worst. She took matters into her own hands and departed for home. When she arrived in Litchfield, Kate poured out her heart to her friend Louisa, who was in the midst of her own romantic crisis with her fiancé William. It was a combustible situation. Kate and Louisa could surmise no reasonable explanation for Alexander's behavior. They summarily declared the courtship ended. Kate was emotionally wounded and anticipated the gossip that was certain to follow. She put on a brave face and made it known to her friends in Litchfield that her courtship with Alexander was finished.[15] When Lyman's letter finally arrived, it was too late to change direction. Having publicly terminated her courtship without contacting Alexander, Kate had painted herself into a corner. There was no way to gracefully extricate herself. The date on which Lyman's letter actually arrived in Litchfield is unknown. The exterior of the envelope showed that it was forwarded to Litchfield from New London on October 26, 1821. By then, Kate was already back in Litchfield.[16]

Lyman finally arrived in Litchfield on November 6 and discussed the delicate situation with Kate.[17] The contents of these conversations have never come to light. Whether Lyman met with Alexander on his way back through New Haven is doubtful but unknown. The situation in the Beecher household after Lyman returned was more chaotic than ever. Kate wrote to her grandmother Foote, "Papa is much out of health. Charles is confined with blisters on his knee . . . Aunt Esther will live here this winter; but her health is feeble, so that we are a pretty miserable company; and while I was the only grown person in the whole family servants and all, that was really well." She offered in jest "if you are lonesome for want of children, we could easily spare Henry or Harriet."[18] Matters had reached rock bottom, and under the circumstances, it was unlikely that Lyman had the emotional energy to reach out to continue his conversations with Alexander.[19]

The month of October was torture for Alexander as well. He was completely at the mercy of Lyman to deliver his invitation to Kate, and the silence was deafening. He unfortunately had the luxury of more time to ruminate. Starting in October 1821, for the first time in six years, Alexander no longer had the responsibilities of a tutor.[20] Without the distraction of constant student recitations, he had more time to consider his future. That made the emotional uncertainty of his relationship with Kate harder to manage. Alexander was a celebrated Yale professor who had been admitted to elite levels of society. His pride was wounded by being ignored. Although he usually hid his feelings, Alexander felt them intensely. He didn't understand why Kate had not accepted his plan to come visit New Haven.

Alexander wrote his parents in mid-October about two significant decisions he faced. First was the prospect of an accelerated departure for Europe. His good friend Professor Eleazar Fitch was suffering health issues, perhaps hay fever, that required an imminent journey to Europe for relief. Eleazar wanted a travel companion. Alexander was the logical choice since he was already well advanced with his planned trip to France. Alexander explained his existing commitments to his parents and concluded it would be "very difficult to get away." He chose to wait until April 1822 as originally scheduled.[21] If he had gone to Paris sooner, any hope of winning Kate's hand would have been lost. Alexander found himself stuck in limbo until he got a response from Kate or Lyman. It was a mistake not to have told Kate about his voyage to Europe, which was less than six months away. Alexander was running out of time.

His second major decision was whether to accept a lucrative, unsolicited offer to become a professor at Princeton. Alexander's visit to Princeton in 1820 had borne fruit. He was offered twice as much money to take his same role at Princeton, professor of natural philosophy and mathematics. He explained his considerations to his parents: "If I had no object in view but merely to lay up money I should certainly go; but I feel too much attachment to this [Yale] Institution . . . Although Princeton ranks high among the Colleges in the U. States, Yale College ranks higher . . . At the same time, I should be twice as far off from home and could not see you more than half as often."[22] He diplomatically turned down the job offer. The proposal was flattering, but Alexander was committed to Yale, his trip to France, and Kate.

Kate's dramatic announcement ending their courtship reached Alexander through the grapevine sometime in November. It was the talk of Litchfield, and there was constant communication with people in New Haven. Gossip of that sort was a hot item. How and where he heard the news is unknown, but he was blindsided and embarrassed. If his pride was wounded by Kate's silence, it was doubly injured by her backdoor dismissal.

He was in a dark frame of mind as he pondered the collapse of his relationship with Kate. He wrote a letter to his sister Nancy in early December that perhaps mirrored his frustrations with Kate. His tone was uncharacteristically harsh with his sister, who was only fifteen:

> You must know that when two persons correspond, a considerable part of every letter is made up of things in answer to the one which preceded it; but as I have nothing from you to reply to, you must expect that I shall be short. In fact, what is there for me to write about? Shall I go into the old tack of exhorting you to write oftener ... and what is worst of all it does no good. You are as deaf to my advice as if you were sure your fingers would be burnt off by touching a pen.[23]

1821 TROUBLE TIMELINE

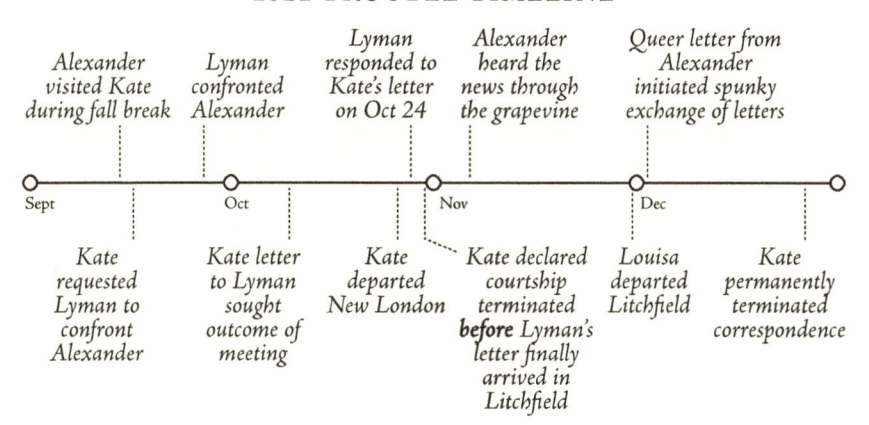

Sept	Oct	Nov	Dec	
Alexander visited Kate during fall break	Lyman confronted Alexander	Lyman responded to Kate's letter on Oct 24	Alexander heard the news through the grapevine	Queer letter from Alexander initiated spunky exchange of letters
Kate requested Lyman to confront Alexander	Kate letter to Lyman sought outcome of meeting	Kate departed New London	Kate declared courtship terminated **before** Lyman's letter finally arrived in Litchfield	Louisa departed Litchfield	Kate permanently terminated correspondence

In late November or early December, Louisa Wait departed her teaching position and left Litchfield permanently. Kate lost daily contact with her closest confidant. In an odd turn of events,

Louisa moved to Philadelphia rather than following her fiancé, William, to South Carolina. Part of the reason may have been to help care for her sister, who had consumption.[24]

Shortly after Louisa's departure, Kate received a "queer" (odd) letter from Alexander in which he confronted her about their relationship. Alexander wrote in anger. A bipolar episode may have unleashed his pen to express his feelings. His earlier diary written "under derangement" was notably confident and expressive. Kate wrote to Louisa that she responded to Alexander's letter with "a queer answer." Their correspondence continued "with an abundance of spunk on both sides." Alexander clearly struck a raw nerve, for "spunk" implied that Kate needed to stand up for herself. After two or three fierce exchanges, Kate permanently terminated their correspondence.[25]

Both Kate and Alexander had made mistakes in what had become a battle of wills. Neither was in a forgiving mood. It appeared to be the end of the road for Kate and Alexander, unless one of them was willing to bend.

8

Romance

> My love is like a melody,
> that's sweetly played in tune.
> —Robert Burns, "A Red, Red Rose"

January 1822–March 1822

Alexander made the first move to resolve the crisis. He wrote a letter to Kate in January 1822 proposing a private meeting in Litchfield. They had not met face-to-face since September 1821. Their last correspondence had been in December. It was unlikely that Alexander sought or received input from friends on how to proceed. But he must have considered his options carefully before he extended his offer. Perhaps he realized there was truth in Kate's complaints. Any rendezvous promised to be volatile following their spirited exchange of "queer letters." Kate might have taken advice from her family and friends. Lyman would have predictably counseled her to agree to accept Alexander's suggestion. She may have discussed the matter with Lucy or John P. Brace. Or perhaps Kate simply followed her heart. The emotional connection of musical memories may have been the tonic that caused both parties to compromise just enough to meet. Whatever the case, she agreed to Alexander's proposed meeting. The fateful encounter was set for Tuesday, January 22, 1822, at the Beecher residence in Litchfield.[1]

Alexander undoubtedly pondered his situation as he rode alone on his horse toward Litchfield that wintry January day. The trail was thirty-seven miles, and the journey took between six and seven hours, giving him plenty of time to think.[2] Alexander detested the gossipy whispers at Yale about his failed courtship. His pride had been gravely wounded by Kate's painful rejection through the grapevine. Seeing her brother Edward, a senior at Yale, was an awkward daily reminder of what might have been. And more importantly, Kate had broken his heart. Alexander had started to fall in love with her the first time they sang together at the piano. But his difficulty expressing feelings and his strict adherence to propriety had driven her away. His faults, not hers, were the root of the problem. He needed to change and share his affection openly if he wanted to win her back. He arrived by midafternoon at the inn where he had stayed during his two previous visits to Litchfield. There was just enough time to freshen up before his late-afternoon meeting with Kate. This encounter would settle things honorably, one way or the other.

Kate likely searched her feelings as she anticipated Alexander's arrival. He was a desirable match, but she could never be pushed into a relationship without romance. She had felt an initial spark as she experienced his passion through music. But his measured sentiments didn't match the fiery intensity of her own. He failed to express his emotions for her directly. A woman like Kate couldn't live that way. Her intuition eventually settled on the prejudice that he had the cold heart of a scientist.[3] That wasn't true, but he would have to open his heart to prove it. By the time

Alexander arrived at the Beecher house, it was probably near Kate's favorite romantic time of day . . . sunset. It was the hour of reckoning.

The Beecher family was aware of Alexander's visit and appreciated that this was a pivotal moment. They sensed Kate's tension as Alexander approached the house and knocked on the door. They hoped for the best, but knowing Kate's quick temper, they were prepared for fireworks. Imagine the serious young man as he was welcomed into the parsonage following his arduous winter journey to Litchfield. After removing his overcoat, he was ushered into the parlor, where Kate was waiting. There would have been a fire burning, which provided warmth and light as daylight faded. Despite the rules of propriety, they were allowed to close the door to maintain a semblance of privacy.

Exactly what transpired next was never fully revealed. Both must have been candid as they clarified their previous actions and misunderstandings. But their honesty was tempered with more kindness than their "queer" letter exchange. Alexander's heartfelt apology for his odd behavior apparently elicited one from Kate for rejecting him behind his back. Most importantly, Alexander somehow managed to summon the intimate words and actions to express his love. His affection was genuine, and it was evident to Kate. It was the thing her heart most desired. She had found her romantic hero at last. Whatever the specifics of the encounter, the outcome was clear. Kate declared in a letter to Louisa, "You cannot think what a long string of misunderstanding there was <u>all</u> <u>around</u> but we finally found out that we both loved each other too well to quarrel any longer & we soon met on such terms as all lovers should meet."[4] Given Alexander's lack of experience, their first kiss was probably sweet but a bit clumsy. They likely played the piano and sang a romantic duet.

The music from the parlor signaled good news to the family. It was the end of Kate and Alexander's courtship and the beginning of their romance.

Alexander most likely proposed that evening. His failure to declare his intentions earlier had been a sticking point in their relationship, and he wouldn't make that mistake twice. Once he asked, Kate was gratified to accept. He already had Lyman's permission to court Kate, but she may have counseled him to ask her father's consent to marry her. Alexander would have trudged upstairs to Lyman's third-floor study, where he received an enthusiastic blessing. Alexander must have stayed for dinner that evening. Kate announced their engagement to the delight of her family. The Beechers would have insisted that Kate's new fiancé spend the night with them. He probably declined because his horse and bag were already at the inn. But Alexander eventually would have accepted their hospitality.

The following day, the newly engaged couple had time for a private conversation about their future. This was probably when Alexander revealed, for the first time, his plans for a journey to France. It was a significant surprise coming so soon after their engagement. Her shock at the news made it difficult to focus, but the implications were inescapable. There were several alternatives to consider. Was there enough time to marry before Alexander departed in April? If so, would the new Mrs. Fisher stay behind or travel with him? Was there a way Alexander could postpone his departure, marry Kate, and then take her with him? From his logical perspective, it was complicated to change professional plans at the eleventh hour. From her emotional perspective, it was distressing not to adjust to their changed romantic circumstances. It would have been interesting to be a fly on those walls. In the end, they agreed to marry when he returned. But Kate was disappointed that they would be separated so soon after falling in love. Worse yet, he could be gone for a year. Alexander softened the blow when he allowed that perhaps he might return in eight months.[5]

Alexander agreed to stay two more nights before returning to New Haven to complete preparations for his journey. Word of their engagement spread like wildfire through Litchfield. People in town were pleased but surprised because Kate had previously announced the demise of their courtship. Kate would have taken Alexander to call on Headmistress Sarah Pierce at Litchfield Female Academy and Tapping Reeve at Litchfield Law School so that they could meet her new fiancé. Both were close to her family, and they were two of the most prominent people in town. It was the start of a process that would establish Kate's new identity. She was known as a fun-loving, extroverted poet. She had special religious status in Litchfield as the oldest daughter of Rev. Lyman Beecher. None of that changed, but her distinction was enhanced as the fiancé of the brilliant young professor at Yale. Kate naturally acquired some of his academic prestige. Perhaps she was more intellectual and complex than general opinion previously allowed. Kate relished the limelight as the new "bride-to-be."

Kate and Alexander spent hours each day reciting poetry and making music in the Beecher parlor. The magic of music and romance filled the air. Since Alexander's first visit to Litchfield, Lyman had acquired a new upright piano from Aunt Jane, one of Roxana's relations in Guilford.[6] It was far superior to the Beechers' previous instrument. Alexander adored listening to Kate play and carefully observed her fingers as they "danced" upon the keys.[7] As a pianist, he was particularly interested in watching the technique of her hands. But as a lover, her hands had gained intimate, new significance. There was something seductive about seeing her fingers stroke the piano keys while the melody touched his soul.

Considerable time was spent acquainting Alexander with Kate's immediate household. Shared meals and conversation forged new bonds with Alexander. Among those residing in the Beecher home, the person most like Alexander was Kate's dear friend John P. Brace. Alexander and John P were only one year apart in age. They were both scientists who respected the intellect of women. Alexander was more distinguished in academics, whereas John P was better versed in the ways of love. Brace was ideally positioned to advise both Kate and Alexander as their relationship evolved. Alexander would have profited from John P's romantic experience and understanding of Kate's personality. Kate would have benefited from John P's willingness to share insights about pleasing a man like Alexander. Kate and John P had never been shy about such matters. Perhaps one or both mentioned to him how much Alexander enjoyed watching Kate play the piano. John P was a Shakespeare aficionado and would have directed them to the bard's 128th Sonnet. In it, Shakespeare expresses envy for the keys as they "kissed" the fingers of his mistress as he watched her play the harpsichord.[8] The sensuous image, once implanted, would have been difficult to forget and would have continued to arouse the lovers each time Kate played the piano.

Sunset was the time when Kate and Alexander could be alone to share their passion. The Beecher house was packed with prying eyes, so it was only natural that a newly engaged couple would seek privacy for their intimate moments. They likely took evening sleigh rides during those first few blissful days to watch sunsets on a private wooded lane. It was a winter alternative to the summer practice of walking to Prospect Hill for kissing. They would have lingered in the relative darkness under the season's crescent moon.[9] People saw them headed out of town and gossiped about their passionate trysts.[10] But what happened out of sight during those evenings strengthened the cords that bound their hearts.

Too soon, the day came for Alexander to return to New Haven. Work remained to finalize his trip. He needed to put his affairs in order for his approaching absence. And he needed to visit his family in Franklin before his departure at the beginning of April. Fortunately, his official duties at Yale were limited since he would be gone for the majority of the remaining school year. Alexander promised to return to Litchfield near the end of March. Kate and Alexander agreed to exchange weekly correspondence while they were apart. The separation was painful for Kate, but it was only temporary. Their parting embrace on January 25 would have been passionate and decidedly more experienced than their initial kiss four days earlier.

Kate beamed in a letter to Louisa a few days later:

> I am an engaged woman ... I did feel wondrous queer till I got a little used to it, but now I feel just as I used to only a little more happy than common ... [I]felt no doubt that I had gained the whole heart of one whose equal I never saw both as respects intellect & all that is amiable & desirable in private character. I could not ask for more delicacy & tenderness.[11]

The next seven weeks provided Kate with a vivid preview of her future as a married woman. Her stepmother, Harriet, was bedridden in her ninth month of pregnancy. The joy of bringing new life into the world was tempered by the physical changes to a woman's body and the considerable risks and suffering of childbirth. Kate's engagement evoked empathy for Harriet's suffering. She took charge of Harriet's household duties, and every chore was a reminder of what lay ahead. But the work was a welcome distraction during her separation from Alexander. Kate's maternal instincts were awakened when a new little sister, Isabella Beecher, arrived on February 22. Kate wrote to Louisa, "She is a sweet wee thing & as good & quiet as ever a child was & I never saw Mama look so well & so pretty as she now does, in my life."[12]

Alexander was fully occupied in New Haven, making final arrangements for his journey. He gathered letters of introduction to the universities in Europe; booked passage on a Black Ball packet ship, which sailed from New York to Liverpool, England; and arranged to take two chests of specie to pay his expenses while in Europe. Alexander sorted his possessions, determining what to take and what to store. He shipped his piano to Franklin for Kate to play during an extended visit he planned for her with his family during his absence. He determined which academic and personal papers to take with him and which to leave in the custody of his friend Professor James Kingsley. And he spent his final weeks in New Haven polishing his French language skills with his landlord, Monsieur Bonfils.[13] Alexander's engagement was particularly good news for Edward Beecher at Yale. The prospective brothers-in-law were free to share their hopes for a future together.

Lyman recovered from his deep depression, which had sapped his strength. He jubilantly wrote to his brother-in-law George Foote, "We have lately had a visit from Professor Fisher, which has terminated in a settled connection, much to my satisfaction as well as of the parties. He goes to Europe in the spring, returns in a year, and then will expect to be married."[14] Lyman used his restored energy to launch a new campaign for Kate's religious conversion. Now that she was engaged and soon to be separated from her fiancé, it provided an opportunity to focus attention on her salvation.

While Kate and Alexander were apart, they exchanged weekly correspondence.[15] These seven love letters were different in character than their courtship correspondence. Surely, they would have continued to provide newsworthy items. But the emerging Victorian concept of romance called for them to share intimate secrets about their character, both good and bad. This appealed to Kate's desire to build a deep relationship. Lyman had pressed Kate to resume her conversion process once she was engaged. Her ongoing failure to achieve religious conversion was an obvious character flaw to share with Alexander. She was unwilling to reject herself as hopelessly depraved. In response to her confessed failure, Alexander related his own fruitless attempts. He had ended his conversion efforts in September 1819. Even during the religious wave that swept New Haven in 1820, he had remained notably unconverted. But in 1821, he drew closer to God. As a college student, he had determined that conversion was neither logical nor supported by the Bible. He apparently returned to his belief that repentance was the sole requirement for salvation.[16]

In part of a love letter that Kate later shared with her friend Louisa, Alexander expressed his romantic dream of one day meeting Kate in heaven:

> How consoling, how blessed must be the hope that can cheer, in that heavy hour which to <u>one</u> of us must one day come, that will appease us, that the eyes that are closing on all that is dearest below, are about to open

> on the glories of immortality & tho' lover & friend are for awhile put far away, a few revolving years, shall see them restored to each others arms & a reunion never more to be dissolved.[17]

Alexander's integrity would never have allowed him to write this passage unless he honestly believed they could get to heaven by some other means than the traditional conversion process.

Alexander made a final visit to Franklin before his journey. He told his family the exciting news about his engagement to Kate. He described his talented and outgoing fiancée to his parents. Eliza provided the feminine impressions of Kate that rounded out the picture of their future daughter-in-law. Caleb and Sally Fisher were thrilled that Alexander was getting married. They insisted that Kate should come stay with them in Franklin for several months while he was abroad. That would give them ample opportunity to welcome her into the family. It's unclear if Alexander ever sought or received relationship advice from his parents. It's doubtful they would have confessed that he was conceived out of wedlock. His father would have simply urged caution during his final visit to Litchfield. But Caleb urgently warned against making the journey to France.[18] Travel by ship was dangerous, and he feared for his son's life.

Once Alexander's preparations were complete, he made a final visit to Litchfield on March 18, 1822. He spent three nights at the Beechers' house and departed on March 21. The visit was a bittersweet moment for Kate. She had finally found romance with Alexander, but she was called to part from him so soon. Alexander was sad to leave Kate, but she would wait for his return to establish the family his heart desired. They had just four days to say goodbye.

Kate and Alexander continued their conversations about his travels and her plans while he was away. She wrote to her friend Louisa a few days after his departure:

> He has recommendations to all the Universities in England + Scotland + to the great scientific characters there + in France . . . I have given up the plan of going to New L[ondon] . . . I intend to remain at home till the fall . . . I shall probably visit Boston & Mr. F[isher] has planned that his [family] should meet me there & that I shall spend a month or two with them. He has sent his Piano & plenty of books home & his sister [Eliza] with whom I became acquainted in New L[ondon] will correspond with me this summer so that I shall anticipate a pleasant time there.[19]

1822 ROMANCE TIMELINE

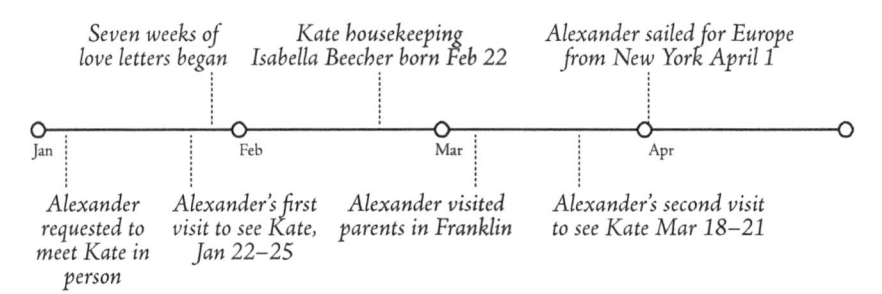

Above timeline:
- Seven weeks of love letters began
- Kate housekeeping Isabella Beecher born Feb 22
- Alexander sailed for Europe from New York April 1

Timeline months: Jan — Feb — Mar — Apr

Below timeline:
- Alexander requested to meet Kate in person
- Alexander's first visit to see Kate, Jan 22–25
- Alexander visited parents in Franklin
- Alexander's second visit to see Kate Mar 18–21

Religion continued to be a point of discussion. It was difficult for Kate to accept Alexander's belief that repentance was sufficient for salvation. Her father had taught her that conversion was the only sure route to heaven. But Kate's heart didn't feel sinful, and she sincerely doubted her ability to achieve conversion.

Although she was happily engaged, she continued to fear for her soul. She wrote to Louisa:

> I have as flattering a prospect of future happiness as often falls to someone, but my heart sinks within me when I think that this may be <u>my all</u>, + that Heaven + immortal happiness may be forever lost.[20]

Although Alexander stayed only a few days, what wonderful days they must have been. Their daylight hours were spent much as they had been during his previous visit: eating meals with her family, visiting friends, sharing intimate discussions, reading poetry, and making music together. Kate had practiced piano "for <u>his</u> sake who loves to hear me play so well."[21] Their evenings were spent viewing sunsets, just the two of them in a carriage on a private wooded lane. They witnessed the splendor in the sky unfold before them. It was her poem about a sunset that had first brought them together. There was no need for conversation as their bodies spoke to each other. They shared feelings they would treasure for a lifetime. Each moment cemented their romance but brought them closer to his departure. Kate wrote to Louisa that she had "just begun to find out how much I could love him."[22]

Alexander departed the morning of March 21. He had ten days to gather his belongings in New Haven, attend to final details, and make his way to New York to board his ship. Perhaps they performed a final duet at the piano or recited poetry one last time, anything to delay his departure. Kate composed a special poem[23] for their parting:

> <u>Once</u>, must the morning of the year
> And Summer sun pass oer

And Autumn fill her golden horn
And Winters tempests roar

Then when gay Spring again returns
So blithe along the vale
And spreads her mantle on the trees
Her breath upon the gale.

One constant heart, that followed still
The Wanderer on his way
Shall Joyful welcome his return
And bless the happy day.

It was never told what Alexander presented as a token of his affection in return. Hopefully, he was drawn to something written by Kate's favorite romantic poet, Robert Burns. "A Red, Red Rose"[24] was a suitable poem about parting lovers. The man compared his love to music, promised to always love his sweetheart, and pledged to return. It would have expressed Alexander's confident and optimistic emotions:

A Red, Red Rose
My love is like a red, red rose
That's newly sprung in June;
My Love is like the melody
That's sweetly played in tune.

So fair art thou, my bonnie lass,
So deep in love am I;
And I will love thee still my dear,
Till all the seas gone dry.

Till all the seas gone dry my dear,
And the rocks melt with the sun;
I will love thee still, my dear,
While the sands of life shall run.

And fare thee well my only love!
And fare thee well awhile!
And I will come again my love,
Though it were ten thousand miles.

Kate and Alexander shared a parting kiss and shed a few tears, and then he was gone. Kate wrote to her friend Louisa four days later, "You my dear Louisa well know about these things & can realize how I felt when called to part from one so particularly dear."[25]

Music and poetry were the essential elements of Kate and Alexander's romance. Music allowed him to share the emotions he had always felt but found difficult to express. Once she understood that his sentiments were genuine, her romantic heart embraced him without reserve. They were both in love for the first time. But they would be separated for nearly a year by a vast ocean. Enduring emotional memories created by music and poetry would sustain their love until they met again . . . They had no idea just how long that might be.

PART III

Metamorphosis

9

Tempest

The raging of the waves against the precipice on which we were driving brought back from the caverns and the rocks the hoarse and melancholy warnings of destruction and death.
—William Everhart, surviving *Albion* passenger

April 1822

Alexander was excited to embark on his ship to Liverpool. Fair weather and a seasoned captain promised a favorable journey. He intended to take full advantage of his time at sea. There was so much to discover from nautical observations. Perhaps he might learn interesting things from other passengers. But this voyage was only the first leg of his quest. His ultimate destination was Paris, where he would meet the great French mathematicians. He was on the cusp of his academic ambition. But his enthusiasm was tempered by the prospect of being so long separated from Kate. Back in Litchfield, she practiced the piano for Alexander's sake, which provided hours of delight and kindled fond memories of their romance. She adored the attention brought by her new identity as Alexander's fiancée. It was a pleasant diversion from the tedious strain of her father's relentless religious exhortations. Kate missed Alexander dearly and counted the days until she received his first letter from Europe.

Alexander's journey began as the *Albion* pushed away from its dock in Lower Manhattan before sunrise on April 1, 1822. The sky was clear, and the waxing gibbous moon had just set.[1] The temperature was in the low forties, so he probably wore a coat as he stood on deck. He would have observed a few lights on shore as the gentle current of the East River carried the 447-ton vessel past the artillery battery off the tip of the island.[2] The ship relied on water currents and sails for propulsion. It was important to depart just after high tide to take full advantage of the outgoing current. High tide that morning was at 4:02 a.m., and sunrise was at 5:43 a.m., so the *Albion* would have sailed early to take advantage of daylight and exit the harbor before low tide at 10:41 a.m.[3] Fortunately, the south wind had shifted to become westerly overnight, which allowed them to travel a bit faster as they departed New York.[4]

It took roughly four hours to travel some thirty miles to reach the open waters of the Atlantic Ocean. Alexander had plenty of time to write letters while he observed the ship's progress. The East River merged into the Hudson River, which carried them past Governors Island into the upper harbor. Navigating the Narrows, which separated the upper harbor from the lower harbor, was relatively easy with help from the receding tide. The greatest danger was crossing the shallow water over the bar of Sandy Hook that connected New Jersey to Rockaway on the tip of Long Island. Ocean-going ships employed pilots with local knowledge of the shoals, currents, and tides to guide them safely in and out of the harbor. It was a fascinating process that Alexander studied with great interest. Once the *Albion* was safely out of the harbor, the pilot returned control of the ship to the captain. A small boat came alongside and transported the pilot to the next inbound ship that needed assistance.[5] Alexander handed three letters he had written during their harbor passage to the departing pilot and asked him to post them.

The first letter was to Alexander's father, Caleb, who was apprehensive about the journey. Caleb had sent him an anxious note prior to the ship's sailing, urging him to reconsider. "I hope, however, you will count the cost before you fully make up your mind to undertake so hazardous an enterprise . . . Should 30 men be placed in a situation where it is certain one of them must be killed, would you for a trifle be one of that number?"[6] Initially, Alexander scoffed at his father's worries, but as departure approached, he expressed concerns about the danger to his colleagues. The risk was small but mathematically inescapable. When one of his fellow tutors, William Chauncey Fowler, attempted to minimize Alexander's concerns, he listened thoughtfully and then ended the conversation with, "Well, this is all very true, but a certain percentage is lost."[7] Alexander ultimately dismissed his father's warning about the 3 percent who were lost. But as he departed New York, he penned a precautionary letter to his father. He enclosed it in an envelope to Yale's President Day. The envelope inside for Caleb provided clear instructions:

>Mr. Caleb Fisher
>Franklin, Mass
>
>To be sent only in case of my decease abroad; otherwise to be returned to me.
>—A. M. Fisher[8]

The second letter Alexander sent was a short note to his Yale colleague Professor James Kingsley:

> We have apparently everything to promise a quick, safe and comfortable passage. Capt. Williams is considered as the first commander from this port, and his ship has no superior. As soon as I get well seated in some coffee-house in Liverpool you may expect to hear from me.[9]

The third letter was a love note for Kate. He had sent her one soon after he left Litchfield eleven days earlier. His correspondence dated April 1 was his last until he reached Liverpool. He had received a recent letter from Kate before he left New Haven, but if she had written a second, he had probably missed it. Love letters between Kate and Alexander would be difficult while he was away. Mail was carried by ships that took at least twenty days eastbound to England and thirty days for the westbound return to America. He promised to send Kate a letter the day he arrived in Liverpool. But if his first note from England managed to get on a ship departing for the United States the day after he arrived, the earliest it could be expected to get to New York was on May 23. So Alexander's next letter might arrive in Litchfield as soon as Saturday, May 25. Kate marked the date on her calendar and anxiously began a countdown for its arrival.[10]

The *Albion* was a packet ship operated by Wright, Thompson, Marshall & Thompson. Prior to the establishment of packet operations, ships departed for Europe from New York whenever they had sufficient cargo. Actual departures could differ by weeks from estimated dates. Wright, Thompson launched its packet service in January 1817. The company's aim was to depart on a

Replica of the Albion. *Courtesy of New York Historical Society, New York, NY.*

fixed day of the month, regardless of cargo or passengers. This schedule was designed to attract lucrative contracts to deliver the mail. The certainty of dates also attracted more passengers. In 1822, Wright, Thompson's successful packet service from New York to Liverpool was expanded to twice each month, departing on the first and the fifteenth of each month. The *Albion* was built in 1819 specifically for packet service. It was a handsome ship, 114 feet long and 29 feet wide, fitted with three masts and commanded by a thirty-seven-year-old veteran captain, John Williams.[11] The crew of twenty-five included its captain, First Mate Henry Cammyer, a second mate, a boatswain, a carpenter, fifteen seamen, plus two cooks and three stewards. When the *Albion* departed on April 1, 1822, it carried twenty-three cabin passengers and six steerage passengers.[12] Although packet service had significantly reduced the cost of a ticket, the price for cabin passage to Liverpool was 35 guineas, or roughly $5,000 in current terms. This price guaranteed Alexander a private cabin, three daily meals, and an elite group of fellow passengers.[13] Cargo for the voyage included cotton, turpentine, rice, beeswax, time-sensitive mail, and a considerable sum of gold and silver coins. Wealthy passengers traveled in the nineteenth century with precious metal coins as an internationally accepted means of payment.[14]

Alexander soon befriended a cabin passenger, William Everhart, who was a businessman from Chester, Pennsylvania. Chester was a thriving center of textile manufacturing located midway between Philadelphia and Wilmington, Delaware. Everhart was tending business ties in the heart of the textile industry just north of Liverpool. Seasickness was a common problem among passengers, and Everhart suffered for most of the journey. While he sat on deck to minimize his discomfort, Everhart had a perfect opportunity to observe Alexander, whose mind was never at rest. Everhart described Alexander as follows:

> [He was] the most industrious man I ever saw. He seemed eager to gain information from everybody and everything. When not engaged with his journal or books or calculations, he was making observations on the temperature of the water & various phenomena of the ocean and frequently in conversation with the captain & more intelligent passengers. He seemed to know something upon every subject & had a peculiar talent for drawing out the recourses of others. Even when walking on the deck he was in a hurry & it appeared to be a matter of business with him.[15]

Alexander became acquainted with many of his fellow passengers as the days progressed. Three weeks on a ship only twenty-nine feet wide made it hard to remain anonymous. There were several interesting individuals on board. An intriguing group of six French cabin passengers was led by the dashing Monsieur Gravez. The French travelers included three men, two women, and one boy. Alexander was excited to have so many people to help him practice his language skills before he went to Paris. But they were probably reticent to speak to him at first for reasons that were soon discerned with the help of another friendly cabin passenger, British Major William Gough. Alexander learned from Major Gough that Monsieur Gravez was actually comte General Charles Lefebvre-Desnouettes. The notorious French general was married to a cousin of Napoleon and had avoided a death sentence in 1815 by escaping to America. Desnouettes was traveling incognito in a romantic bid to rejoin his wife in France. He had been separated from his spouse and daughter for seven years and risked death to be reunited with them. Major Gough, who had fought under Wellington against Napoleon, would have recognized his former adversary immediately.[16] Presumably, the other French cabin passengers were traveling under assumed names as well. One of the other two men in the group was apparently the general's nephew. The most mysterious member of the group was a beautiful young woman, the alluring Madame Garnier.[17] It was curious that an attractive young woman was traveling with her eight-year-old son but without her husband. Crossing the Atlantic was a dangerous and costly journey. It is unclear how she was connected to the other French passengers.

Among the remaining cabin passengers, the most infamous person was undoubtedly Anne Powell from Toronto. She was the sophisticated thirty-five-year-old daughter of William Powell, chief justice of Upper Canada (Ontario). But Anne had been spurned by her lover, John Robinson, the attorney general of Upper Canada. After Robinson married another woman, Anne began to stalk the couple. Ultimately, she was deemed to be deranged. When Robinson was dispatched on government business to England in 1822, Anne begged to travel with him. He refused, and Anne was confined to her parents' home to give Robinson and his wife a head start in case she chose to follow. But Anne escaped her captivity and pursued them to New York. There, she attempted to board the March 15 packet ship with Robinson, but in the interest of his safety, she was refused passage. So Anne had waited two fretful weeks to board the *Albion*, hot in pursuit of the man she passionately desired.[18] It would be interesting to know how she introduced herself and explained her travel plans to Alexander.

The *Albion* had favorable winds and weather for its first twenty days at sea.[19] Alexander made the most of his voyage by taking scientific measurements and conversing with the captain and fellow passengers. Although Alexander was an introvert by choice, when he met an intelligent person, he could be quite engaging. Perhaps the French allowed him to discuss ordinary matters if not their personal stories. During those three weeks, Alexander pried whatever useful knowledge he could from the more interesting of his fellow passengers. In the evenings after dinner, he retired to his private stateroom to review his daily observations recorded in his travel journal. It was a productive and pleasant routine. He probably ended each day rereading a love letter from Kate. April 20 was a special milestone. It was exactly one month since his final evening with Kate. His dreams that night would have aroused fond memories of their passion.

Kate had intimate memories of her final sunset with Alexander. She would have marked the evening of April 20 as she counted the days until his first letter arrived from Europe. Perhaps she reread his love letters, sensed his presence, and pictured his smiling face. As the days passed, sunsets and playing the piano were bittersweet reminders of Alexander's absence. Fortunately, she was quite busy, and the activity was a helpful distraction from her loneliness. She played an important role in supporting the Beecher household since her stepmother, Harriet, was busy with an infant daughter, Isabella. Harriet apparently became friendlier once Kate was engaged and had concrete plans to exit the household. Kate initiated correspondence with her future sister-in-law Eliza Fisher and began to feel comfortable in her new role as Alexander's fiancée.[20] She was introduced to Litchfield Law School student Horace Mann, a hometown friend of Alexander's from Franklin. Mann described his meeting with Kate in a gossipy letter to his sister in Boston:

> You may have heard that Professor Fisher of N. Haven has been making <u>love</u> to a Litchfield Lady, Miss Catharine Beecher... I had a little conversation with her; we exchanged a few diversions on Scott's novels ... she is a lady of superior intellect, she writes very good poetry & will probably make the professor a very good helpmate.[21]

Just after Alexander's departure from Litchfield, Lyman received spiritual news that was as welcome as Kate's betrothal. His son Edward Beecher achieved conversion after four years of obedient prayer. Lyman responded with a letter to Edward in late March 1822, noting, "However unexpected and wonderful it may seem that a thing regarded as so difficult as your conversion should at last become a reality, you are not the first who has felt so."[22] Lyman used Edward's success to ratchet up the pressure on Kate. On April 1, 1822, the date Alexander's ship sailed, Lyman wrote to Edward, "Catharine has been sick three days, the first in acute distress. I had been addressing her conscience not twenty minutes before. She was seized with agonizing pain. I hope it will be sanctified . . . We must not sleep, but try now to have our family converted."[23] Lyman was hopeful that Kate's distress was a sign of religious progress. But Kate's agony was more likely due to the heartbreak of Alexander's ship sailing for Europe.

At about one o'clock on the afternoon of April 21, Alexander's ship made land, coming within ten miles of Fastnet Rock, a lighthouse off the southwest shore of Ireland. At 2:00 p.m., they were headed east and passed within seven miles of Cape Clear Island, about sixty miles southwest of Kinsale. At that point, the weather turned foul, with heavy squalls headed toward them from the south. At 4:00 p.m., a violent gale struck. It split the foresail and broke the horizontal foreyard to which the mainsail was attached. As the wind intensified, the crew was ordered to repair the damage, and the sails were trimmed to weather the storm. By 8:00 p.m., the decks were cleared, and it was hoped the worst of the storm was over. They had avoided calamity thanks to the quick action of the captain and crew. All on board expected that the *Albion* would arrive comfortably at Liverpool the next day.[24]

Then, at about 8:30 p.m., a savage tempest struck with minimal warning. A giant wave swept over the *Albion*, throwing it on its beam ends, which means it was tipped almost ninety degrees to the side and nearly capsized. Imagine the ship had just passed diagonally over the crest of a huge wave and was headed to the bottom of the trough. The bow was tipped down at a steep angle, and the stern was dangerously exposed as it rode high out of the water. A sudden gust of wind from the starboard must have caught the stern and sails at precisely the wrong moment. The ship tilted violently to its port side as it plunged helplessly into the trough between the waves. This allowed the wind to wreak havoc on its sails, and the huge wave the ship had just crossed came crashing down on top of the *Albion*. The violent destruction must have happened in a matter of seconds. Neither the crew nor the passengers would have had any warning to take precautions as they and everything around them were powerfully cast about. Six crewmen and one cabin passenger were carried overboard to their watery graves.[25]

Alexander was injured when the ship nearly capsized. One can picture him seated comfortably at his writing desk, working on his travel journal. The rocking motion of the ship never bothered him, even when the waves were a bit larger than normal. The next moment, the cabin was turned sideways, and Alexander was hurled violently, headfirst, into the wall. His candle was snuffed out, and the room was suddenly flooded with seawater. After what must have been a frightening pause, the room tilted back, and the rocking of the waves resumed. He found himself dazed, sitting in perhaps a foot of water. Slowly, he regained his bearings and realized he had sustained a painful blow to his head. As he sat in his darkened chamber, Alexander gradually realized from the smell and taste that the liquid covering his face was not water but his own blood.[26]

When the ship righted itself, Captain Williams surveyed the wreckage and quickly realized they had suffered catastrophic damage. The ship had three masts. The main mast had been brought down, plus the mizzen and foremasts had been broken aloft, so the deck was a tangled mass of ropes and canvas. The water had swept everything else off the decks, including the lifeboats, cookhouse, compass, railings, and unfortunately, the axes required to clear the sails and broken rigging from the deck. Most importantly, the wheel had been torn off, and without a means to turn the rudder, there was no way to steer the ship. They were helpless against the fury of the storm. The giant wave had battered in the hatches and smashed some of the stateroom walls, so there was nothing to prevent the churning seawater from flooding the ship. The captain quickly marshaled the crew to break out the pumps. But the flooded decks below made it difficult to maintain footing. Members of the crew and several passengers lashed themselves to pumps as they valiantly strove to keep the *Albion* afloat. The deranged Anne Powell was determined to survive so that she could pursue her lover. She was later described as the most ardent volunteer at the pumps.[27]

The ship was unmanageable, helplessly adrift, and driven inexorably by the strong south winds toward the rugged Irish cliffs to the north. If they managed to avoid sinking, they faced the harrowing prospect of being battered against the rocky coast of Ireland. Although Captain Williams was well aware of their dire predicament, he did his best to reassure the passengers that they were in no danger. He optimistically predicted that the winds would soon shift and come from the north, which would keep them away from the hazardous coastline. Despite Alexander's injury, he was given the remaining ship's compass. As he sat on a chair below deck, his feet in water, he called out the ship's heading to the captain above. There was nothing Captain Williams could do with the information, but it allowed him to monitor the ship's position and pray that the winds changed direction. As a scientist, Alexander must have recognized the fatal implications of the physics and geography involved. Unlike his fellow passengers, who were still optimistic, he understood that they were headed for tragedy. A few of the crew were similarly aware. They began to refuse the captain's orders and broke out the rum to mourn their dismal fate.[28]

Alexander had both the luxury and curse of knowing that he was about to die. His misery was protracted for seven hours between the time the giant wave swept the ship and the moment they reached the rocky Irish coast. This provided him with plenty of time to contemplate his fate. What thoughts must have passed through his mind? He was a man of faith. Surely, he would have asked God for forgiveness of his sins. Contrary to his Calvinist denomination, he believed that repentance alone was sufficient for salvation. He must have hoped he was right. Having dismissed his father's prophetic warning about the dangers of sea voyages, he would have lamented being among the small percentage of those who were lost at sea. Fortunately, he had left letters for Caleb and Kate with the pilot. His family would be devastated. But what must have anguished Alexander the most was a future that he would never experience with Kate. He would never marry and have children of his own. Kate would be left to chart a new course in life. She would be heartbroken, and there was no way he could console her. That task would fall to her family and his. Alexander must have hoped that he would meet Kate in heaven as he had lovingly predicted. His thoughts would have returned to their parting kiss.

Shortly before dawn on April 22, Captain Williams and First Mate Henry Cammyer realized that the *Albion* was caught between two points of land near Kinsale. They were entering the treacherous Courtmacsherry Bay. The ship was being driven inexorably by howling south winds toward a sixty-five-foot precipice of stone. A jagged reef at its base rose from the sea and ran parallel to the cliffs about thirty feet in front of them. This ominous formation was like a spine of small mountains. The tidal shifts in the bay were extreme, and the water level could have risen fifteen feet as high tide approached. The combination of tide and winds running in the same direction would have amplified the size and fury of the waves as they pounded the coast.[29] With imminent doom certain, the captain summoned all passengers on deck. They were roused from their cabins and had only moments to hastily prepare. The beautiful Madame Garnier appeared on deck wrapped only in a blanket.[30] Apparently, she had removed her bulky wet clothing in a bid to swim ashore. William Everhart, the cabin passenger from Chester, Pennsylvania, who had been seasick for most of the journey, had to be helped to make it topside.

Loss of the packet ship the Albion. *The picture was based on survivor accounts but improperly shows passengers on shore before the ship split in half. Courtesy of the Mariners' Museum and Park, Newport News, VA.*

View of the Albion *shipwreck site from cliff at low tide. The ship was lodged across the sharp ridge shown in the center. Photo by author.*

He noticed that Alexander chose to stay below. "[Alexander] was standing at his stateroom door, the blinds down so as to expose the upper half of his person, one side of his face bloody, nothing in his hands, his head down and his countenance exhibiting deep and anxious meditation."[31] There was nothing Alexander could do to escape his predicament, and he was apparently resigned to his fate.

From his cabin, Alexander could have heard the captain as he shouted the fatal news over the sounds of the tempest, "The ship will strike within minutes and there is nothing we can do to save her." Some passengers, "particularly the females, expressed their terror in wild shrieks. Major Gough of the British army declared that 'death, come as he would, was an unwelcome messenger, but we must meet him like men.'"[32] Very little was said by most as they awaited their demise in shocked silence.

A surviving passenger later painted the dramatic scene as it unfolded:

> It is not possible to conceive the horrors of our situation. The relentless blast impelled us towards the fatal shore; the ship was a wreck; the raging of the [waves] against the precipice on which we were driving, brought back from the caverns and the rocks the hoarse and melancholy warnings of destruction and death. The stoutest heart amongst us must have quaked now in utter despair, and just at the grey of dawn the *Albion* struck.[33]

Throughout the night, passengers and crew had borne the terror as their ship was buffeted among the waves by the fierce winds. What they had endured was beyond their worst nightmares. But they were unprepared for the horror that was about to descend upon them. The movement of the ship abruptly stopped as the *Albion* was violently lodged atop the jagged reef. The vessel came to rest, perched diagonally across the sharp ridge of rocks that dug into its hull. They were saved from crashing into the cliff but trapped too far from it to scramble ashore. Survival was tantalizingly close but just beyond their grasp. There was an eerie moment when the ship was completely still . . . And then a giant wave crashed over the top of them.

Roughly a dozen souls, including Captain Williams, were swept from the deck. Their bodies were hurled violently against the rocky cliffs. The lucky ones were killed by the blunt trauma of the rocks or were knocked unconscious and drowned quickly. The less fortunate were swept off the boat but survived the first wave. They attempted to swim, but as the waves continued to thunder ashore, their bodies were hurled against the rocks again and again until they all succumbed.

On board, fifteen people lost their footing and became tangled in the ropes and canvas on the deck. They were submerged by the first wave. The shock of the fifty-degree water caused them to gasp for air, but instead they swallowed seawater. Several drowned before the wave receded. The trapped survivors vainly tried to extricate themselves from their entanglements before the next wave struck. But soon, the deck was littered with corpses.

The remaining survivors clung to whatever they could find to keep themselves erect and held their breath until each wave passed. But destiny had more terror in store for them. With each wave, the ship was being hammered mercilessly downward by the weight of the waves, and the teeth of the rocky reef bit deeper into the hull. Slowly but surely, the rocks were cutting the ship in half.[34]

The relentless waves continued for half an hour, at which point a party of local people appeared on top of the cliff. But the ship was too far away for them to attempt any rescue. Their ropes were too short to reach the survivors. They saw four people clinging to the bow of the ship. One was a woman, perhaps Anne Powell, who shrieked wildly for help. The rescuers watched helplessly for several minutes as the waves continued to engulf the survivors. Then, to the horror of those on shore, another giant wave broke over the *Albion*, and with a wrenching groan, the ship split in half. They could only watch as the bow of the boat rolled into the sea and took the poor woman and three others with it. They looked in vain but never saw any of them return to the surface.[35]

Sixteen people were perched dangerously on the stern of the ship, but fortuitously, the back half of the severed vessel floated in toward the cliffs. As it came to rest on a ledge beneath the precipice, thirteen people scrambled onto the rocks. They frantically sought toeholds and crevices to cling to before the next towering wave came crashing down upon them. Seizing the opportunity, the rescuers from above tossed ropes to those below and began to haul some of them to safety. It was a desperate race against time. As the waves continued to batter the survivors, one by one, they began to weaken and lose their grip, falling to certain death. Ultimately, seven of the thirteen were saved. This was how Everhart and Cammyer escaped death.

Meanwhile, three passengers remained on the stern, which balanced precariously on a rock ledge. A steerage passenger, Stephen Chase, clung to a mast and was hauled to safety when he managed to catch a rope that was thrown to him. A crew member caught another rope and was hoisted aloft just before a giant wave carried the hull and the third individual back into the sea.[36]

There were three consequential turns of fate that day, or things might have ended quite differently. First, the high tide that amplified the giant waves, fortunately, carried the *Albion* safely over the dangerous rock formations in Courtmacsherry Bay. If the ship had broken apart in open water, it is doubtful anyone could have survived. Second, the manner in which the ship lodged on the reef ultimately caused it to split in half. But when the back half floated near the cliffs, it allowed people to scramble ashore, and nine were ultimately rescued. The third bit of chance was, unfortunately, cruel. Just east of where the *Albion* struck, there was a gap in the cliffs. If the winds had blown them just three-quarters of a mile to the east, the *Albion* would have landed on the sandy Garretstown Beach, and most likely, everyone on board would have survived.

Albion *wreck site near Garretstown Beach. Courtesy of Google Earth.*

The tempest that wrecked the *Albion* was a monstrous two-day event off the coast of Ireland. It sealed the doom of fourteen ships, including the *Albion* and two British Navy vessels, one being an eighteen-gun brig, the HMS *Confiance*.[37] Both British naval ships lost all hands. (See the accompanying map.) There must have been tremendous gusts of wind to cause such massive destruction. The *Albion* became the most notorious shipwreck of the era because of the graphic eyewitness accounts of its survivors. The stories provided by two survivors, passenger Everhart and First Mate Cammyer, plus those from John Purcell of the rescue party, offered terrifying glimpses of the human tragedy. Only nine of the fifty-four people aboard the *Albion* survived, two passengers and seven members of the crew.[38] Among the forty-five casualties, the bodies of only sixteen were ever found. They were buried in the cemetery of the new Templetrine Church, not far from the site of the shipwreck.[39] To conceal his identity, General Desnouettes was buried without a marker just outside the church's front door. Three prominent passengers had stone

Major Shipwrecks, April 21–22, 1822

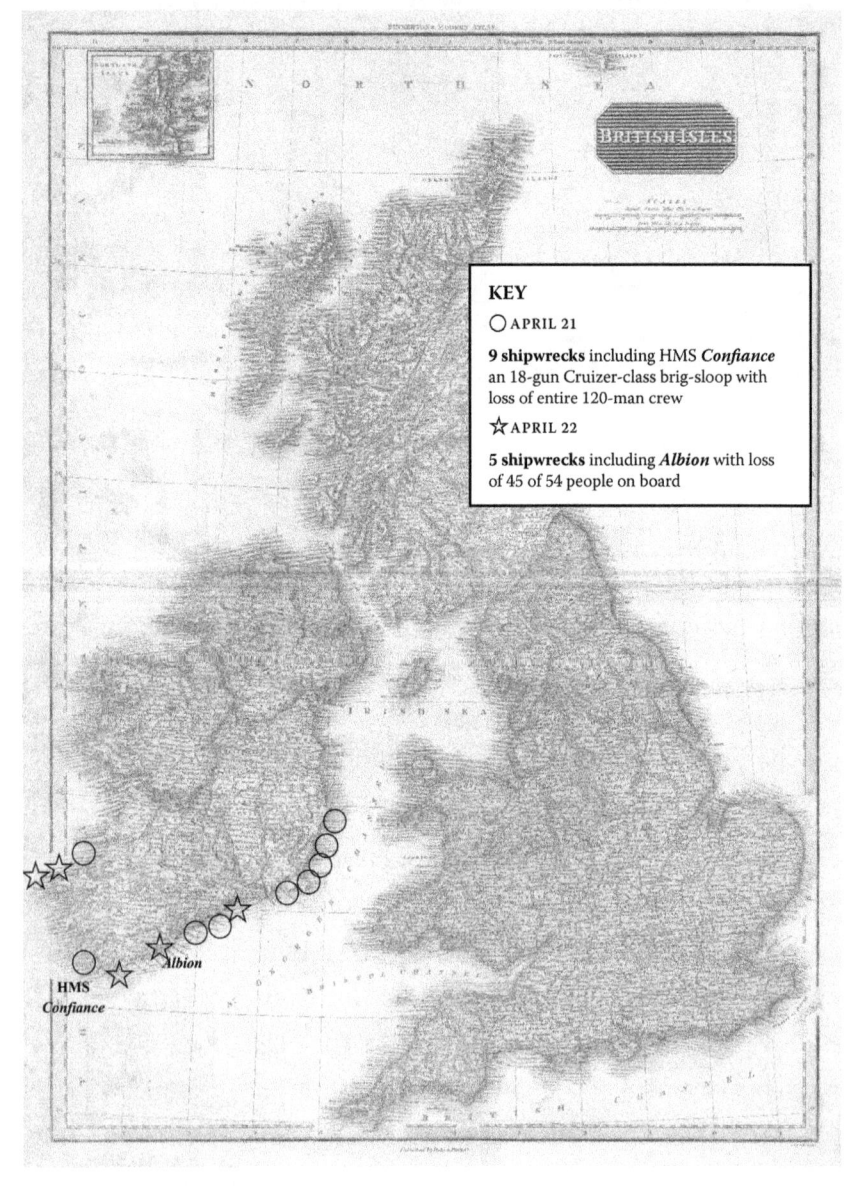

KEY

○ APRIL 21

9 shipwrecks including HMS *Confiance* an 18-gun Cruizer-class brig-sloop with loss of entire 120-man crew

☆ APRIL 22

5 shipwrecks including *Albion* with loss of 45 of 54 people on board

1818 map of the British Isles. Courtesy of Geographicus Rare Antique Maps. Locations of shipwrecks added by author.

memorials behind the church. Major Gough's was elaborate and surrounded by an iron fence. A wealthy Boston businessman; William Dwight; and Anne Powell, the daughter of the chief justice of Upper Canada, each had a stone slab placed over them. The remaining twelve bodies were buried in a row of unmarked graves between Dwight and Powell.

There is no way to know if Alexander's cabin remained intact after the initial impact. Hopefully, it did not. Because if it did, he probably traded a quick, violent death for a terrifyingly slow one. At first, he would have heard the anguished cries on deck from his cabin below. He would have been safe from being swept off the ship. As each wave crashed over the boat, his cabin would have alternately flooded and drained. But as the ridge dug deeper into the hull and the ship sank lower, his cabin would have flooded permanently. He would have been trapped in a dwindling pocket of air. His eventual drowning could have been clearly anticipated as he desperately gasped to breathe. If he lasted that long, he would have had to control his panic as he made his final peace with God and bid Kate adieu. It would have been an agonizing death.

The body of Alexander Metcalf Fisher was never recovered. He died at the age of twenty-seven. It was a tragic end to Kate and Alexander's touching romance. It would take over a month for news of the *Albion* to reach the States. When word arrived, it would shock America and particularly Kate Beecher. For five weeks after the tragedy, she counted the days, waiting for Alexander's letter to arrive, blissfully unaware.

10

Forlorn

> Hell is empty and the devils are all here.
> —William Shakespeare, *The Tempest*

May 1822–September 1822

Kate was lonely, but she was pleased to mark the four-month anniversary of her engagement to Alexander on Wednesday, May 22, 1822. She was twenty-one years old and enjoyed the celebrity of her new status as his fiancée. The weather got warmer in May, and the beautiful mountain laurels and rhododendrons started to bloom. Kate loved the natural beauty of Litchfield. She had asked Sarah Pierce if she could help at Litchfield Female Academy, and most likely, work was beginning to occupy Kate's days. At home, she enjoyed the company of her family and friends, including Lucy and John P. Brace. News of Alexander's tragic death, exactly one month earlier on April 22, had yet to reach America. But each sunset was a sentimental reminder of her last evening before parting from Alexander two months earlier. Piano practice had a sensuous but lonesome effect as well. He had promised to send her a letter as soon as he arrived in Liverpool. Based on cross-Atlantic travel times, he had told her that Saturday, May 25, was the earliest she could expect to receive his letter.[1] That was only three days away, and the anticipation focused her eager emotions.

Mail had to be picked up in Litchfield, so Kate probably checked for a letter on May 25 by walking the short distance to the post office. It was located in the general store operated by Moses Seymour Jr., who also served as Litchfield's postmaster for twenty years.[2] There was no letter from Alexander that day, which was disappointing but not a total surprise. Kate's engagement had been the talk of the town. Once Mr. Seymour, who was a married man with nine children, understood that she was expecting a letter from her fiancé, he would have promised to keep an eye out for it. Fortunately, the stage brought a delivery of mail from New Haven every day except Sunday.[3] Kate would have returned to the post office on Monday, May 27, with high hopes, but there was still no letter from Alexander. She understood that ships crossing the Atlantic could be delayed a few days, but nevertheless, she was disappointed. She likely would have continued her daily visits to the post office on Tuesday, Wednesday, and Thursday, with the same result. Her hopes would have grown each day and proportionately increased her distress when no letter arrived. It was surely disheartening to visit Mr. Seymour each day without any success.

When Kate checked the mail on Friday, May 31, there was no letter from Alexander, but one had arrived from her father, Lyman.[4] He had gone to New Haven for business two days earlier on Wednesday. It was rather curious; her father didn't usually write so soon after his departure. But Kate was distracted and apparently didn't open it immediately. She prepared to endure another sunset without a letter from Alexander. She entered the Beecher residence, and everyone was either out or busy upstairs. She sat down in the parlor and must have glanced again at the letter from Lyman. Kate broke the seal and began to read. The first few sentences told the grim news: Alexander was dead! The letter fell from her hand, and Kate collapsed unconscious on the floor. It is unclear whether someone heard her fall and how long it took for help to arrive, but when they found her, Kate was described as "insensible."[5]

Kate's family helped her into bed, where she remained until she regained her mental faculties. The shocking reality was that her fiancé, Alexander, was gone. She would never see him again. Her romantic engagement had turned to ashes. Perhaps later that day or the next, she read the rest of her father's letter with a combination of agony and disbelief:

> May 30, 1822
>
> My Dear Child,
>
> On entering the city last evening, the first intelligence I met with filled my heart with pain. It is all but certain that Professor Fisher is no more.
>
> Thus have perished our earthly hopes, plans and prospects. Thus the hopes of Yale College, and of our country, and, I may say, of Europe which had begun to know his promise, are dashed. The waves of the Atlantic, commissioned by Heaven, have buried them all.[6]

What sort of a person could deliver such shattering news in a letter rather than in person? Was Lyman's business so pressing that he couldn't come himself? If so, why didn't he send her brother Edward? As soon as Kate learned of Alexander's death, she needed someone to put their arms around her and console her. Lyman's letter was either a case of bad judgment or a complete lack of sensitivity. Either way, such news coming from her beloved father made it even more hurtful. Kate must have felt totally abandoned.

It was hard to imagine a more devastating emotional blow for a romantic person like Kate. But the deepest cut was about to come in the rest of the letter. Lyman analytically plunged the knife of Calvinist doctrine into Kate's heart as he discussed Alexander's eternal state. The question was whether Alexander's soul was burning in hell. According to church doctrine, that was the fate of anyone who died unconverted. This may not have been the first concern that popped into Kate's head. But Lyman quickly planted that malignant fear. This was the opening salvo in what would become an epic theological battle between father and daughter. Lyman speculated that Alexander might have achieved conversion in those final hours.[7] At that moment, Kate needed clarity, not just "hope." Although Alexander had expressed confidence that they would meet in heaven, her father was a trusted man of God. Lyman cast significant doubt on Alexander's fate. When her mother died seven years earlier, Kate had the immediate consolation that Roxana was in a better place. That was not the case with Alexander.

Finally, Lyman forcefully twisted the knife he had plunged into Kate's heart. Without a pause to let her process the news and grieve, he seized the opportunity in his letter to urge her religious conversion and told her to forget Alexander:

> And now, my dear child, what will you do? Will you turn at length to God, and set your affections on things above, or cling to the shipwrecked hopes of earthly good? Will you send your thoughts to heaven

and find peace, or to the cliffs, and winds, and waves of Ireland, to be afflicted, tossed with tempest, and not comforted?[8]

Lyman used Alexander's death as a teaching moment. He must have sincerely believed that Kate could find true comfort from God only through conversion. But while Lyman may have meant well, his timing was incredibly heartless. He failed to give her space to absorb the initial blow. He told her to forget Alexander in the same letter where she learned about his tragic death. It was a watershed moment between father and daughter. Although Kate never wrote how she felt about Lyman's letter, her feelings for her father were shaken.

While still in New Haven after sending his letter to Kate, Lyman met with James Kingsley, the Yale professor who had custody of Alexander's papers. The two men made decisions about the disposal of these materials. Kingsley appropriately retained Alexander's professional papers, such as lecture notes. But with questionable judgment, they divided his personal papers between them. Lyman took possession of Alexander's travel and religious diaries, and Kingsley kept Alexander's personal correspondence. They did this prior to the arrival of Caleb Fisher later in June. The disposition of the personal papers was apparently withheld from Caleb when he came. It seems unlikely that a father would knowingly surrender his son's most confidential personal items to strangers.[9]

Lyman read Alexander's diaries and discovered that the young man had meticulously recorded his inability to achieve conversion and had seemingly abandoned this process in 1819.[10] Lyman decided to keep the existence of Alexander's journals secret from Kate. He feared that access to Alexander's personal thoughts in these materials could have an unfavorable influence on her prospective conversion. Perhaps as a father and clergyman, he presumed the discretion to suppress information from Kate, but he had no right to withhold the diaries from Alexander's parents. Ironically, Lyman never suspected Alexander's more recent religious awakening, which would have been even more damaging to his cause.[11] Professor Kingsley's behavior was even worse. Although he was an officer of Yale College and considered himself to be Alexander's good friend, he had no right to withhold Alexander's private correspondence from his parents. Such a moral lapse was something Kingsley would not willingly admit, and it was kept secret for the remainder of the year.

Yale Professor James Kingsley. Courtesy of Yale University Art Gallery.

Rev. Lyman Beecher. Courtesy of the Litchfield Historical Society, Litchfield, CT.

Edward Beecher. Courtesy of Boston Athenaeum, Boston, MA.

Shortly after receiving her father's letter, Kate received a comforting letter from her brother Edward and responded to him on June 4.[12] In her response, she expressed her anxieties about Alexander's soul and her failure to find solace through religion:

> Your letter came at a time when no sympathy could soothe a grief "that knows not consolation's name."

> Yet it was not so much the ruined hopes of future life, it was dismay and apprehension for his immortal spirit. Oh, Edward, where is he now? Are the noble faculties of such a mind doomed to everlasting woe, or is he now with our dear mother in the mansions of the blessed? . . .
>
> My dear brother, I am greatly afflicted. I know not where to look for comfort. The bright prospects that turned my thoughts away from heaven are all destroyed; and now that I have nowhere to go but to God, the heavens are closed against me and my prayer is shut out.

Edward had achieved conversion only two months earlier, in March. He encouraged her conversion and managed to offer a bit more hope for Alexander's soul in his response: "Though your loss is great I cannot feel that your hopes are all blasted. Oh, why cannot hopes of immortal happiness rise in your mind? Then although you would feel that this world was not your home, it would not be a comfortless abode to you . . . Mr. Fisher I hope and believe is not lost. This is the belief of all who knew him."[13]

When Lyman returned home in early June, he met privately with Kate. Her young brother Henry, only ten at the time, witnessed the heartbreaking scene as he peeked into his father's study: he saw tears running down the cheeks of his father as he sat next to Kate, who was sobbing.[14]

Sunsets became a poignant daily reminder of Alexander's passing. Kate missed the poetry and joyful music they had shared. She longed for his gentle touch and would play the piano, not "for his sake" but to connect with him. The sensation of her fingers as they stroked the keys may have made her hair bristle. But the mournful tempo of her songs betrayed Kate's painful sorrow.

Initial newspaper accounts of the tragedy began to reach Litchfield by early June. Two ships from England, the *Criterion* from London and the *Martha* from Liverpool, had both arrived in New York on May 28, 1822, bearing the sad news about the wreck of the *Albion*. By the following day, unpublished word had spread to New Haven and greeted Lyman when he arrived on business.[15] By the first of June, the word was all over Litchfield. Printed accounts appeared in town within days. On June 4, the *Connecticut Journal* in New Haven reprinted the story first broken by the New York *Daily Advertiser*.[16] It included a graphic eyewitness account by John Purcell, the Irish steward who managed to save some of the crew, plus early comments by the surviving first mate, Henry Cammyer. There were reports of recovering $20,000 of US currency and over £3,500 of gold coins. A letter from Jacob Mark, US representative in Ireland, stated that recoveries included two boxes of specie for Professor Fisher. By June 8, lurid details were reprinted in New Haven's *Columbian Register*:

> Among the bodies washed ashore, is that of the French Lady; she was extremely beautiful; when first discovered [among the rocks] by some respectable persons it was entirely naked. It is mentioned to us as a fact which we think ought to be mentioned, that a country boy, who saw the body, took off his outside coat and covered it.[17]

From the description, the nude body was that of Madame Garnier, who had come on deck wrapped only in a blanket.

It is uncertain when and how the news of Alexander's death reached his family in Franklin. It may have been through word of mouth or news accounts; no personal letter announcing it is found among the somber materials meticulously collected by the family. Following an appropriate interval, Jeremiah Day, the president of Yale would have mailed Alexander's letter, which had been forwarded to him by the pilot.[18] Caleb Fisher's hands would have trembled as he held the envelope addressed in his son's familiar handwriting.

> Mr. Caleb Fisher,
> Franklin, Mass
>
> To be sent only in case of my decease abroad; otherwise to be returned to me.
> —A. M. Fisher

He must have choked back the tears as he adjusted his spectacles and began to read aloud to his wife, Sally:

> Honored Parents:
> I have not thought it necessary in taking my departure for Europe to dispose of my property with the formality of a will; yet as accidents may occur, and my life may possibly be taken away too suddenly to admit of making any arrangements of my affairs, I leave with President Day, to be handed to you in case of my decease, my wish in regard to my money at interest and funds. I think you will

admit it to be a reasonable distribution and will comply with it.

This is, that my friend Catharine E. Beecher should receive two thousand dollars and you the remainder. I should hope this last would be about equal to the sums you have charged against me for my education. Although I cannot devise exactly what would be the amount of my salary yet payable. It will of course be continued to the time of my decease; and I should hope that in consideration of the personal expenses I am about incurring for the benefit of College, the Corporation would be willing to make the salary of the college year, in the event of my decease, complete.

Your affectionate son,

A. M. Fisher

Alexander probably didn't expect to die. Otherwise, he might have offered some consoling words in his letter. But his first priority was to provide a substantial gift to Kate in the event of his demise. That demonstrated his commitment to and affection for her. Two thousand dollars in 1822 would be approximately $50,000 in today's terms.[19] As a matter of context, Kate had cleared only $100 after working in New London for six months.[20] Two thousand dollars was equivalent to ten years of earnings as a teacher and was effectively a grant of financial independence. The balance of his estate fulfilled his commitment to repay the investment his parents had made in his education so that it could be used for his siblings. Alexander's top two priorities were Kate and his siblings' education.

Caleb traveled to New Haven in late June to deal with

Alexander's estate. He brought Alexander's letter and presented it to the court in New Haven. A probate bond was filed Tuesday, June 25, and was signed by Caleb Fisher and Professor James Kingsley. Edward was authorized to act as Caleb's agent for the estate, so he would have been present that day in court. As a result, both Kingsley and Edward became aware of Alexander's bequest to Kate on June 25, if not earlier. Edward was authorized to advertise for claims against the estate and sell Alexander's personal property. He also was given control of all the financial accounts.[21] That was a position of great responsibility for such a young man. It would have been an appropriate point to mention what had happened to Alexander's personal papers, but he apparently did not disclose their whereabouts to Caleb.

The next day, a memorial service for Alexander was held in Yale's chapel. Presumably, Caleb timed his court visit so that he could be in New Haven to attend. It doesn't appear that he brought any of his family with him. Professor Kingsley delivered a celebrated eulogy that told the story of the shipwreck and extolled Alexander's virtues. He asserted hopefully that "those who knew him well, most easily believe, that the last feeling of his heart, as the [waves] closed around him, that the last aspiration as he sunk into the opening gulph was—'Father, not my will, but thine be done.'"[22] In other words, he speculated that Alexander had a last-minute conversion. Prints of the eulogy were advertised for sale within weeks, and it was favorably reviewed in the August issue of the *Christian Spectator*.[23]

Unfortunately, Professor Kingsley totally ignored Kate in his eulogy. He didn't even mention that Alexander was engaged. He expressed no sympathy for her grief. As a woman, she must have been particularly wounded by this slight to her status by the male establishment. She was incensed at Kingsley's lack of respect and compassion. From that point forward, she loathed Professor James Kingsley. He supposedly didn't mention her because he sought to maintain the solemn dignity of the occasion by "avoiding personal sentiments of the bereaved."[24] But an additional motive may have been envy, caused by Alexander's sizable bequest to Kate. An important clue was captured in a handwritten note on the last page of a surviving printed copy of the eulogy:

> Professor Kingsley has (very appropriately) omitted to state the fact that his lamented colleague was engaged to be married to an interesting young woman of Litchfield, Connecticut and that in the will which he left behind him, he bequeathed her what little property he possessed. JG

The mystery of the eulogy program, which is in the archives of the Litchfield Historical Society, is that the initials JG do not match the handwritten name on the front, Lydia Dillwyn. The identities of both JG and Lydia are unknown, but there must have been an insider connection to Kingsley to be privy to Alexander's bequest.[25]

The theological debate launched by Lyman in his initial letter to Kate on May 30 raged through the summer and into the fall. Kate expressed her hopes for Alexander's soul and pointed out inconsistencies in Calvinist doctrines. Lyman and Edward defended their beliefs and fought to save Kate's soul. Enough of the letters among Lyman, Edward, and Kate have survived to provide the gist of the battle. It was the fight of a young woman trained at Litchfield Female Academy pitted against two Yale-educated men. Kate clearly benefited from hearing her father's kitchen table theology discussions. But she was smarter and had stronger reasoning than either man. These were traits she inherited from her mother, Roxana.

Kate was probably unaware at the time that Roxana, who was raised as an Episcopalian, had once sparred with Lyman about conversion. It happened before Kate was born. Lyman had applied the standard approach for Roxana's conversion before they were married. He tried to get her to accept her wickedness and submit to God's will. But it had never occurred to Roxana that she was totally depraved and unworthy of God's affection. She wrote Lyman, "To love God because he is good to me you seem to think, is not a right kind of love, and yet every moment of my life I have experienced his goodness."[26] At one point when they were together, Lyman posed the ultimate Calvinist test to Roxana: Would she be prepared to rejoice should God choose to damn her for his own honor and glory? "She retorted that if to be damned meant anything it meant to be horribly wicked. The idea that for her to be horribly wicked would contribute to the honor and glory of her Heavenly Father was unthinkable! With a bewildered look, Lyman exclaimed, Oh Roxana, what a fool I've been!"[27] Roxana's superior intellect had bested Lyman.

Ultimately, Roxana professed to have achieved conversion, and there is no reason to doubt her word. But once they were married, Lyman claimed that she became a submissive wife. In reality, Roxana was an intellectual woman living in a man's world. She was a pragmatist and apparently decided to pick her battles. She let Lyman be the boss, but she asserted her authority when it mattered. Although Roxana knew Kate was smart, she never pressed her intellectually like she did with William and Edward.[28] Perhaps Roxana wanted to spare Kate some of the anguish that awaited an educated nineteenth-century wife.

In July, Kate demonstrated rhetorical talent that would have made Roxana proud. She channeled her struggle to convert into a debate with her father and brother Edward about religious doctrines and possible misinterpretations of the Bible. She wrote her brother:

> Sometimes I think the Bible is misunderstood . . . I see that my feelings are at open war with the doctrines of grace . . . I can more easily doubt the truth of these doctrines than the rectitude of God.[29]

As Kate argued the fine points of religious doctrine with her father, her logic against conversion hardened. In frustration, Lyman took Kate in July to Rev. Joel Hawes in Hartford. Hawes had a double incentive to help Kate since he was Lyman's colleague and one of Alexander's friends from Andover Theological Seminary.[30] Lyman wrote to Edward to describe her case:

> Catharine's Letter will disclose the awfully interesting state of her mind. There is more movement than there ever existed before, more feeling, more interest, more anxiety; and she is now, you perceive, handling edge-tools with powerful grasp. Brother Hawes talked with her, and felt the difficulties and peculiarities of her case. I have at times been at my wit's end to know what to do.[31]

The debates continued into August. Kate was a natural fighter, but she was emotionally drained by the intellectual battles with the father who had once been her playmate. At some point, she left a note on Lyman's desk.[32] It was a plaintive cry for help. In it, she was speaking about God, but it could have applied equally to her father:

> I am like a helpless being placed in a frail bark, with only a slender reed to guide its way on the surface of a swift current that no mortal power could ever stem, which is ever bearing to a tremendous precipice, where is inevitable destruction and despair . . .
>
> There is One standing upon the shore who can relieve my distress, who is all powerful to save; but He regards me not.

Lyman was frustrated by his religious debates with Kate. She had exhausted him. Rather than speaking to her in person, he wrote a cruel response on the opposite side of the page. He left it for Kate to find:

> I saw that frail boat with feeble oar, and that rapid current bearing onward to destruction of an immortal mind, and hastened from above to save . . . While the stream prevails and her oar bends, within her reach is my hand, mighty to save, and she refuses its aid. What shall I do? . . . If she refuse, the stream will roll on, and the bark, the oar, and the voyager be seen no more.[33]

Kate had not found the comfort she desperately needed from her father. Lyman had been the model for affection that Kate had once applied to disparage Alexander's supposedly cold heart. How ironic that in her hour of greatest need, it was Lyman who lacked a warm heart.

Lyman's unrelenting pressure on Kate to convert became

unbearable. She needed to get out of Litchfield. She had planned to stay with the Fisher family in Franklin for a few months starting in late October. But when she received an invitation to visit her Boston relatives, Aunt and Uncle Homes, in September, she accepted the opportunity to escape. Despite Edward's plea, she declined to stop along the way in New Haven to attend his graduation at Yale. She refused to be in the presence of that devil, Professor Kingsley, even to see her brother celebrated as valedictorian.[34] In Boston, Kate found comfort in reading John Newton's works, which stressed Christ's compassion. She established a friendship with her distant in-law Julia Porter, "another young woman, who like herself, felt forsaken. 'She is homeless and forlorn,'" Catharine wrote to Edward. She took pleasure in comforting Julia.[35]

Kate had not heard from Louisa since she received the news of Alexander's death almost four months earlier. Shortly after Kate arrived in Boston in late September, she got an anguished letter from her dear friend. Louisa had not written earlier because she had gone to care for her sister Marcia, who was "fading away beneath consumption's deadly hand." Kate acknowledged Louisa's sorrow but could not hold back the flood of her own anguished emotions:

> I am changed. I am not what I was. I never shall be again. You have known what it is like to have the first, best, ardent love of a generous heart. What it is to feel that there is <u>one</u> that ever loves you, thinks of you & <u>prays</u> for you, but you know not, you cannot know till you have felt it, the desolation of soul, the bitterness of spirit that turns even Heavens blessed light to darkness, when such a friend is forever lost.[36]

Kate's heart was broken. She was tormented by men who tried to analyze her rather than empathize with her. She was hounded by devils, and her faith failed her. She was forlorn, with nowhere to turn.

11

Renewed

> Should auld acquaintance be forgot
> and never brought to mind?
> —Robert Burns, "Auld Lang Syne"

October 1822–March 1823

Kate traveled to Franklin in October 1822 to live with Alexander's family for the winter. The sight of her lover's home and the memories of his parents and siblings reopened painful wounds. Lyman had counseled against the visit, fearing it would distract her from conversion. But that was a risk she was willing to take. It couldn't be worse than the torment in Litchfield. The Fishers welcomed her like a daughter. Fortunately, Kate found the unconditional love and support she needed from Alexander's mother, Sally. The bond that developed between Kate and Sally would prove to be important.

She was embraced by Alexander's family upon her arrival in Franklin. Kate had previously met his sister Eliza in New London. Caleb introduced himself and the rest of the family; his wife, Sally; his son, Willard; and his other daughter, Nancy. Everyone wanted to smile, but the initial gathering was more conducive to tears. As Kate entered the house, the first thing she saw was Alexander's piano, which he had sent for her to play. She must have paused as memories of making music with him and their sad farewell flooded back. She described the situation in a letter to her friend Louisa:

> Your feeling heart can in some measure imagine what were my feelings when first introduced to scenes so calculated to renew & aggravate grief. Here [were] his bereaved parents, who had lost their hope & comfort & his brother & sisters, whom he had guided in the paths of knowledge with affectionate & unwearied care.[1]

The Fishers and Kate gathered in the parlor near a portrait of Alexander that evoked mourning. Kate listened intently as each person shared their stories about him and testified how much he loved her. Caleb was a modest fifty-six-year-old farmer who was proud of all his son had accomplished. He was determined to carry out Alexander's wishes for Kate. Sally was fifty-one and the source of Alexander's warmth and intellect. She radiated motherly affection for Kate. Sally showed Kate the decorated box where she enshrined her memories of Alexander. It contained all his letters.[2] Sally expressed the wish to share these treasures with Kate. Willard looked enough like Alexander's portrait hanging on the wall that it must have been eerie for Kate. He was twenty-six, only twenty months younger than Alexander. Willard was smart, but because he was destined to take over the family farm, he had not been educated to the level of his brother.[3] Eliza was Alexander's nineteen-year-old sister with an outgoing personality like Kate. They had already met and corresponded about Kate's visit. Eliza welcomed Kate, who had just turned twenty-two, like a beloved older sister. Nancy was the youngest child at sixteen. In several ways, she would have reminded Kate of Alexander. She was a bit shy, quite smart, and musically gifted.[4] Nancy would have smiled bashfully at Kate.

The Sunday after Kate's arrival in Franklin, she attended church with the Fisher family. They traveled almost four miles each way by carriage to attend Sabbath services. The minister was the widely acclaimed Dr. Nathanael Emmons. He was a kindhearted man but staunchly orthodox in his doctrinal views.[5] He had personally instructed Alexander in theology and chose to eulogize him for Kate. He addressed her feelings directly. If she was hoping for comfort, she was sorely disappointed. After offering that there was "ground for hope that [Alexander] had experienced a saving change before the end," he asserted that Alexander's death was God's will:

> God may and certainly will do more good by his sudden and unexpected and alarming death than he could have done by his life. They know not to how many his death may be sanctified. It may have a happy effect upon a very sensible and highly polished person who may imagine that she has the largest share of sorrow in this instance of mortality . . . God has answered all his benevolent purposes by his death and all is well.[6]

Emmons's message was that Alexander's death was part of God's plan to save Kate's soul . . . if she would only seek conversion. It was a harsh warning that did not have its intended effect. Kate bridled at the suggestion. One can only imagine how it made the Fishers feel.

Kate's visit to Franklin required an adjustment in her behavior. Life on the Fishers' farm was the antithesis of the lively Beecher household in Litchfield. Everything was a short walk from the parsonage in Litchfield, and social opportunities abounded. Farm life was much slower. Social activity was limited to church and going to the post office in Medway, both of which required a horse for transportation. When Kate arrived in October, the harvest was in, but the animals had to be tended all winter, and household chores continued. Presumably, Kate did her fair share to help. The combination of isolation and sorrow may have made Kate wonder, at first, if visiting the Fishers was a wise decision.

Lyman continued his correspondence with Kate when she arrived in Franklin. In an October 27 letter, he appeared to soften his approach. He allowed for the first time that there might be different paths to conversion. Perhaps in a weak moment, he wrote:

> Some need one sort of discipline, some another; one to be driven by the flaming sword of Christ, another to be drawn by the cords of love. One heart to be melted, another to be broken.[7]

But about a week later, in early November, he returned to his earlier tone. He responded to a "sad" letter written by Kate. Lyman warned that "the renewal of your sorrows by so many touching associations as you find at Franklin has brought you a flood of temptation"; he worried that these would block "the mercy and justice and goodness of God."[8] He dispensed with the cords of love as he pressed the theological debate.

The constant reminders of Alexander were initially difficult for Kate to bear. But the love shown by the Fisher family gradually began to bear fruit. Kate developed a particularly close relationship with Alexander's mother during her stay in Franklin. Sally Fisher became the nurturing maternal influence that Kate's heart required. Strong emotional bonds were forged by their shared love and memories of Alexander. Sally apparently managed her grief by creating a memorial box containing her cherished bits of Alexander. She had saved every letter her beloved son had written to his parents and siblings. They were stored in her small chest that she had covered and lined with remnants of wallpaper from their home. The outside was green with a gold pattern; the interior contained gray octagons.[9] Over the course of several months, Sally asked Kate to read each of his letters aloud to her. The series started when he entered college in 1809 and ended with his final letter in 1822. At the appropriate junctures, Sally must have shared her recollections and little stories to round out Alexander's character. Mother and fiancée created new connections while spending countless hours together sharing memories of Alexander.[10] Kate developed a deep appreciation for Alexander's kind heart, love of family, and sense of humor.[11]

As their friendship blossomed, Sally's guidance helped Kate appreciate her own intellectual potential. Sally was an intelligent woman who was the source of Alexander's genius. She shared the math textbooks Alexander had written as a boy. She began to teach Kate mathematics the way she taught Alexander, who was a math prodigy. Her arithmetic instruction kindled Kate's interest in a subject that had always eluded her.[12] Kate began to realize how much she loved to learn. With gratitude, Kate began to tutor Willard, Eliza, and Nancy, like Alexander had done earlier.[13] She probably started with subjects she had mastered, such as literature and poetry. Kate began to read the books Alexander had sent for her enjoyment. These included works by his favorite authors, Jonathan Swift and Alexander Pope, quite different fare than her favorite works by Scott, Austen, and Burns.

Perhaps the most difficult emotional hurdle for Kate to overcome was playing Alexander's piano. She loved music, and he had sent his instrument to Franklin specifically for her enjoyment. But touching the keys that his fingers had graced aroused a thirst for passion that she had no way to quench. At first, she must have shared her two bound music books with Eliza and Nancy as they regularly practiced. There was a certain detachment possible as a music instructor. Eliza was an acceptable pianist, but Nancy was quite gifted, like her brother. Listening to the sisters must have inspired Kate to play herself. It may have felt strange to commune with Alexander's spirit through his instrument. But eventually, it was comforting and helped deepen a relationship with Nancy as Kate became a mentor.[14]

At some point in October, Caleb Fisher decided to collaborate with Yale on a monument to enshrine his son's memory at the local cemetery. Professor Kingsley was selected to compose a formal epitaph, which, in academic style, was to be written in Latin. Kate was asked to write original poetry that would grace the other side of the gravestone. She was excited at the prospect. It was the perfect opportunity to engage her poetic skills to help reach closure with her deceased lover. Kate had memorialized her sentiments when her mother, Roxana, died. But this time, her verses would be etched in stone to stand the test of time. By November, she had composed several different versions and sent them to her brother Edward, seeking his comments. He was enthusiastic about her creation. "As to the epitaph I like it. It is better than anything that I know of, especially the part from O Dark the scene." He went on to "suggest some verbal alterations" but allowed that whatever she chose, he approved.[15] After several revisions, she arrived at her final version,[16] which notably ended with Alexander safely in heaven:

> Thy grave, O Fisher, is the rolling flood
> Thy urn, the rock reared by God!
> Yet near thy home raised by affection's hand
> To speak thy name, this simple stone shall stand.
> How dark the scene, till Faith direct on high
> Beyond those orbs that charmed thy youthful eye.
> There now thy noble mind, expanding glows
> In floods of light nor pain nor darkness knows.
> Youth, Genius, Knowledge, Virtue past away
> From Earth's dim shores to Heaven's eternal day

Kate would have been curious to understand what would be chiseled on the other side of the stone slab. Edward translated Kingsley's proposed Latin inscription and included it in his letter to her:

> Sacred to the memory of Alexander Metcalf Fisher who was a graduate of Yale College, afterwards tutor + then Professor of Mathematics and Nat. Philosophy in the same. Possessing great talents + a very discriminating judgment, he applied himself so attentively to the requisition of knowledge that whilst he was but a youth he had nearly attained the highest summit of literary distinction. He possessed besides, all the virtues which adorn the character of a good man, affable manners, benevolence, integrity, the greatest fidelity in the performance of every duty, + supreme

reverence for God. Led by the love of service + the desire of seeing other countries, he sailed for Europe + was wrecked in his passage on the coast of Ireland + perished on the 22 of April in the year 1822 aged 27.[17]

But by December, Edward began to foreshadow a brewing controversy over her verses among his colleagues at Yale. "I like & approve the alterations which you have made because although some lines were very good which are omitted, yet they refer more to feelings peculiar to us."[18] What he was alluding to was the academic establishment's conviction that Kate's poetry would mar the dignity of the monument. The prevailing opinion at Yale was that Kate should keep her personal sentiments to herself and off Alexander's gravestone. This was an echo of the Kingsley eulogy controversy, a side effect of the male hierarchy's disdain for women. Edward's earlier encouragement had gotten him in the middle of a fight between Kate and her nemesis, Professor James Kingsley.

As the conflict ripened, a member of Yale's Dwight family sent letters to leaders of the college that attacked Kate's poetry. Word of his criticism reached her, and she was wounded. Kate was proud of her work and was offended that her sentiments were deemed inappropriate. In a subsequent letter, Edward diplomatically sought to downplay the hurtful comments. He wrote, "Mr. Dwight's letter was in true Dwight style. They are none of them overstocked with taste, but he supposed of course that he should be on the safer side if he praised Professor Kingsley . . . Moreover, it seems to me that in his criticisms of your verses he criticized technically & not from any true feelings of propriety."[19]

Yale exerted serious pressure on Caleb to omit Kate's poetry. But in the end, Caleb chose to have her verses inscribed as written. The memorial provided a public display of Kate's sentiments. Her poetry graced the front of the four-foot granite monument in what is now known as the Union Street Cemetery in Franklin, Massachusetts. Her poem was chiseled beneath this epitaph:[20]

In Memory of

Alexander Metcalf Fisher AM

Professor of Mathematics and Natural Philosophy

in Yale College, New Haven

Who on a voyage to Europe, perished in the

wreck of the Albion on the coast of Ireland

April 22, 1822 AE 27

Front of Alexander's monument bearing Kate's epitaph. Photo by author.

Rear of the monument bearing Kingsley epitaph. Photo by author.

In an act of true justice, the epitaph of Professor Kingsley was relegated to the back of the stone slab.[21] Kingsley had trifled with Kate's emotions a second time, and the misogynist behavior of the male establishment had earned her deep resentment.

Sometime during December, Kate finished rereading Alexander's family correspondence aloud to Sally. But as they finished his letters, Sally realized that some of Alexander's personal papers were missing. She wanted Kate to read his travel and religious diaries to her before she departed. Kate wrote to her brother Edward asking about them. He responded without hesitation, "Mr. Fisher's Private papers are all in father's hands except the letters to him which Mr. Kingsley has."[22] Edward knew that the documents had been withheld but didn't feel the need for an apology. He was most likely following Lyman's direction. Presumably, Alexander's personal correspondence was mostly of a professional nature. But one can imagine what thoughts must have raced through Kate's mind at that moment. Did Alexander receive Kate's final love letter, or were her intimate sentiments in the hands of her nemesis, James Kingsley?

Kingsley's sins against Kate were threefold. He initially ignored her in his eulogy. He and the Yale establishment had subsequently tried to preclude her verses from Alexander's monument. With Edward's revelation, Kate learned that Kingsley and her father had breached the trust of Alexander's private papers. Men had acted arrogantly, with little regard for her position or feelings. She had no legal status as a fiancée. But she had experienced the ugly side of patriarchal society. Kate had been abused because it was deemed acceptable in the nineteenth century; she was a woman living in a man's world. Her distrust and disdain for the male establishment had been earned by their cavalier exercise of power. She would never forget the lesson. This was a significant turning point for Kate. It was the start of her lifelong fight to improve the lives of women.

Lyman promptly complied with Kate's request to forward Alexander's personal papers. His excuse for not sharing them earlier was that he feared the religious diaries might derail her conversion. As Kate and Sally read Alexander's religious diaries, they would have concluded that he had given up on conversion in August 1819. Kate dismissed concerns about Alexander's religious diaries in a letter to her father. "I learned more from his letters, and in other ways, probably as much as I should have learned from his diary."[23]

Kate and Sally had previously confronted the most delicate matter concerning Alexander: the fate of his soul. They were painfully aware of the frightful implications of church doctrine if he died unconverted. Kate had never achieved conversion, and Sally had experienced it only three years earlier, in January 1820, at the age of forty-eight.[24] The early conversations must have been difficult. Yet Alexander's doubts about the process expressed in his letters from college provided grounds for optimism:

> For my own part, I am unable to reconcile the opinions which prevail here concerning the use of the means of grace [conversion] either with reason or scripture ... Nor do there appear to be any directions in Scripture concerning the use of the means of grace. On the other hand, when the five thousand, the jailor asked what they should do to be saved, they were answered: Repent and be baptized ... Likewise John the Baptist and our Savior preached immediate repentance. They gave no command to use the means of grace and wait for a blessing.[25]

In addition, Kate found credence in conversations with Alexander after their engagement. He had expressed confidence in his salvation. Something had reawakened his faith in God sometime between 1819 and 1822. Kate would have related Alexander's religious convictions to his mother's eager ears. Kate and Sally must have hoped, for his sake and their peace of mind, that Alexander's beliefs about salvation were correct.

There was a second dark secret in Alexander's past that his diaries fully exposed. Sally was well aware of it, and he may have shared it personally with Kate or in one of his love letters. In the summer of 1815, he fell into a deep depression and quit Andover. Caleb brought him home, and on his way to Franklin, his mood changed dramatically from deep depression to euphoric mania. He recorded this at the time in his journal:

> My spirits were unusually buoyant . . . On my arrival at home, my mother perceived from the rapidity of my motions & conversation that all was not right, and as she afterwards told me, was much alarmed by it. —Some of my mental faculties, I seem confident were really elevated.[26]

Alexander experienced a period of intense, exuberant mania, which he documented meticulously in a journal titled "Brief Heads—written under derangement." As Kate read his words, she learned about his elaborate scheme to save the world through the power of science. He was to be God's representative on Earth.[27] Alexander actually enjoyed the manic state and preferred not to be "healed" by the doctor:

> I had a plaster applied to my back and took wine &

anodynes. I would not have been reduced to my ordinary state of mind for the world. Altho' it was repeatedly suggested to me by some of my friends that I was deranged, I was absolutely certain that it was not so, and that my mind was never before in so perfect a state . . . it was more than a month from the time I was taken, before my mind was brought in every respect to its former state.[28]

Kate would have recognized evidence of similar behavior in her father, Lyman, and probably shared that with Sally.[29] Perhaps seeing symptoms of her father's disorder in Alexander provided an additional connection with him.

By January 1823, Sally's influence had significantly increased Kate's desire to learn. Kate asked Caleb to obtain Alexander's written lectures from Professor Kingsley, which he did despite Yale's objections. She enjoyed mastering new subjects, such as the nature of electricity, from his manuscripts. She even posed questions to her brother Edward to help her comprehend some of the more complicated scientific concepts.[30] Kate then used her new knowledge to instruct Alexander's siblings in matters of physics and mathematics. She noted that the Fisher children, "under their brother's care have made good progress in their studies. It is a pleasing mournful task to supply his place to them & it is gratifying to see them improve every day."[31]

Kate gained faith in Alexander's salvation and composed poetry to capture her sentiments. Her friend Louisa requested to see the verses. Kate forwarded the poem in a January letter to Louisa with the caution, "You ask for something original. I will send the last piece I have written not because it has any poetry in it but because it expresses my feelings."[32] It was titled "Jesus saith unto her 'Woman why weepiest thou?'" One of the six stanzas spoke touchingly of Alexander's love for her:

> I weep not that any youthful hopes
> All wreaked beneath the billows rest
> Nor that the heavy hand of death
> Has stilled the heart that loved me best.

She declared her independence and made a clean break from her father's religious views in February 1823. Kate had been living with the Fishers for over four months. Unlike her plaintive cries for help the previous year, she wrote with muscular confidence to her father:

> Should arguments equally powerful with those advanced by you and Edward, and ten thousand times more so, be advanced to prove I had physical strength to move the everlasting hills, it would be to no purpose. Consciousness would be that brow of iron that would resist them all... Now which is easiest to abandon, confidence in my own consciousness or in your interpretation of the Bible?[33]

She asserted that the church misinterpreted the scriptures about salvation. Kate, who was not allowed to attend college, had successfully challenged her Yale-educated father and brother on theological points. Religion had always been male turf, but she proved that a woman could compete. They agreed to disagree. Lyman accepted his failure as a sign that God had chosen a special role for Kate.[34] Roxana would have been very proud that her daughter had matched her husband and son blow for blow.

Kate's self-assurance extended to her newly appreciated intellectual ability. She had acquired a taste for the "higher branches" of education through her studies with Sally and tutoring Alexander's siblings. She had discovered that she loved to learn. Kate wrote to her father about this epiphany. She asserted her intelligence and decried the pitiful state of her education, which she attributed to neglect:

> My memory is quick and retentive, and all the reason my mind is not stored up with knowledge is the neglect of the past. All the knowledge I have has, as it were, <u>walked into my head</u>.[35]

Kate concluded that the education system for women must change. Sally Fisher and Kate's mother, Roxana, were both smart and talented in mathematics. Roxana had been quite interested in chemistry. But neither woman had benefited from the educational opportunities routinely provided to men. Kate realized that educational deficiency was common among women and limited their potential. The male establishment was not going to do anything to change that. She needed to act.

The critical seeds for Kate's mission had been planted. Lyman wrote to Kate about the possibility of starting a school. "I wish to know if it is your purpose to teach school next summer. If so, would it not be best for Mary & you to establish a school of your own in some suitable place rather than be assistants. It would be pleasant for you both."[36] Her brother Edward was now living in Hartford, so it was a logical place for her to share a home. Kate could continue to learn collegiate subjects from Edward. And Rev. Joel Hawes had mentioned the need for a good women's school in Hartford when Lyman had taken her to see him back in August 1822.

Kate put all the pieces together and responded in a February letter to Lyman that she had decided to establish a school in Hartford.[37] It was typical for women and men at the time to create small private schools, but Kate had bigger plans. She wanted to provide women with a higher level of education that would benefit their lives and society. Kate had discerned her new purpose in life. At the outset, she rejected her father's advice to copy the teaching methods of his friend Emerson Saugus.[38] She would found a school where women provided other women the education they deserved.

Emerging from a period of grief is a complicated process that varies from person to person. There is no single process that works. But there are two primary objectives required for success.[39] By establishing a new purpose, Kate had achieved the first prerequisite to emerge from her bereavement. The second requirement was for Kate to settle an ongoing relationship with her deceased lover, Alexander. Although she loved him, she needed to move forward with her life. Her initial wounds had healed with the caring warmth of the Fisher family. Playing on Alexander's piano must have served an important role in finding peace. Yet his love letters bound her firmly to the past. She could keep them and risk ongoing grief or destroy them and erase the memory of the one who loved her best. Neither choice was satisfactory.

Kate apparently chose a compromise and asked permission to place her love letters in Sally Fisher's memorial box. It served as a symbolic means to achieve closure with Alexander. It allowed her to leave him behind and simultaneously keep him in reserve. She wouldn't cling to him but would keep his memory private, buried deep within. The letters were safely stored with his other correspondence and carefully protected by his mother. Kate probably sealed them so that no one would tamper with her precious treasure. She was free to reclaim them at some future date.

Although there is no record of *how* she placed the letters in Sally's box, knowing Kate, it was most likely ritualized and involved music. One can imagine the scene as Kate prepared to depart Franklin in March 1823. She would have privately placed Alexander's love letters in Sally's box by candlelight. Perhaps she sang one of her favorite Robert Burns songs as she played Alexander's piano, in tears, for the last time:

> Should auld acquaintance be forgot
> and never brought to mind?
> Should auld acquaintance be forgot
> and auld lang syne?[40]

It had been almost eleven months since Alexander's tragic death in the wreck of the *Albion* on April 22, 1822. With the help of the Fishers, Kate had established a new purpose in life and had settled her ongoing relationship with Alexander. She was ready to emerge from her bereavement. A consequential career would rise from the ashes of Kate and Alexander's love.

PART IV

Career

12

Crusader

To dream the impossible dream, that is my quest.
—Miguel de Cervantes, *Don Quixote*

1823–1835: Educator
Kate Beecher launched her crusade to improve the lives of women through education when she founded her school for girls in May 1823. Hartford Female Seminary (HFS) had a humble beginning, with just seven students and two teachers in a room rented above a harness shop in downtown Hartford.[1] She offered "finishing studies," such as literature, art, and music. To a casual observer, it may have seemed like any other small female school in America. But her vision was bold. *Women would teach other women those subjects normally reserved for men.* Kate would also teach the "higher branches of education, including Rhetoric, Latin and Chemistry."[2] She was entering uncharted territory and would be challenged at every turn by the male establishment. It might have seemed daunting, but it was a noble quest, worthy of pursuit.

HFS was well received in the community and grew rapidly

from its inception in 1823. Within two years, Kate had to relocate to the basement of North Church in Hartford. The new venue conferred greater institutional stature to Kate and her school. She was pleased with her progress. But she found it exhausting to teach so many subjects to thirty teenage girls while also serving as an administrator.[3] Fortunately, there was always music to raise her spirits during the day. As the school grew, it became the platform for Kate's Hartford success. It provided a legitimate professional role for an independent woman. She was accepted as a peer by the heads of other institutions and welcomed by community leaders. HFS became a laboratory to create an innovative model for educating women. Her pioneering educational ideas included prioritizing communication skills (writing) ahead of memorization; connecting related subjects, such as geography and history, to make them more interesting; emphasizing general principles rather than details in subjects like mathematics; and introducing physical education.[4]

Amid her initial success, Kate considered matrimony sometime during the first part of 1824. Eligible suitors in Hartford would have found her interesting and talented but a bit unorthodox. At the age of twenty-three, she was beyond the average age when women married. It had been two years since Alexander's death, yet she was not deterred from marriage by memories of him. She simply set a high bar for romance that only Alexander had managed to clear. Then, in August 1824, Kate was jolted by the news that Louisa's fiancé, William, had deserted her.[5] They had been engaged for over five years. Louisa had delayed following William when his career took him to South Carolina. Instead, she had loyally gone to nurse her sister, who was dying of consumption. In Louisa's absence, William found someone else. Kate was incensed at what she viewed as William's treachery and lashed out at him. She impugned his integrity in a series of heated letters to Louisa and their friends. But her correspondence changed nothing, and William married the other woman. By the end of September, Kate wrote to Louisa about the end of her own marriage prospects: "What I said about a home of my own in one letter had not much meaning to it. If I meant anything it was a matrimonial home but I have pretty much concluded not to take one."[6] What role, if any, William's betrayal played in Kate's decision to stay single was unclear, but it did nothing to enhance her opinion of men. It was apparently the last time Kate ever seriously considered marriage.[7]

In February 1825, Kate learned that Louisa was suffering from consumption. She had contracted it while nursing her sister. It was the curse of the female caregiver. Kate wrote a tender letter professing her love and hoping that her friend was "yet to be spared." She lamented Louisa's condition as "frail + ready to sink like a bruised flower." She asserted "a sister's love could smooth your pillow & comfort your heart." Kate offered, if and when Louisa's days were numbered, to "take the place which your sisters would have taken if they were still on earth."[8] Kate attempted to arrange a meeting in Litchfield when Louisa traveled to Connecticut to spend her final days with relatives. But based on several letters they exchanged, it appears they were not able to meet. In Kate's final letter to Louisa in November 1825, she wrote:

> Louisa I think <u>good friends</u> are unquestionably the first + greatest blessings in life—without these what is wealth or beauty or fame or any earthly good—it is the sympathy of friends that give relish to all our comforts + consolation in all our troubles—I shall always

feel thankful I have so many <u>real good friends</u> + that I may count <u>you</u> among my <u>dearest + best</u>.[9]

Louisa Wait died early in 1826 at the age of thirty-two.[10]

During 1825, Kate provided increasing spiritual leadership at HFS in addition to her academic guidance. It seemed like a logical extension since she was the daughter of the well-known evangelist Lyman Beecher. Despite her theological battles with him, she had not rejected the Congregational Church. In fact, she even asked to join his church in Litchfield and later joined Rev. Joel Hawes's First Congregational Church in Hartford.[11] Kate incorporated prayer into the daily HFS routine and encouraged her students' faith. Teachers and pupil assistants who were more devout were paired with students who were just beginning their religious journey.[12] In 1826, this approach evolved into a religious revival like those her father conducted. It was an extraordinary undertaking for a woman, especially one who was unconverted. Lyman had mixed feelings about his daughter's spiritual activity and was not very supportive. Her revival was initially limited to students, but it eventually spilled into the greater Hartford community. Although Rev. Joel Hawes had been a good friend of Alexander's, when Kate asked for help, he declined and blamed travel plans. But as the fervor spread, Hawes was apparently caught off guard and stepped in to reassert male control. Kate's efforts were a notable success, with numerous "converts" among her students and the community.[13] Her experience instilled self-confidence and created a strong base of support among grateful parents.

The growth of HFS soon provided an opportunity for Kate to employ her leadership skills through fundraising. Her school required money to construct a more suitable physical structure for a growing student body and faculty. She engaged Daniel

Wadsworth, a wealthy banker and the leading financial supporter of First Congregational Church, to design the facade of her proposed building. She recruited key figures in the Hartford community to become trustees and support her subscription drive. These deft fundraising tactics were an indication of Kate's growing sophistication. But the Hartford city fathers found her plans for a school building "overly ambitious." When their sentiments threatened to derail her efforts, she marshaled support from the satisfied mothers of students converted during her revival. These women influenced their husbands to raise $4,850 through a stock subscription for the newly incorporated HFS. Kate built her new edifice in 1827, four years after founding her school. The building included a study hall large enough for 150 students, a lecture hall, and six recitation rooms.[14] HFS was well on its way as a professional educational institution.

New Hartford Female Seminary building. Courtesy of Harriet Beecher Stowe Center, Hartford, CT.

Kate kept in touch with Alexander's family and friends while she was in Hartford. She took his brother, Willard, and sister Eliza to visit Litchfield in 1824.[15] About that time, Alexander's eighteen-year-old sister, Nancy Ann Fisher, followed Kate to Hartford to attend HFS. Nancy, who was known in Hartford as "Ann," eventually became a music teacher at HFS, and in 1829, she roomed with Kate's sister, her fellow teacher Harriet Beecher.[16] Nancy became Kate's primary link to the Fisher family. She would have shared the wedding news when Willard Fisher was married in 1828 and when Eliza Fisher was married in 1829.[17] In an interesting twist of fate, Willard married the younger sister of Alexander's hometown crush, Eliza Wheeler. Kate was in constant contact with Rev. Joel Hawes, who lived in Hartford. She established contact with Alexander's good friend Denison Olmsted when he returned to Yale in 1825 to take Alexander's prior position as professor of natural philosophy and mathematics.[18] She would have learned that Denison named his first son, born in 1822, Alexander Fisher Olmsted.

Hartford and later Boston became magnets for the Beechers as they began to depart Litchfield. Edward ran a school in Hartford after he graduated from Yale in 1822. When Kate founded her school in 1823, he became her tutor for Latin and other academic subjects. Mary joined Kate as one of the two teachers at HFS in 1823 and continued until 1827, when she retired to marry a wealthy Hartford lawyer. Harriet followed her sisters as a student at HFS in 1824 at the age of thirteen. Kate's brothers Henry and George were sent to live with the other Beecher siblings in 1825 when the health of their stepmother, Harriet, faltered after a stroke. At various times, Kate, Edward, Mary, Harriet, Henry, George, and Aunt Esther lived together in a rented house in Hartford. Then, in 1826, the family center of gravity shifted east to Boston. Lyman accepted a call from the Hanover Street Church in Boston. Edward became a tutor at Yale in 1826, but he moved to Boston when he was called as a minister by the Park Street Church later that year. Harriet, Henry, and George followed the family to Boston. Henry eventually departed for boarding school in Amherst, Massachusetts. Harriet returned to HFS in 1828 as a teacher.[19]

In 1828, Kate made two significant changes to her vision for HFS. The first was her decision to pursue a source of permanent financial support for the school. She wrote to Edward about her bold plan to turn HFS into an "endowed Seminary of 130 to 140" students.[20] She wanted to shape it along the lines of men's colleges, which were supported by endowments. HFS was totally dependent on tuition paid by students each term. She needed a stable source of additional funding to professionalize the education provided for women. Kate's second change was a subtle shift away from her earlier religious revival activity to emphasize a more universal morality. This would broaden the appeal of HFS to women of all religious denominations. She intended to educate women academically and morally so that they could become a force for social change. By early 1829, Kate presented her new vision, "Suggestions Respecting Improvements in Education," to the HFS trustees. She concluded, "Education in this country will never reach its highest end, till the care of the physical, social, and moral interests take precedence of mere intellectual developments and acquirements."[21] To achieve her aims, she envisioned a distinct school department with someone charged with focusing on "moral character and habits." She called for the construction of a "boarding home" for teachers and students, for it was in the home that she believed morality was appropriately shaped.[22]

But Kate suffered two significant defeats in 1829 that soon

ended her quest for an endowed HFS. The community rejected Kate's ambitious plan to raise a $20,000 endowment. Her timing was unfortunate because it coincided with a campaign to raise funds for a men's school in Hartford, which ultimately created Trinity College. An exclusive affiliation with the Congregational Church might have been a pragmatic approach to raising money. But it would have compromised her nondenominational approach to morality. Ultimately, putting the moral development of students in the hands of women rather than male clergy was a bridge too far for the town fathers.[23] The second failure was Kate's attempt to recruit Zilpah Grant to HFS. Grant was a devout and highly talented woman, a cofounder of Ipswich Female Seminary. Kate offered her the role of running the new department of moral character with a huge salary of $1,000. But Grant thought that Kate's substitution of morality for religion and her vision of social change were too worldly. She rejected the offer, and with this second defeat, Kate's campaign to endow HFS came to an end. Her twin failures triggered a nervous collapse that caused Kate to cease work at HFS for the next seven months. This was the first of a series of professional withdrawals after Kate suffered a career setback. The bright spot was that her eighteen-year-old sister Harriet stepped into the breach and skillfully managed the institution during her absence.[24]

When she returned, Kate began to shift her focus from building HFS to launching a broader crusade for women's education. She needed a bigger platform to achieve her vision for women. As she honed her ideology, she nearly drove her family crazy. She engaged them in such intense debate that they came to dread her visits. Her sister Harriet, who was in Boston for part of 1830, wrote a friend, "Catharine has been here and we are thoroughly metaphysicated . . . At breakfast we generally have the last evening's argument hashed through and warmed over; indeed they served us with an occasional nibble the whole day."[25] Kate's siblings apparently preferred her earlier leadership, which focused on music and merriment.

In 1830, Lyman Beecher articulated the vision that captured Kate's imagination and turned her gaze westward. He considered an offer to head Lane Theological Seminary in Cincinnati. Lyman was enthusiastic about their mutual prospects in the West. The "West" was what people called the Northwest Territory, which primarily included the present states of Ohio, Indiana, Illinois, Michigan, and Wisconsin. He sent Kate an inspirational letter calculated to appeal to her interests: "The moral destiny of our nation, and all our institutions and hope, and the world's hopes, turns on the character of the West, and the competition now is for that of preoccupancy in education of the rising generation in which the Catholics and infidels have got the start of us."[26] Lyman ultimately rejected Lane's offer because of his commitment as a minister to help rebuild the Hanover Street Church, which had burned in 1830. But the seed was planted in Kate's mind. Following her recent reverses in Hartford, the West offered a bigger stage as she expanded her crusade for women's education. Edward was the first Beecher to heed his father's advice when, in 1830 at the age of twenty-seven, he became the president of Illinois College in Jacksonville.[27]

By 1831, competition with men as peers had toughened Kate's exterior. She had pursued a noble crusade for women's education that was worthy of romantic writers like Cervantes and Sir Walter Scott. She traded romance with Alexander for that of a crusader. She embraced her pioneering role as an unmarried woman. Yet an incident that summer demonstrated that her feelings for Alexander remained strong. Young Angelina Grimké

Angelina Grimké. Courtesy of Library of Congress.

came to visit HFS as a possible student. Grimké was enchanted by the school, but at one point, she read a piece of poetry that struck a deep chord in Kate. The poem was written by a young woman whose fiancé had died. Kate was "convulsed by agitation" and told the story of her engagement and Alexander's death. Angelina wrote in her diary that Kate:

> went on to say how this affliction had been blessed to her and how completely the whole course of her life had been changed by it . . . [that] she had been uncommonly wild and thoughtless, living without a thought of religion but since that time had been an altered character.[28]

But Kate's characterization of Alexander's death as a "blessing" did not square with her emotional reaction. A tender nerve had been touched.

In September 1831, Kate resigned from her position at HFS, and a year later, the trustees put it in the hands of her old friend John P. Brace. He gave up his fight to save Litchfield Female Academy and moved with his wife, Lucy, to begin a new life in Hartford. Prior to Kate's departure, she had allowed only women to teach at HFS as a matter of principle. She believed that women were more effective than men as teachers of women. Unfortunately, this practice limited the ability of HFS to offer an expanded science curriculum. Only so much could be done without college-educated men, and women were not allowed to attend college yet. Brace's presence brought an infusion of science expertise to the school's faculty.[29]

No longer employed at HFS, Kate focused on putting her emerging vision into print as *The Elements of Mental and Moral Philosophy*. During the winter of 1831, Kate anonymously published the book out of her own funds. She arranged to have copies sent to leading religious thinkers through a third party to gauge their response. The Unitarian Henry Ware "found much to admire and approve" but thought its doctrines "far from my own views of religious truth." She sent a copy to Archibald Alexander, a conservative Presbyterian professor at Princeton. Although in his case, she not only revealed her identity but also invited herself to stay at his house to discuss the book. He accepted her offer, which was the beginning of a lifelong pattern where Kate, as a self-proclaimed intellectual, insinuated her way into the homes of notable public figures. Professor Alexander found some of the passages too unorthodox, and she later removed the offending pages.[30]

By 1832, when Lane Seminary came knocking a second time, Lyman accepted the position. It had been two years since the initial offer. Kate and her father traveled to Cincinnati that spring to survey the community. Lyman was to head both Lane Theological Seminary and the Second Presbyterian Church. Kate was charmed to find her uncle Samuel Foote, her mother's brother, living in a magnificent Cincinnati home. Uncle Samuel had founded the prestigious Semi-Colon Club that sponsored evening soirees of intelligent conversation, music, and poetry, similar to what Kate had enjoyed in Litchfield. Edward King, her stepmother's cousin who had attended Litchfield Law School, was also in town. He had established the Cincinnati Law School, the first of its kind in the West. King was married to Sarah Worthington, daughter of the former Ohio governor; at thirty-two, she was the same age as Kate. It was almost like Litchfield had been transplanted on the Ohio River. Kate wrote her sister Harriet, "I have become somewhat acquainted with those ladies we shall have the most to do with, and find them intelligent, New England sort of folks."[31] She was thrilled to be connected to the pinnacle of society in Cincinnati. But what she failed to appreciate was that kinship connections could only open doors. Social status in the West was driven by economic relationships. The power and influence of eastern politicians and the Litchfield network were declining as economic growth shifted westward. In 1810, when Kate moved to Litchfield, the state of Connecticut ranked ninth in population among states, and Ohio was thirteenth. In 1830, just before she moved to Cincinnati, the state of Connecticut ranked sixteenth in population, whereas Ohio had risen to fourth.[32]

US CITIES IN 1830[33]

Rank	City	Population
1	New York	202,589
2	Philadelphia	93,665
3	Baltimore	80,620
4	Boston	61,392
5	New Orleans	46,082
6	Charleston	30,289
7	Cincinnati	24,831
	Hartford	7,074

Kate moved from Hartford, with a population of seven thousand, to Cincinnati, which was 3.5 times larger. Cincinnati was a booming metropolis of almost twenty-five thousand people on the banks of the Ohio River in 1830. It was the seventh-largest city in the United States and the largest city in the West. The Ohio and Mississippi Rivers provided cheap water transportation that brought immigrants to the West seeking inexpensive land for farms. Boats took their corn and hogs to the port of New Orleans for sale. The US government sold land that originally belonged to Native Americans, who were being forcibly removed, for $1.25 per acre. Purchases were funded by loans from hundreds of small banks that sprang up to support the real estate boom. Cincinnati became a prosperous manufacturing center where hogs were turned into salted meat, soap, and brushes. The city was nicknamed "Porkopolis." It was said that its residents used every part of the pig except the squeal.[34] Cincinnati was four times the size of Saint Louis, the second-largest western city, with a population of 5,832, in 1830. Chicago had barely one hundred inhabitants in 1830; its growth was driven later by the advent of railroads in the 1850s.[35]

Rapid growth in the West created enormous economic opportunity, which is what Kate's uncle Samuel was pursuing through investments. But when the Beechers arrived in November 1832, Cincinnati also suffered from social upheavals. The city struggled with waves of immigrants who faced religious and ethnic discrimination. It attracted radical abolitionists and became a key station on the Underground Railroad. Religious denominations began to split along North-versus-South lines over the issue of slavery. Public health suffered from waterborne disease as the river became the only waste-disposal system for the city's burgeoning population.[36] Business leaders worked hard to keep the lid on these challenges. The polite society that Kate embraced in Cincinnati was the result of a conscious effort by elite citizens to maintain civic order amid a boiling cauldron of social issues. It was a delicate balance the civic leaders did not want disturbed.

Cincinnati in 1841. This lithograph shows a view of the city looking south, with the Miami and Erie Canal in the foreground. The Ohio River and Kentucky are in the distance. Courtesy of New York Public Library, New York, NY.

Kate soon identified the need for a new school to educate women, and by the spring of 1833, she founded Western Female Institute. Her plan was to establish and lead a school based on what she had created in Hartford. But this time, she did not teach. She persuaded one of her favorite students, Mary Dutton, and some of the teachers from HFS to move west and run her school. Kate was active in society and accepted by Cincinnati's leading families.[37] Her position near the top of the social ladder in Cincinnati facilitated the growth of her new school. Western Female Institute prospered in 1833 and 1834. It was in Cincinnati that Kate introduced her innovative program of calisthenics set to music.[38] She was nearly two centuries ahead of her time. She appeared headed for success in the West.

Unfortunately, student activity at Lane Seminary later in 1834 caused problems in Cincinnati. That fall, a group of antislavery students at the seminary started to mix socially with Black residents. Lyman advised against interracial gatherings because they might stir trouble with conservative elements in town. He understood the range of sentiments. Although the Beechers later became strong abolitionists, Lyman had once employed Black indentured servants.[39] But the students ignored his warning and persisted in social interactions with Black Americans. When Lyman traveled east to raise money for the school, the Lane trustees seized the opportunity to disband the student antislavery society. That prompted a mass student exodus.

But matters got worse after Lyman's return. Word of his fundraising speech in Boston followed him back to Cincinnati. He had spoken of westerners' "limited means of education, and of the importance of introducing the social and religious principles of New England among them"; his condescending tone was not well received.[40] In December 1834, James Hall, an influential Cincinnati publisher, ridiculed Lyman. Daniel Drake, the powerful founder of both the local medical college and the local hospital, supported Hall. He published an essay that predicted the rise of independent western institutions free from the corruption of eastern influences. Most leading citizens would have preferred to have the controversy fade away. But Kate loyally jumped to Lyman's defense against Hall and Drake. Her reflexive response was similar to her defense of Louisa Wait when her fiancé, William, deserted her. She launched an aggressive campaign to exclude Hall and Drake from important social circles.

Kate traveled to New York in the spring of 1835 for her pivotal speech at the American Lyceum. In it, she boldly expanded her vision for women in education. She identified the need for ninety thousand teachers in the West. Her remarks were published in *An Essay on the Education of Female Teachers*. When she returned during the summer of 1835, Kate's uncle Samuel and her King "cousins" rebuffed her efforts to exclude Hall and Drake. Kate found herself shut out of society. Her aggressive tactics had backfired and turned the Cincinnati elite, whose daughters were the lifeblood of her school, against her. Later that summer, when she launched a campaign in Cincinnati to raise half of the $30,000 for her plan to identify and train thousands of new teachers, it was rebuffed by the citizens she had battled. Kate may have sensed her blunder, but she defensively claimed the "Committee were absorbed in their own affairs."[41] Kate repeatedly ignored Mary Dutton's warnings about the declining fortunes of Western Female Institute. Two years later, the school finally closed when the property it rented was foreclosed during the financial Panic of 1837. But the true cause of its failure was that Kate "alienated her constituency."[42]

The summer of 1835 was full of emotional distress for Kate. Her father was charged with heresy by Rev. Joshua Wilson, a southerner who had been the most prominent minister in Cincinnati prior to Lyman's arrival. Wilson saw Lyman as a rival and had resented him from the beginning. He brought Lyman to trial within the Presbyterian Church. Lyman aggressively defended himself and was acquitted.[43] But during the trial, the health of his wife, Harriet, declined, and she died in July at the age of forty-five. Kate had never been fond of her stepmother, so few tears were shed. A year later, however, her father, at the age of sixty-two, married forty-seven-year-old Lydia Jackson from Boston. The third Mrs. Beecher proved even less popular than the second.[44] Just one month after Harriet died, Alexander's mother, Sally Fisher, who had nurtured and mentored Kate, passed away at the age of sixty-four. Custody of Alexander's love letters to Kate moved to Caleb Fisher. It might have been a wise time to retrieve them. But Kate apparently made a conscious decision to leave them in Franklin.[45] Nancy "Ann" Fisher had already retired from HFS and subsequently married Rev. Thomas Kidder. In 1839, at the age of thirty-three, Nancy Fisher Kidder gave birth to her first daughter, whom she named Catharine Beecher Kidder.[46] Kate's bond with the Fisher family endured seventeen years after his death.

1835–1869: Philosopher Author

Amid Kate's distress during 1835, an opportunity emerged that helped launch her career as a feminist thinker. Angelina Grimké started a public letter campaign to enlist northern women in the fight for abolition. She was the same person whom Kate had met in 1831 when Angelina considered attending HFS. Kate's views on women were an outgrowth of her campaign for female education. She believed that it would be a mistake for northern women to support abolition and sent a letter of response to Grimké.

Kate opposed slavery as evil, but she supported gradual elimination rather than immediate abolition. Her differences with Grimké were over tactics, not the objective. Kate believed the measures employed by radical abolitionists were counterproductive. She noted that people generally responded better to suggestions that were made diplomatically by those from within their community. She pointed to the success of the British approach, which first outlawed the slave trade in 1807 and then provided the gradual elimination of slavery in 1833.[47] She contrasted that with radical broadsides by northern abolitionists like William Lloyd Garrison, which raised anger and defensiveness among southerners. She lamented that Garrison's attacks on southern character were similar to the sorry-state politics in America.[48] In terms that still ring true today, Kate declared that the objective of political parties had become to destroy the opponent's character rather than debate the issues on their merits.[49] She argued that humility and diplomacy were required to reduce passion and achieve success. She believed that women were uniquely qualified to provide such leadership:

> It surely has become the duty of every female instantly to relinquish the attitude of a partisan, in every matter of clashing interests, and to assume the office of mediator, and an advocate ... promoting a spirit of candor, forbearance, charity and peace.[50]

Over the next two years, her letters evolved into the 151-page *An Essay on Slavery and Abolitionism*, which was published in 1837. The purpose of the essay was to rebut Grimké's call for women to support abolition. But its logic outlined Kate's emerging "sphere of domesticity" ideology and the important role of women in society.[51] Kate noted that hierarchy was a natural state of human life—teachers over students, parents over children, and bosses over workers. That didn't mean that those on top were smarter or better. It was often the reverse. Women who ruled the domestic sphere were deemed subordinate to men who dominated the public sphere. But like a damsel in distress, the position of wives and mothers furnished them with moral authority. Theoretically, that allowed them to sway their husbands and instill morality in their children for the good of the nation. If northern women publicly supported radical abolition, they would forfeit their privileged influence. She believed it could lead to war.[52] Kate's vision was to educate women so that:

America will be distinguished above all other nations, for well-educated females and for the influence they will exert on the general interests of society.[53]

Kate's biographer Kathryn Kish Sklar noted that with her essay, "the core of the feminist dilemma took shape." Grimké and later supporters of suffrage thought female leadership was properly derived from natural rights as *equals* of men. Kate believed that women's leadership appropriately stemmed from *differences* with men. Although she accepted the existing sexual hierarchy, Kate asserted that the future of democracy depended on moral character developed in the home, where *women* were dominant. She sought to elevate the role of mother and homemaker within a "sphere of domesticity."[54] Kate became a crusader like her father, but not for religion. She sought to save her sisters and the nation through morality.

To support her new doctrine of domesticity, Kate wrote *Treatise on Domestic Economy*, which brought widespread name recognition and significant financial rewards. Her book effectively launched the professional discipline of home economics when it was first published in 1841. It was designed to improve the quality of life for female homemakers and their families. For example, she promoted the nutritional value of whole-grain flour and stressed the importance of proper ventilation. That was more than a century before modern experts deemed white bread an issue and demanded carbon monoxide detectors.[55] The accompanying figures were taken from her book and illustrate a professional approach to health and home.[56] She explained health issues using scientific diagrams of the vital organs and described why good exercise and nutrition were critical to their proper function. She did the same for the muscular, skeletal, and nervous systems. Kate asserted that almost half of American women had some curvature of the spine, which she attributed to lack of exercise, tight-fitting dresses, and long periods of improper posture during female work and activities. Likewise, Kate provided practical suggestions for the home, such as the floor plan for a well-functioning home. She shared useful suggestions for managing insects such as bed bugs, cockroaches, fleas, and ants. She even

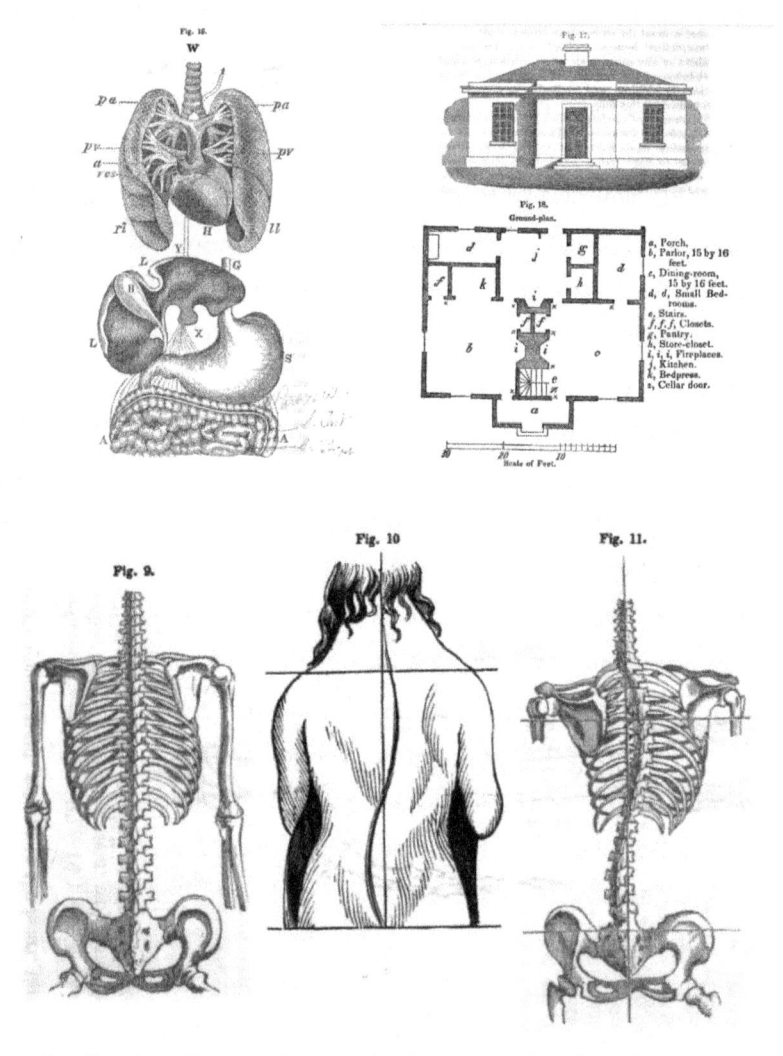

Figures from Treatise on Domestic Economy *(1843). Courtesy of Google Books.*

gave gardening advice for planting perennial and annual gardens, with flower suggestions organized by color and height.

Treatise succeeded because it met an urgent need for self-help by the masses of women who left their hometowns to head west. Although there were advice books available on various individual topics, Kate combined the information conveniently in a single volume at a reasonable price.[57] Alexander Fisher would have been pleased with its utility and Kate's application of the latest scientific research. Her book was updated annually and was followed five years later by a popular cookbook, *Miss Beecher's Domestic Receipt Book*. Kate became one of the most famous women in America. As a result of her popularity, some have dubbed her the "Martha Stewart of the 1840s."[58]

Kate traveled east during the summer of 1843. At the end of June, she stopped along the way to visit her brother George. He was a thirty-four-year-old minister in Chillicothe, Ohio, with a wife and two small children. George was passionate about ideas, and in 1836, he was the first Beecher to join the antislavery society. Gardening and music were his escape from intellectual excitement.[59] He entered the ministry to satisfy his father's expectations, but he was shy and not comfortable in the role. He suffered more than one nervous breakdown and may have been bipolar like his father, Lyman. The day after Kate's arrival, George died from a gunshot wound in an apparent suicide. The coroner ruled it an accident. His death was a horrible shock for Kate. She and George had both suffered religious pressure from their father. She gathered her brother's papers as she searched for answers. Ultimately, she used her connections to publish *The Biographical Remains of Rev. George Beecher*. Kate resolved to succeed where her brother had fallen short. But Kate's relationship with Lyman was never the same in the aftermath of the tragedy. The distance introduced by her clash with Lyman over Alexander's soul was increased.[60]

During her trip east in 1843, Kate returned to her plans for an organization that would find, train, and place qualified women teachers in the West. Her initial efforts had been spurned in Cincinnati in 1835. But when she arrived in New York during 1843, she visited the wealthy Cortlandt Van Rensselaer and his wife, Catharine, who had been a student at HFS. Kate used her new celebrity as an author to help establish herself as an expert who linked the needs of the West with the resources of the East. She won the Van Rensselaer's backing, which was instrumental in gaining wider financial support.[61] But she returned to Cincinnati convinced that political realities required a male figurehead for her organization to succeed. She found her man in Calvin Stowe, a professor of biblical studies at Lane Theological Seminary. He was conveniently the man her sister Harriet had married in 1836.[62] For the next three years, Calvin served that function as Kate continued to gather endorsements to launch her organization. She channeled her book earnings to support her fundraising efforts.

Horace Mann, the notable champion of education and hometown friend of Alexander, became a supporter. Mann became the first secretary of the Massachusetts Board of Education in 1837.[63] He was instrumental to Kate in 1846 when he helped her recruit William Slade, the former governor of Vermont, as the nominal head of her organization. Slade's role was to travel west to find locations for teachers and support them. Kate would stay in the East to recruit and train teachers. When he arrived in Cincinnati, Slade discovered that she had overstated the level of support he could expect from the community. He subsequently reorganized her committee as the National Board of Popular Education and effectively took control from Kate. She was outraged that he presumed to lead the organization she had created.[64]

Calvin Stowe. Courtesy of George Eastman House Collection.

Horace Mann. Courtesy of Library of Congress.

Gov. William Slade. Courtesy of Vermont Historical Society, Barre City, VT.

Shock from the fiasco with Slade caused Kate to seek water cures in Brattleboro, Vermont, to regain her health. The treatments involved a combination of wet bandages and ice-cold water to painfully flush out "bad humors." The treatments lasted for several weeks. Following a suitable period, she returned to her crusade renewed. This process of renewal became a regular pattern of Kate's behavior. Her nervous breakdowns tended to come when she faced failure.[65] She saw herself as a romantic, selfless crusader like Don Quixote, fighting against insurmountable odds for her impossible dream.

In one of her escapes, Kate invited Delia Bacon, a talented former HFS student, to join her at Brattleboro. Miss Bacon was thirty-five, single, and a Shakespeare scholar. She was also the sister of prominent Congregational clergyman Leonard Bacon. Since 1845, Delia had had a close personal relationship with a minister named Alexander MacWhorter. He was ten years younger than Bacon and had studied at Yale. Based on their

Kate Beecher, circa 1858. Courtesy of Schlesinger Library, Harvard Radcliffe Institute.

Delia Bacon. Courtesy of Wikimedia Commons.

behavior, Kate had assumed they were engaged, but when she asked one of his friends, he "scoffed" at the possibility. Delia insisted that MacWhorter had proposed, and her family demanded a clerical trial to clear her name. The charges were defamation, falsehood, and disgraceful conduct. The church establishment, led by Lyman Beecher's close friend Nathaniel Taylor, strongly backed MacWhorter and attempted to prevent the trial. Kate identified with Delia as a woman whose rights were being abused by the male clergy. Kate met with Taylor, who attempted to browbeat her over the issues. But his misogynist attitude was reminiscent of the male establishment after Alexander's death. It provoked her wrath and elevated the trial to a matter of great importance.

Kate took this controversy to a new level when she launched public attacks on Taylor and the church establishment. MacWhorter's supporters engaged in a "whisper campaign ... to smear Delia's reputation." During the trial, they exploited confidential information gained when Delia sought spiritual guidance from her minister, Rev. Joel Hawes.[66] In the end, MacWhorter was found not guilty by a vote of twelve to eleven.[67] Kate had taken notes and was determined to make a martyr out of Delia and herself. She wrote a book called *Truth Stranger Than Fiction*, in which she exposed the sordid details. Lyman was appalled and attempted to obtain and destroy her manuscript, which simply stiffened her resolve to publish. When Kate's book was released in 1850, it received poor reviews, but Horace Greeley called it "a deed of noble self-sacrifice and moral heroism." Delia fled to England and ultimately returned to America in 1858, where she died in an insane asylum.[68] Although Kate's crusade was just, she lacked a trusted advisor who was her intellectual equal, someone who could help moderate her temper.

The 1840s began the return of the Beecher clan to centers of power in the East. Edward returned to the pulpit at Boston's Salem Church in 1844 at the age of forty-one. Henry Beecher, who had done well as a minister in Indiana, was recruited in 1847, at the age of thirty-four, to become the minister of the prestigious Plymouth Church in Brooklyn. Harriet, at the age of thirty-nine, followed her husband, Calvin, to Brunswick, Maine, in 1850 when he became a professor at Bowdoin College. Lyman resigned his ministry at Second Presbyterian in 1846 at the age of seventy-one and toured England to lecture on temperance. He resigned from Lane in 1851 and settled in Brooklyn to be near his son Henry.[69]

As the 1840s drew to a close, Kate's career had peaked, and her world had changed. She toured the West, seeking locations for schools to train women as teachers. Two were established briefly in Quincy, Illinois, and Burlington, Iowa. But she was unable to attract the funding and staff to make them succeed. Facing the failure of her newest schools, Kate once again retreated for water cures.[70] John P. Brace resigned from HFS in

1847 at the age of fifty-four to take a job teaching in New Milford before he became editor of the *Hartford Courant*. Lucy Brace, his wife and Kate's friend, had died in 1841. She was the last survivor of Kate's inner circle of female friends from Litchfield. Sadly, she lived only forty-four years, but her son Charles Loring Brace provided a proud legacy when, in 1852, at the age of twenty-six, he founded the Children's Aid Society of New York.[71]

In the early 1850s, Kate settled on two institutions that were the focus of her remaining career. She took over Milwaukee Female Seminary and, in 1851, incorporated it as Milwaukee Normal Institute and High School. Kate found supporters among Milwaukee's German immigrants. In 1852, she founded the American Women's Education Association, which became her ongoing platform for advocacy. She used it to raise money for her school in Milwaukee.[72] Without a permanent home, she shuttled between Milwaukee and her relatives on the East Coast. She believed that what set her new school apart from other schools like Mount Holyoke or Vassar was that in addition to a collegiate curriculum, it "provided practical training" critical to a woman managing a home.[73] She grew it successfully until 1856, but her tenure ended in controversy. She took offense when the board wouldn't provide funds for a building project where she offered to invest $3,000 of her own money. Kate resigned in protest. When the school ultimately completed the building in 1861, she declined to accept a position that was offered.[74] But her school prospered and later became Milwaukee College, an institution that outlived her. In 1895, it merged with Downer College to form Milwaukee-Downer College. In 1964, its property was sold, and its students and faculty were merged into Lawrence University, which still claims its legacy.[75]

Kate's fame was eclipsed by two of her talented siblings in

the 1850s. Her brother Henry's career soared after he moved to New York. He became a popular and highly paid speaker based on his engaging oratorical style. He rebelled against his father's notion of a wrathful God and popularized the now-prevalent notion that "God is Love."[76] But he became famous politically for his heated opposition to the Compromise of 1850, which had strengthened the Fugitive Slave Act.[77] Then, a few years later, he became a fighting abolitionist after the Kansas–Nebraska Act of 1854 opened those states to slavery based on "popular sovereignty." He raised money for guns, termed "Beecher Bibles," to be sent to Kansas to defend its settlers against marauding proslavery bands.[78] During 1851, Kate took time off near the peak of her own career to help manage the household of her sister Harriet Beecher Stowe. This provided Harriet the time necessary to finish her groundbreaking novel *Uncle Tom's Cabin*. Kate tried unsuccessfully to influence her publisher to print Harriet's book, but it was deemed too controversial. When the book was eventually published in March 1852, it propelled Harriet, at the age of forty-one, to national fame and a more comfortable life. Harriet toured Europe on speaking tours and vacations.[79]

Kate's two famous siblings—Harriet Beecher Stowe and Henry Ward Beecher—with their father, Rev. Lyman Beecher. Courtesy of New York Public Library, New York, NY.

Harriet's son Henry tragically drowned in July 1857 while swimming in the Connecticut River. He was a student at Dartmouth College. Harriet and her husband, Calvin, were stricken with grief. She was tormented by the fact that young Henry had died without being converted. She faced the same emotional struggles about the fate of Henry's soul that Kate had faced with the death of Alexander.[80] Two years later, Harriet published a novel called *The Minister's Wooing*. It was the story of a young sailor, James Marvyn, who left his sweetheart, Mary Scudder, behind when he went to sea. He was thought to have died unconverted while at sea. When he returned alive rather than drowned, he found Mary engaged to the elderly minister in town. Fortunately, the minister bowed out so that James and Mary could be happily married. The novel was clearly inspired by the death of Harriet's son.[81] But it bore a startling similarity to the story of Kate and Alexander. Thirty-five years after the wreck of the *Albion*, Harriet understood the scars Kate still bore. Some family members saw the novel as an allegory of how Kate's life might have turned out if Alexander had lived.[82]

Harriet Beecher Stowe's son, Henry, who drowned at age nineteen. Courtesy of New England Historical Society, Boston, MA.

Kate's life was dedicated to improving the lives of American women. But as the women's rights movement picked up steam in the 1850s, she fervently opposed it. She shared the objective of fighting for women with younger leaders like Elizabeth Cady Stanton and Susan B. Anthony. But she differed with them on the appropriate tactics. She favored education and petitions to help women, whereas Stanton and Anthony focused on suffrage as both a right and a means to improve the lives of females. Kate published *The True Remedy for the Wrongs of Woman* in 1851, in which she opposed Stanton and Anthony's efforts.[83] Kate feared that women would be corrupted by politics. It was a corollary to her earlier arguments about the role of women in abolition.

Susan B. Anthony. *Courtesy of History of Woman Suffrage.*

Elizabeth Cady Stanton *and daughter Harriot. Courtesy of Library of Congress.*

During the Civil War, the Beecher siblings collaborated on their father's two-volume *Autobiography* to cement his legacy before he died in 1863. Kate's brother Charles served as editor as the Beechers created a monumental, if slightly self-serving, tribute to Lyman.[84] The writing process helped reorient Kate's sense of identity. It rekindled her memories about her debates with Lyman over the fate of Alexander's soul. She must have read with interest Roxana's debates with Lyman about conversion. She had always identified more with her father's emotional side. But as she explored Roxana's intellect, Kate began to identify with her mother.

During the 1850s, Kate's interest shifted from morality back to religion. She may have been spurred on by her brother Edward's book *The Conflict of Ages*, published in 1853.[85] She authored two books that summarized her beliefs, *Common Sense Applied to Religion* in 1857 and *An Appeal to the People in Behalf of Their Rights as Authorized Interpreters of the Bible* in 1860.[86] While she found fault with all Christian denominations, Kate admired the way the Episcopal Church included children as full members. Her mother, Roxana, was raised as an Episcopalian, and Kate found the church more welcoming to a diversity of beliefs. In 1862, she officially joined the Episcopal Church.[87]

In 1864, she published *Religious Training of Children in the School, the Family, and the Church*, another work about her faith. It was an intellectual tour de force. She believed that one should interpret the Bible and live accordingly rather than rely on doctrines developed by expert theologians.[88] The Bible should be used to guide one's life to create the best good for humankind.[89] A memorable way to summarize her pragmatic approach to life and salvation would be as follows:

> Faith is a journey and God will judge us more for the direction we pursue in life than for the mistakes we make.[90]

Kate lived with her sister Harriet during 1869 as they collaborated on an updated collection of domestic advice in *The American Woman's Home*.[91] As Kate turned sixty-nine that year, her thoughts turned to securing her legacy. She was a weary crusader who wanted to retire in peace to write her memoirs. She had no warning of the challenges ahead.

13

Legacy

> She was the mother of more children than any other woman in all parts of the country that gratefully remembered her as teacher and guide.
> —Henry Ward Beecher

1870–1878
Kate returned to Hartford Female Seminary (HFS) during the fall of 1870 in an attempt to revive the fortunes of the school she had founded. One of the students recalled her as a "strange old lady . . . whom we both made fun of and at the same time respected and admired"; she played the piano and addressed the assembled students in the main hall.[1] The school still had one hundred students and offered a total of forty-four courses, including geometry, trigonometry, chemistry, botany, Latin, French, history, composition, English literature, instrumental music, and gymnastics. But growing competition from public schools threatened the existence of HFS. In 1870, thanks to pioneers like Kate Beecher, Emma Willard, and Mary Lyon, public high schools provided most of these subjects to young women

for free. HFS was not an endowed institution, and to make ends meet, it had to charge a tuition higher than that for some men's colleges.[2] Kate returned at the request of the school's trustees and lent them money for needed renovations. Seven months later, when the trustees refused to repay her loan, Kate resigned and relinquished the reins of the school to Miss Mary Beecher.[3] It was time to settle down and write her memoirs.

When Kate returned to Hartford near the end of her career, it was a different city than the one she had left in 1832. By 1870, Hartford had a population of 37,180, which was only half the size of Milwaukee and less than 20 percent of the size of Cincinnati.[4] But Hartford was perhaps the richest city in America. During the 1850s, Samuel Colt had revolutionized the manufacturing of guns by using interchangeable parts. The Civil War provided funding for profitable growth in the arms industry. Colt's innovation and the trained workers from his factory attracted competitors like John Browning and spawned numerous machine tool shops. The infrastructure and skilled workforce gave rise to the manufacturing of sewing machines and typewriters using Colt's concept of interchangeable parts. As a result, vast wealth was created in Hartford, which became America's "Silicon Valley" of its day. The artistic community thrived in Hartford, and a residential neighborhood called Nook Farm attracted authors like Harriet Beecher Stowe and Mark Twain. Describing Hartford in 1868, Twain declared, "Of all the beautiful towns it has been my fortune to see this is the chief."[5]

Kate was a notable character in Hartford. Music and drama were constant parts of her life. She sent invitations to a "door step concert at Nook Farm with Miss Beecher at the guitar." She entertained leading Hartford intellectuals like Horace Bushnell with her theatrics and parodies of sermons.[6] Kate enjoyed mingling with the cultured inhabitants of the community. She joined Trinity

Episcopal Church and humorously cajoled a free ride home after church by telling the driver that she was a friend of the carriage owner.[7] It was a comfortable environment where Kate could live while she composed her memoirs during 1872 and 1873.

Beecher–Tilton Scandal

Isabella Beecher Hooker. Courtesy of Wikimedia Commons.

Victoria Woodhull. Courtesy of Fine Arts Library, Harvard University.

Elizabeth Tilton. Courtesy of Museum of the City of New York, New York, NY.

Henry Ward Beecher. Courtesy of Library of Congress.

While Kate wrote her memoirs, a sex scandal engulfed her brother Henry. Victoria Woodhull had attracted Kate's half sister, Isabella Beecher Hooker, to the suffrage movement. Woodhull was criticized by the Beechers for her notorious advocacy of "free love." In 1871, Isabella wanted Kate to get to know Woodhull and arranged for the two of them to take a New York carriage together so that they could meet. During the ride, Woodhull disclosed to Kate that her brother Henry was having an affair. He had committed adultery with a parishioner, Elizabeth Tilton, who was the wife of one of Henry's friends. Woodhull demanded that the hypocritical attacks on her cease or she would expose the sordid details. Kate instinctively declared her brother innocent and reportedly threatened to strike Woodhull dead if she went public with the story. When Woodhull eventually published the lurid story, she incurred Kate's wrath. The Beecher–Tilton scandal captured newspaper headlines and the public's imagination as it unfolded over the next four years. When a church trial predictably exonerated Henry, Tilton's husband pursued him with a civil lawsuit. Kate and most of the Beecher siblings loyally supported Henry's innocence, with the notable exception of Isabella. Although Henry was found not guilty, it was clear to many that the affair was real. The Beecher name was tarnished by the matter.[8]

Kate positioned her legacy in *Educational Reminiscences and Suggestions*, which was published in 1874. The pointed tone of her work was probably accentuated by the Beecher–Tilton scandal, which unfolded as she wrote. As with most memoirs, she accentuated the positives and downplayed her mistakes. Although she attributed many of her failures to men, the misogynist behavior of the male establishment throughout her career justly deserved her contempt. She particularly despised male control of the purse strings: "Be it understood, however, that in all these transactions

I was guided by the counsels of the best business men. Where I was in error it was by following 'good advice.'"[9] Men had denied HFS the endowment it required, and Kate blamed men for her school's decline.

One of the delicate issues Kate had to address was her long-standing opposition to suffrage. Her position had evolved significantly between 1850 and 1870. What started as a philosophical disagreement became a debate about practical considerations. She predicted that suffrage would not be possible during the nineteenth century and that improvements in women's rights and health demanded immediate remedies. Despite her tactical objections to suffrage, she declared her shared principles with the women's movement in an address delivered in Boston in December 1870:

> We agree, then on the general principle that women's happiness and usefulness are equal in value to those of man's and consequently she has the right to equal advantages for securing them.
>
> We agree, also that woman, even in our own age and country, has never been allowed such equal advantages, and that multiplied wrongs and suffering have resulted from this injustice.
>
> Finally, we agree that it is the right and duty of every woman to employ the power of organization and agitation, in order to gain those advantages which are given to the one sex, and unjustly withheld from the other.[10]

That was a significant change from her earlier position. Kate did not include these principles in her memoir, but she did support suffrage for educated women.[11]

The other ticklish question was how to treat Alexander in her memoir, which was designed to cement her independent legacy. Excluding him would demonstrate her consistency of purpose as a role model for single women. Including him would complicate her storyline. She chose to exclude the saga of her engagement and Alexander's tragic death entirely. Yet there was an unmistakable, though nameless, reference to Alexander, whom she credited for her interest in "Mental Philosophy." Describing her early years in Hartford, she wrote, "Soon I became deeply interested in this study; for I had been led to my profession by most profound and agitating fears of dangers in the life to come, not only for myself, but for a dear friend who, according to the views in which I had been trained, had died unprepared."[12] She also paid unnamed homage to Alexander's mother, Sally, as the mentor who introduced her to arithmetic, writing that at "twenty-two . . . [she] was favored by most thorough instruction from a friend in the family where I spent the winter."[13] The inclusion of references to Alexander and Sally revealed deep connections. It was a testament to their influence on her purpose to help women through education. Her relationship with Alexander was Catharine Beecher's untold story.

• ♦ •

Three intertwined strands of achievement ran through Kate's evolving career. First and foremost, she was a pioneer advocate for women's education. She raised the academic bar and expectations for the education of females. Her innovative curriculum provided a framework for women's higher education in America and established her place in the Pantheon of Pioneer American Female Educators, some of whom are discussed here.

Sarah Pierce *(1767–1852), Litchfield Female Academy, 1792. Courtesy of Litchfield Historical Society, Litchfield, CT.*

Emma Hart Willard *(1787–1870), Troy Female Seminary, 1821. Courtesy of Schlesinger Library, Harvard Radcliffe Institute.*

Catharine (Kate) Beecher *(1800–1878), Hartford Female Seminary, 1823; Milwaukee Normal Institute, 1851. Courtesy of Schlesinger Library, Harvard Radcliffe Institute.*

Zilpah Grant Banister *(1794–1874), Ipswich Female Seminary, 1828. Courtesy of Fran Simpson.*

Mary Lyon *(1797–1849), Mount Holyoke Female Seminary, 1837. Courtesy of Wikimedia Commons.*

Catharine (Kate) Beecher notably founded HFS in 1823 and the Milwaukee Normal Institute in 1851. Although HFS lasted only sixty years, her school in Milwaukee became Milwaukee College in 1853 and later Milwaukee-Downer College in 1895. In 1964, it merged with Lawrence University in Appleton, Wisconsin, which still claims its heritage.[14]

Sarah Pierce founded the Litchfield Female Academy in 1792. The school started by teaching women ornamental subjects like art, needlework, and music. But it added academic subjects such as chemistry, history, botany, science, and languages. Pierce espoused the post–American Revolution philosophy of Republican motherhood, which emphasized the importance to democracy of the moral and intellectual training of children. Kate Beecher attended LFA as a student and later served as a teacher.[15]

Emma Hart Willard founded the Troy Female Seminary in 1821. She believed that women could learn the higher branches of education just as well as men. Troy was the first school in the United States to offer a higher education curriculum for women, including mathematics, philosophy, geography, history, and science. It was likely the pattern for Kate Beecher's school in Hartford.[16]

Zilpah Grant Banister cofounded the Ipswich Female Seminary in 1828. She attended the Byfield Academy around 1811, where she studied under Rev. Joseph Emerson, who believed that women should be educated more like men. She remained to teach at Byfield, where her most famous student was Mary Lyon. While at Byfield, Zilpah may have taught Alexander Fisher's sisters, Eliza and Nancy, who attended the school. Zilpah rejected Kate Beecher's offer to join HFS in 1829.[17]

Mary Lyon cofounded Ipswich Female Seminary in 1828 and founded Mount Holyoke Female Seminary in 1837. She had been educated at Byfield, where rigorous academics were combined with religious commitment. She followed Zilpah Grant Banister to Ipswich, where she became a teacher. In 1834, she helped found Wheaton Female Seminary. When she founded Mount Holyoke Female Seminary in 1837, she hoped that her school would appeal to a broader socioeconomic group of women.[18]

Kate's students and teachers were living proof of her importance as an educator. Countless American women were educated at schools she founded or were taught by teachers she trained. These women are but a sample of her profound impact.

Harriet Beecher Stowe became an author and abolitionist. She was Kate's younger sister. Harriet was one of the first students to attend HFS and later served as a teacher. She was the author of many novels, including *Uncle Tom's Cabin*, which established her credentials as an abolitionist. She was also a prolific writer of short stories, nonfiction books, and articles.[19]

Sarah Payson Willis, "Fanny Fern," became a popular columnist, humorist, and novelist. Kate Beecher described Sarah as one of the "worst-behaved" students at HFS but also "loved her the best." Sarah published her first article in 1851 under the pen name "Fanny Fern." Her first book, *Fern Leaves* (1853), was a bestseller. By 1855, she was the highest-paid columnist in America.[20]

Sarah Walker Davis became an adviser to her husband, David Davis, who was Abraham Lincoln's campaign manager in 1860 and later a Supreme Court justice. She attended HFS and was a dedicated intellectual. Sarah married David Davis, a prominent lawyer, in 1838 and followed him to Bloomington, Illinois. She and her husband became close friends of Lincoln, and he was a frequent visitor to their home.[21]

Mary Hawes Van Lennep became a missionary and memoirist. She was the only daughter of Rev. Joel Hawes. She graduated

Select HFS Students and Teachers

Harriet Beecher Stowe (1811–1896). *Courtesy of Francis Holl.*

Fanny Fern (1811–1872). *Courtesy of Wikimedia Commons.*

Sarah Walker Davis (1814–1870). *Courtesy of McLean County Museum of History, Bloomington, IL.*

Mary Hawes Van Lennep (1821–1844). *Courtesy of Wikimedia Commons.*

Rose Terry Cooke (1827–1892). *Courtesy of Wikimedia Commons.*

Virginia Thrall Smith (1836–1903). *Courtesy of Connecticut Women's Hall of Fame, New Haven, CT.*

Annie Trumbull Slosson (1838–1926). *Courtesy of JSTOR.*

Kate Foote Coe (1840–1923). *Courtesy of Wikimedia Commons.*

from HFS in 1838. She kept a journal (1841–1843) of her life and character, which was published in 1847. She became a missionary and departed for Turkey with her husband in 1843 and died abroad of dysentery in 1844.[22]

Rose Terry Cooke became a poet and author. She attended HFS at the age of ten and received instruction from Kate's friend John P. Brace. Her first published poem appeared in the *New-York Daily Tribune* in 1851 and was highly acclaimed. She contributed articles and stories to *Putnam's Magazine*, the *Atlantic Monthly*, and *Harper's*.[23]

Virginia Thrall Smith became a pioneer advocate for children. She attended HFS in the late 1830s. She became interested in local charities and was appointed administrator of Hartford City Mission in 1876. She was devoted to helping the poor, and in 1881, she started a free kindergarten at the Hartford City Mission. In 1892, she organized the Connecticut Children's Aid Society.[24]

Annie Trumbull Slosson became an author and entomologist. She attended HFS after her wealthy merchant family moved to Hartford in 1852. She was best known for her short stories, which were published in the *Atlantic Monthly* and *Harper's*. She collected insect specimens during her frequent travels, and late in life, she was known as "the old bug lady."[25]

Kate Foote Coe became an educator and journalist. She was Kate Beecher's first cousin and served as a teacher at HFS in the early 1860s before heading south to teach former enslaved people after the Civil War. She traveled the West and became an advocate for Native American education and health. Kate served for fifteen years as the Washington, DC, correspondent for the *Independent*.[26]

The second strand of Kate's achievement was moral philosophy. Kate was an original feminist thinker who crystallized the view that women should capitalize on their differences from men to assert leadership. She articulated an important role for educated women as mothers and teachers to change America for the better. She also developed a spiritual philosophy that individuals should pattern their lives on a commonsense understanding of the Bible rather than the abstract doctrines devised by theologians. She believed that God would judge a person's faith by its "abiding, controlling purpose" more than its frequent "failures and shortcomings."[27] She published numerous books and essays, including *The Elements of Mental and Moral Philosophy* (1831), *An Essay on the Education of Female Teachers* (1835), *An Essay on Slavery and Abolitionism* (1837), *Common Sense Applied to Religion* (1957), and *Religious Training of Children in the School, the Family, and the Church* (1864). It was an intellectual body of work worthy of a PhD by a woman who was never allowed to attend college.

The third strand of Kate's achievement was as a bestselling author. For three decades in the nineteenth century, Kate Beecher was a household name in America. She was widely popular as a dispenser of practical advice that affected the lives of millions of people. She employed the latest science on health and nutrition to provide guidance. She founded the discipline of home economics, but her books took these lessons beyond the classroom, directly to the home. Her influence is sometimes likened to that of Martha Stewart. Her books *Treatise on Domestic Economy* (1841) and *Miss Beecher's Domestic Receipt Book* (1846) were reprinted for decades. They were bestsellers and perennial sellers. Kate plowed all of her earnings back into her crusades for women. She reprised these works in 1869 as *The American Woman's Home* with her sister Harriet. Her success as an author demonstrated her relevance to women in the nineteenth century.

No one is perfect, and Kate had significant weaknesses. Her early success made it more difficult for her to admit and learn from her mistakes. She had no trusted sounding board with sufficient intellect to challenge her opinions. It was unfortunate that her gifted mother, Roxana, died when Kate was only sixteen. Kate developed an authoritative style as her career progressed, which sometimes grated on men and women alike. But she was also skilled at using charm to get her way.[28] At times, Kate's inability to recognize barriers helped her accomplish things beyond all expectations. Yet it also caused spectacular failures, like her school in Cincinnati. Kate was a noble crusader who picked too many fights. Many of her battles were provoked by the misogynist behavior of the male establishment. But some, particularly those with rival feminist leaders about suffrage, could have been curtailed. She was a powerful stick of dynamite with a short fuse. As noted earlier, her aunt Mary once cautioned Lyman in a letter, "She has so much intellect that it is your duty to pay the utmost attention to the temper so that we may love what we are compelled to admire."[29] Kate would have benefited from following more of her own advice about the need for diplomacy.

Kate's life can be confusing to people in the twenty-first century. Her crusading career embraced a peculiar mixture of progressive ideas wrapped in a set of conservative principles popular in her day. She was a talented and complicated individual who was not always perfect. But her accomplishments were extraordinary for a nineteenth-century woman. They were achieved in the face of great adversity as an independent woman. Catharine

Beecher should be recognized and appreciated as a significant leader of progress for women.

• • •

Educational Reminiscences and Suggestions was Kate's last major work; it was published in 1874. She continued to attend conferences and do charity work, but her career was complete. In 1876, she moved to Elmira, New York, to live with her half brother, Thomas, who was a minister. He was talented like his siblings, but he lacked their ambition. His life was a series of contradictions. One of his parishioners in Elmira said of him, "When I see Mr. Beecher in the pulpit, I think he should never come out of it, but when I see him out of the pulpit, I think he should never go into it."[30] Thomas Beecher notably officiated the wedding of Samuel Clemens (Mark Twain) to Olivia Langdon, the daughter of one of his parishioners, in 1870.[31] He and his wife, Julia, welcomed Kate and did their best to make the remaining years of her life as comfortable as possible. Elmira was a town of less than twenty thousand people and featured Mr. Gleason's water treatments, which probably appealed to Kate.

In 1878, Kate suffered a stroke and never regained consciousness. Her brother Henry eulogized her career at his church in Brooklyn on Friday night of the day she was stricken:

> She determined to do this—to give the whole of her life for the benefit of others ... she was the mother of more children than any other woman in all parts of the country that gratefully remember her as teacher and guide.[32]

She died two days later on May 12. The *New York Times* published excerpts from Henry's eulogy and, a few days later, printed an account of her funeral. Pieces of the story were picked up and printed by newspapers across the country.

Kate was buried in a simple coffin, dressed in a plain nightdress. Three carriages followed the hearse to the cemetery, and there was a small graveside ceremony. Her brothers Thomas and Edward were pallbearers, along with Mr. Gleason and three close acquaintances. Edward was the only sibling who made the journey to her funeral in Elmira. The mourners returned to Rev. Thomas Beecher's Park Church, where a large number of people had assembled. Per her brothers' wishes, there was no great fanfare, only a few flowers at the church. "Rev. Elijah Horr, a Methodist minister led in prayer . . . thanked God for her useful life . . . and prayed that the scattered family might at last be reunited in heaven." Edward Beecher rose to the pulpit and, in deference to Henry, who had already eulogized his sister's career, spoke primarily about her character and personal life. He noted how it was affected by Alexander's death fifty-seven years earlier:

> The news of his death was the turning point in Cath[a]rine's life. It was made different from what it would have been had she married Professor Fisher. Suffering perfected her character into self-sacrifice and devotion to others.[33]

EPILOGUE

> We only see clearly with our hearts. What is essential is invisible to our eyes.[1]
> —Antoine de Saint-Exupéry, *The Little Prince*

1873

Kate Beecher was compelled by her heart in 1873 to bid Alexander a final farewell. She had kept his memory buried deep beneath her crusty exterior for fifty years. Glimpses of him were seen infrequently. Putting his letters in Sally's box allowed her life to move forward. She forged a remarkable career and independent life. But writing her memoirs forced her to examine the choices she had made. Kate could position her legacy for posterity however she pleased. But ultimately, she would have to account to Alexander when and if they met in heaven. She had become elderly and needed to deal with his love letters, which she had so painfully left behind. Her life came full circle.

There was a touching eyewitness account of Kate's romantic farewell to Alexander's love letters. It was told to Lyman Beecher Stowe in the early 1930s. Stowe was gathering material for his upcoming book, *Saints, Sinners and Beechers*. Lyman was the grandson of Kate's sister, the famous author Harriet Beecher Stowe. He was a Harvard graduate and a book editor at Doubleday, Page

& Co. in New York. Stowe had coauthored a biography of his grandmother Harriet with his father, Charles Stowe, in 1911. His new project was to tell the larger story of the Beecher family. As the self-appointed family historian of his grandmother Harriet and the Beecher family, he was privy to inside stories, which he solicited from his fellow Beecher descendants and others closely connected with the family.[2]

The eyewitness account of Kate burning the letters was provided by Willard J. Fisher, grandson of Alexander Fisher's brother Willard, when he responded to Stowe's request for information about Kate Beecher. Willard was a Phi Beta Kappa graduate of Amherst College with a PhD in physics from Cornell University. He spent his career researching meteors at the Harvard Observatory.[3] Willard was ultimately entrusted by his family with Alexander's personal papers, which he donated to Yale's Beinecke Library in 1921. As a young boy, Willard and his family were present during Kate's farewell visit in 1873. His story was published in *Saints, Sinners and Beechers* in 1934.[4] It was retold by Kathryn Kish Sklar, Kate's biographer, and Beecher biographer Milton Rugoff.

Historical records generally support the timing and legitimacy of Stowe's narrative. The boy Willard who related the story was supposedly five at the time. Willard was born in September 1867 and would have been five from September 1872 to September 1873.[5] Stowe asserted that this event happened "not long" after the failure of Kate to revive the fortunes of Hartford Female Seminary, which would have meant sometime after 1871.[6] Kate Beecher's biographer, Kathryn Kish Sklar, placed the event "shortly after the completion of her memoirs," which would have been 1873 or 1874.[7] With those dates in mind, 1873 was a plausible year for a true account by Willard Fisher.

Although the timing of the story was essentially correct, Stowe incorrectly placed these events at the Fisher family farm in Franklin, Massachusetts. Research of real estate deeds proves that the farm was sold to Emerson Bullard before the grandson Willard was born, so that would have been impossible.[8] However, the location was probably speculation on the part of Stowe or Fisher. One understandable mistake does not invalidate the essential truth of the entire story. The event probably took place at the home of Sewall Fisher in nearby Framingham, Massachusetts. Sewall was the final family occupant of the Fisher farm. Stowe's account says that Willard was "there at the time," which makes it sound as if he was visiting. Willard lived in New York, so that makes sense.[9]

While it is quite likely that Willard remembered Kate's visit, his recollection was probably aided over the years by his father, George Fisher, an Episcopal minister, and his uncle Sewall Fisher, who were both present at the event. Stowe ended his account with a tantalizing morsel about a gold engagement ring on Kate's finger, the only piece of jewelry she ever wore.[10] It's less believable that a five-year-old would remember a gold ring on her finger and understand its significance. It might have been a Beecher family memory, but the ring is not referenced anywhere else in Beecher biographies.[11] Although engagement rings did not become common until the middle of the nineteenth century, Kate and Alexander were not average people. So while it is possible, with no further evidence, the ring remains a matter of speculation.

The box kept by Sally Fisher to store and memorialize Alexander's keepsakes was not mentioned in Stowe's account. It was donated in 1921 to the Beinecke Library, along with the rest of the Alexander Metcalf Fisher Papers, which are quite extensive. It contained items from Alexander's papers, and the collection of family letters would have fit nicely inside.[12] Sally's chest has a dome top and is seventeen inches wide, ten inches deep, and nine inches high. It was clearly decorated for some special purpose. It is a reasonable assumption that it was a memorial that housed Alexander's correspondence. So when Kate entrusted her love letters to Sally in Franklin, it was the most likely place to store them. As a result, it is probable that it would have been produced for Kate when she came to retrieve Alexander's letters.

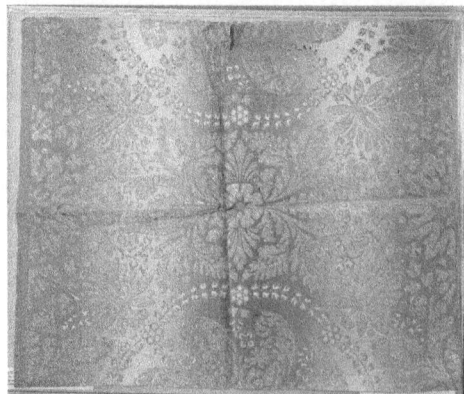

Top: Sally Fisher's memorial box. Courtesy of Beinecke Rare Book and Manuscript Library, Yale University. Bottom Left: Wallpaper from the Fisher home that was used to cover the exterior of the box. Courtesy of Beinecke Rare Book and Manuscript Library, Yale University. Bottom right: Interior of box covered in Fisher parlor wallpaper. Courtesy of Beinecke Rare Book and Manuscript Library, Yale University.

EPILOGUE

Kate waited fifty years to reclaim Alexander's letters because she loved him. She was still conflicted and had just finished her memoirs to position her professional legacy. She had avoided highlighting their romance to cement her reputation as an independent woman. But if historical standing was her sole motivation, she could have returned to Franklin to recover the letters anytime between 1823 and 1873. Sally Fisher's death in 1835 would have been the opportune moment. Without Sally to guard the letters, someone could have opened them and exposed Kate's secrets. The only reason to take that risk was because the evidence of their love was still precious to her. Although in 1873, Kate had run out of time to protect her privacy.

With that context in mind, what follows is a slightly corrected and dramatized version of the published account of Kate's visit to retrieve Alexander's love letters. It is offered as a tribute to their romance.

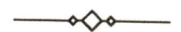

The carriage ride from the train station, with the familiar sounds of the horse's hoofs, was a pleasant respite from the arduous journey for the elderly Kate Beecher and provided her a bit of time to focus on the task ahead. It was 1873, and the past year's strain on her health had solidified her conclusion that she had no choice; the time was now or never. She remembered Sally's decorated box with its small domed top, which she had not seen for fifty years. She had traced its possession to Sewall Fisher, who had taken it when they sold the family farm in Franklin. He had responded promptly to her request to see it, and now the box was nearly in her grasp.

Kate arrived wearing her usual black dress with its flowing

skirt, her white hair braided into those outmoded screw curls, a relic of her childhood. Sewall's brother George and his family happened to be visiting from New York. She enjoyed playing with the children, particularly young Willard, who, at the age of five, was clearly an intelligent boy. She connected with him in an uncanny way as he sat on her lap, telling him stories and playing the finger game, "Here is the church, here is the steeple." It was a pleasant distraction, but soon it was time for the mission she had longed to complete and yet dreaded. As Sewall carried the box with Uncle Alexander's papers to the room set up for his visitor, he wondered what secrets it contained. Alexander had died twelve years before Sewall was born. But he had heard the family stories about the brilliant young professor, his engagement to the equally talented Kate, and his tragic death in a shipwreck before they could be married.

Kate entered the room where the box had been placed with a sense of trepidation. When she saw its familiar shape and covering, it kindled her emotions. She had to pause a moment to catch her breath. But as she sat in a comfortable chair next to a large open fireplace, the cracking sounds and wisps of smoke evoked a comforting nostalgia. Filled with anticipation, she carefully lifted the lid of the box and began her task. Each group of familiar letters and manuscripts was carefully removed and set aside until she reached her objective: a small packet of letters that she had tied with a blue ribbon and sealed with wax fifty years earlier. Thankfully, the seal was still intact. She broke it and immediately recognized that still-familiar script of his. Memories flooded back, stirring feelings she had buried deep within, hidden for all those years. It was as if she was a young woman again, at the piano with her beloved Alexander. Her heart felt the warmth of his love.

After a few minutes, she composed herself and commenced her predetermined task of reading each letter, thoughtfully absorbing its contents, feeling the sensations . . . and then consigning it to the flames in the fireplace. Hour by hour, she immersed herself in the letters, which alternately brought a smile to her face and a tear to her eye. Every now and then, she noticed young Willard peeking at the doorway. She didn't mind the attention; he was only a boy, and glancing at him gave her a much-needed pause from the emotional demands of her endeavor. As Kate advanced the final letter toward the fire, her hand hesitated. She sighed deeply, pondering one last time what might have been . . . and then it was done.

Love is the essential ingredient of life. But for Kate, it was a bittersweet emotion. Alexander's letters were visible reminders of her passion and loss. Eventually, their existence threatened the privacy of intimate moments that were hers alone. By burning them, Kate safeguarded her memories where they had always been—in her heart.

The ultimate reunion of Kate and Alexander would have been in heaven. What people believe about paradise and how one gets there are matters of personal faith. Most find that their concept of salvation evolves as they grow older. What Kate and Alexander wrote or said at any specific time may not reflect where they ended their spiritual journeys. There is no way to know if Kate and Alexander made it to heaven. But one hopes they did and finally found eternal peace and love in each other's arms.

ACKNOWLEDGMENTS

I was first introduced to the amazing legacy of Catharine Beecher in a history course I took from Professor Elizabeth Blackmar at Columbia University twenty-three years ago. She also taught me the incredible value of reading family letters for historical research. For both things, I am deeply indebted to her.

I must thank retired professor Kathryn Kish Sklar (UCLA and Binghampton), who authored the definitive biography of Catharine Beecher in 1973. Her work both inspired me and served as a springboard for my research. She challenged me to understand the evolution of romance during the nineteenth century. While we have different interpretations of Kate's relationship with Alexander, we agree on the importance of Catharine Beecher's legacy.

The research for this book was made possible by the generous support provided by numerous librarians and archivists. Elizabeth Burgess, former director of collections at the Harriet Beecher Stowe Center, provided timely insights and suggestions about the Beecher family. Her successor at the Stowe Center, Cat White, has provided continued encouragement. I must thank all those who provided remote digital access to documents during the pandemic: Linda Hocking and Alex Dubois at the Litchfield

Historical Society, Jessica Tubis and Mary Ellen Budney at the Beinecke Library, Diane Carey and Jenny Gotwals at the Schlesinger Library, and Tracy Tomaselli at the Guilford Free Library. This project would have been impossible without their help.

Field research played a key part in this story. Toni Smith helped me find the Alexander Fisher memorial in Franklin, Massachusetts, and provided permission to clean it to prove that Kate's poetry was actually inscribed. Historian Raymond White showed me the exact site of the *Albion* wreck in Ireland. As a young man, he dove the location and personally saw the black ballast stones and found gold coins. He introduced me to the current owners of the property, T. J. and Liam Barry, who generously provided access to visit.

My family has motivated me to write this book. My parents, Nancy and Bob Wilson, always believed in me. My children and their spouses have been there for me as I completed my research and sharpened my focus. In particular, it was my daughter-in-law, Katlyn Wilson, who saw the potential of Kate's untold story.

I saved the most important thanks for last. My wife, Deb Wilson, has listened to me talk about this project for nearly a quarter of a century. She has read my manuscripts, made great suggestions, and continuously urged me to finish this book. It would not have been possible without her loving support.

APPENDIX

I: KATE BEECHER'S MUSIC

Kate's first Music Book, cover. Cover art by Kate; penmanship by William Beecher. Courtesy of Schlesinger Library, Harvard Radcliffe Institute.

Kate's first Music Book, interior. Index is alphabetical, but page numbers show the time sequence of inclusion. Courtesy of Schlesinger Library, Harvard Radcliffe Institute.

II: KATY BEECHER'S GET-WELL POEM TO HER TEACHER

Katy Beecher's get-well poem to her teacher. Courtesy of Schlesinger Library, Harvard Radcliffe Institute.

APPENDIX   233

III: BEECHER AND FISHER GENEALOGY

DAVID BEECHER FAMILY

5 wives, 12 children, 7 died as infants (not shown)

1. David Beecher (1738–1805) married (1764) Mary Austin (1740–1770)
   - Mary (1766–1806)
2. David Beecher (1738–1805) married (1771) Lydia Camp Morris (1746–1773)
   - Lydia (1771–1801)
   - David (1773–1834)
3. David Beecher (1738–1805) married (1775) Esther Lyman (1749–1775)
   - **Lyman (1775–1863) Raised by Esther's sister Catharine and Lot Benton in North Guilford**
4. David Beecher (1738–1805) married (1776) Elizabeth Hoadly (1742–1777)
5. David Beecher (1738–1805) married (1777) Mary Lewis Elliott (1744–1818)
   - **Esther (1779–1855) Aunt Esther and her mother Grandma Beecher moved to Litchfield to be with the Beechers**

FOOTE WARD ANCESTORS

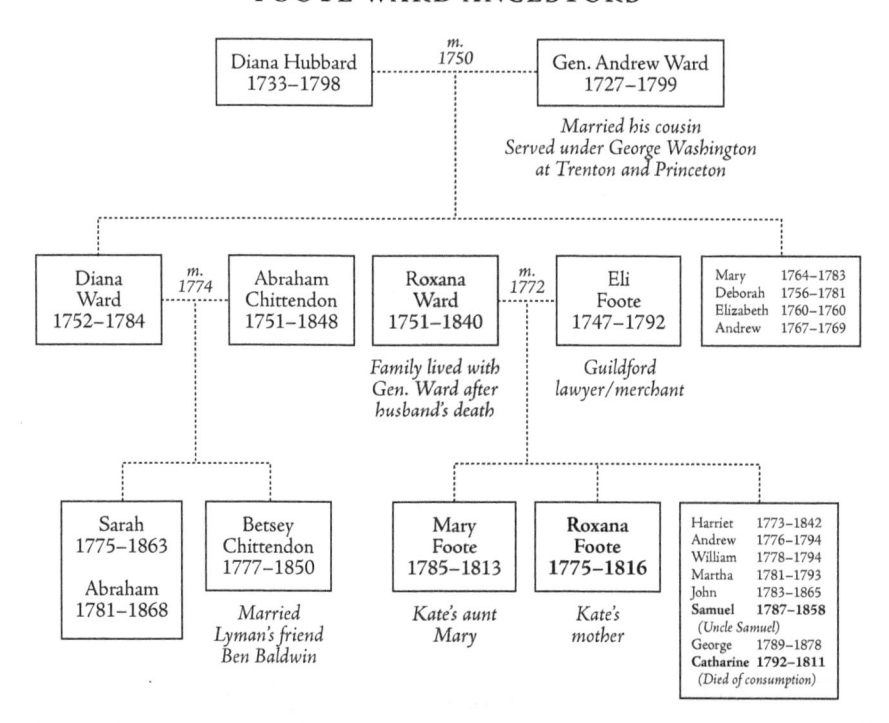

Diana Hubbard (1733–1798) m. 1750 Gen. Andrew Ward (1727–1799)
*Married his cousin
Served under George Washington at Trenton and Princeton*

Children:

- Diana Ward (1752–1784) m. 1774 Abraham Chittendon (1751–1848)
  - Sarah (1775–1863); Abraham (1781–1868)
  - Betsey Chittendon (1777–1850) *Married Lyman's friend Ben Baldwin*
- Roxana Ward (1751–1840) m. 1772 Eli Foote (1747–1792)
  Family lived with Gen. Ward after husband's death   *Guildford lawyer/merchant*
  - Mary Foote (1785–1813) *Kate's aunt Mary*
  - **Roxana Foote (1775–1816)** *Kate's mother*
- Mary 1764–1783; Deborah 1756–1781; Elizabeth 1760–1760; Andrew 1767–1769
- Harriet 1773–1842; Andrew 1776–1794; William 1778–1794; Martha 1781–1793; John 1783–1865; **Samuel 1787–1858** *(Uncle Samuel)*; George 1789–1878; Catharine 1792–1811 *(Died of consumption)*

LYMAN BEECHER FAMILY

3 wives, 13 children, and 56 grandchildren

1. Lyman Beecher (1775–1863) married (1799) **Roxana Foote (1775–1816)**

   - Catharine (1800–1878)—pioneer advocate for women's education
   - William (1802–1889)—minister
     1832 married Katherine Edes (1802–1870)—6 children
   - Edward (1803–1895)—Yale, Andover Theological Seminary, minister, college president
     1829 married Isabella Porter Jones (1807–1895)—11 children
   - Mary (1805–1900)—teacher, Hartford Female Seminary
     1827 married Thomas Perkins (1798–1870)—4 children
   - Harriet (1808–1808) died as infant
   - George (1809–1843)—Yale Seminary, minister, committed suicide
     1837 married Sarah Buckingham (1817–1902)—2 children
   - Harriet (1811–1896)—teacher and famous author
     1836 married Calvin Stowe (1802–1886)—7 children
   - Henry Ward (1813–1887)—Amherst, Lane, minister, scandalous Tilton affair
     1837 married Eunice Bullard (1812–1897)—9 children
   - Charles (1815–1900)—Bowdoin, Lane, minister
     1840 married Sarah Coffin (1815–1897)—6 children

2. Lyman Beecher (1775–1863) married (1817) **Harriet Porter (1790–1835)**

   - Frederick (1818–1820)—died as child
   - Isabella (1822–1907)—suffrage leader
     1841 married John Hooker (1816–1901)—4 children
   - Thomas (1824–1900)—Illinois College, Yale Seminary, minister, friend of Mark Twain
     1851 married Olivia Day (1826–1853)
     1857 married Julia Jones (1826–1905)—4 adopted children
   - James (1828–1886)—seaman, Andover Theological Seminary, missionary, general, minister, committed suicide
     1853 married Ann Morse (1827–1863)
     1864 married Frances Johnson (1832–1903)—3 adopted children

3. Lyman Beecher (1775–1863) married (1836) **Lydia Beals Jackson (1789–1869)**

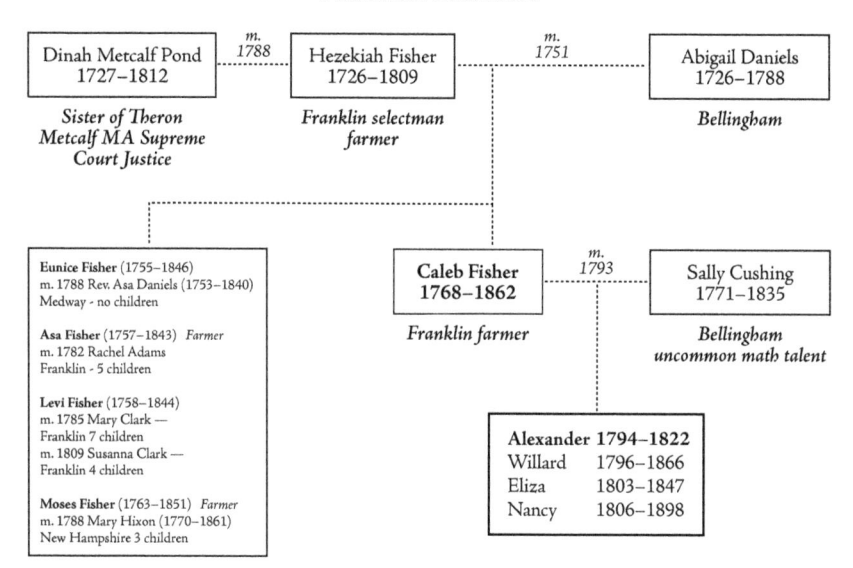

APPENDIX

FISHER FAMILY

```
Dinah Metcalf Pond ──m.1788── Hezekiah Fisher ──m.1751── Abigail Daniels
    1727–1812                    1726–1809                 1726–1788

Sister of Theron              Franklin selectman           Bellingham
Metcalf MA Supreme               farmer
   Court Justice
```

Eunice Fisher (1755–1846)
m. 1788 Rev. Asa Daniels (1753–1840)
Medway - no children

Asa Fisher (1757–1843) *Farmer*
m. 1782 Rachel Adams
Franklin - 5 children

Levi Fisher (1758–1844)
m. 1785 Mary Clark —
Franklin 7 children
m. 1809 Susanna Clark —
Franklin 4 children

Moses Fisher (1763–1851) *Farmer*
m. 1788 Mary Hixon (1770–1861)
New Hampshire 3 children

Caleb Fisher ──m.1793── Sally Cushing
  1768–1862   1771–1835

Franklin farmer   *Bellingham*
                          uncommon math talent

Alexander 1794–1822
Willard   1796–1866
Eliza   1803–1847
Nancy   1806–1898

FISHER BROTHER CONNECTIONS

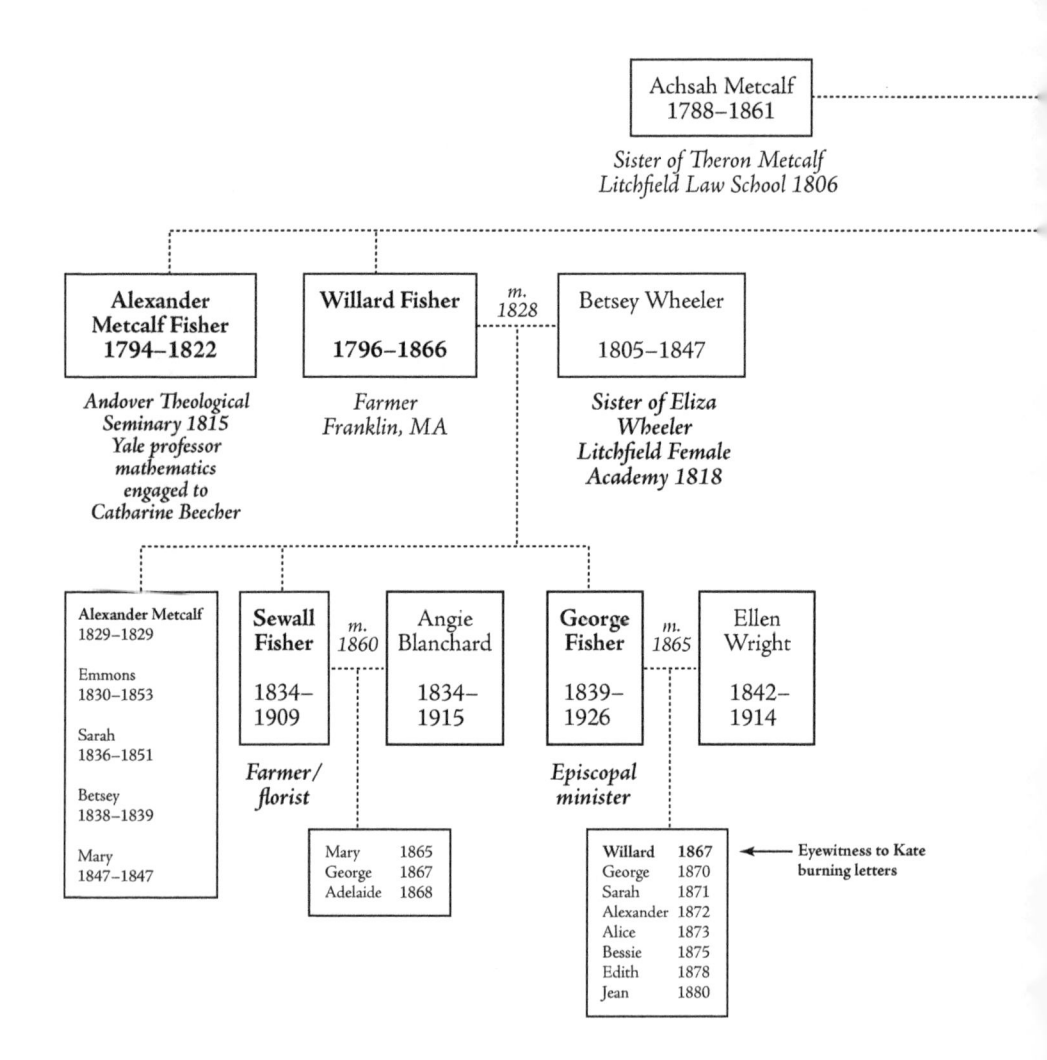

Achsah Metcalf
1788–1861

Sister of Theron Metcalf
Litchfield Law School 1806

Alexander Metcalf Fisher
1794–1822

Andover Theological Seminary 1815
Yale professor mathematics
engaged to Catharine Beecher

Willard Fisher
1796–1866

Farmer
Franklin, MA

m. 1828

Betsey Wheeler
1805–1847

Sister of Eliza Wheeler
Litchfield Female Academy 1818

Alexander Metcalf 1829–1829

Emmons 1830–1853

Sarah 1836–1851

Betsey 1838–1839

Mary 1847–1847

Sewall Fisher
1834–1909

Farmer/florist

m. 1860

Angie Blanchard
1834–1915

Mary 1865
George 1867
Adelaide 1868

George Fisher
1839–1926

Episcopal minister

m. 1865

Ellen Wright
1842–1914

Willard 1867 ← Eyewitness to Kate burning letters
George 1870
Sarah 1871
Alexander 1872
Alice 1873
Bessie 1875
Edith 1878
Jean 1880

APPENDIX

FISHER SISTER CONNECTIONS

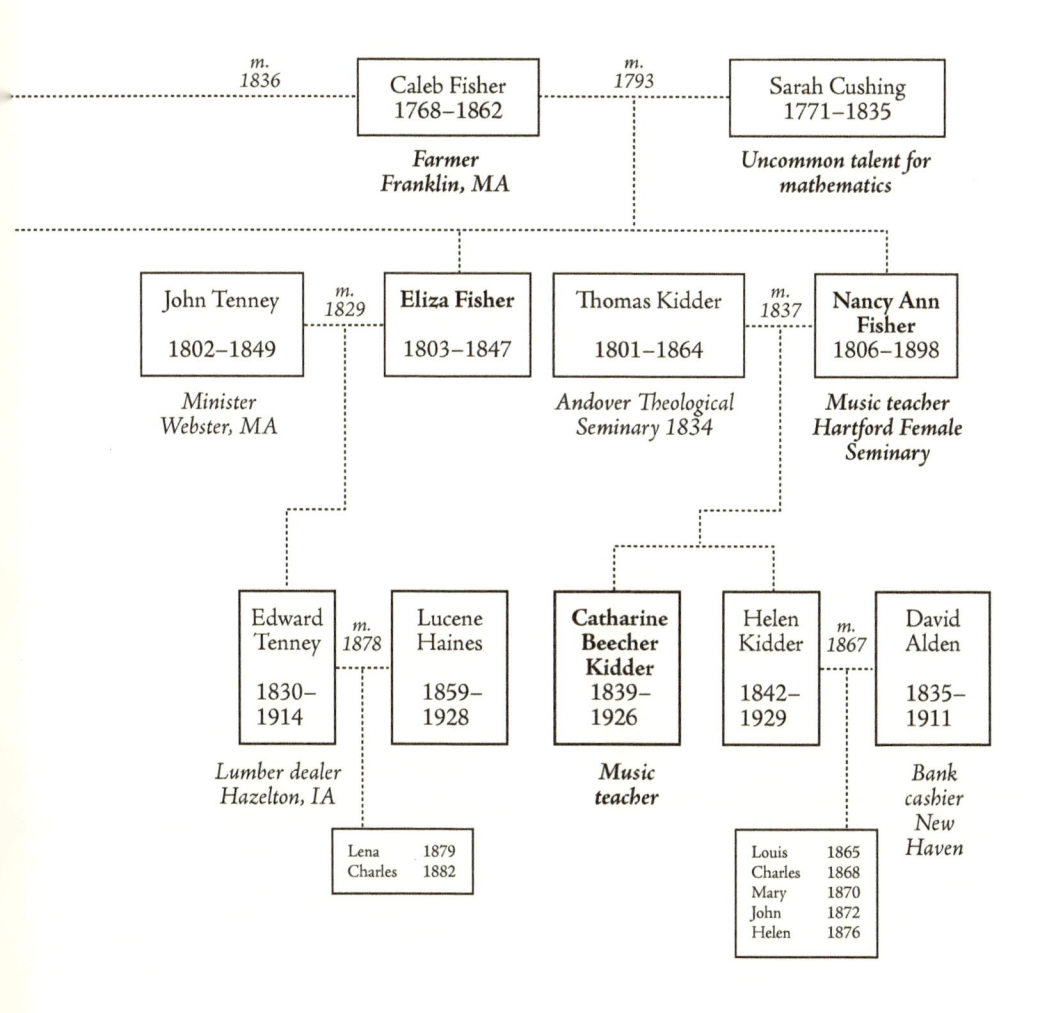

```
                    m.                              m.
          1836                                1793
    --------- Caleb Fisher ----------- Sarah Cushing
              1768–1862                 1771–1835

              Farmer                    Uncommon talent for
              Franklin, MA              mathematics
```

- **Caleb Fisher** (1768–1862) m. 1836 — Farmer, Franklin, MA
- **Sarah Cushing** (1771–1835) m. 1793 — Uncommon talent for mathematics

Children:

John Tenney (1802–1849)	m. 1829	**Eliza Fisher** (1803–1847)	Thomas Kidder (1801–1864)	m. 1837	**Nancy Ann Fisher** (1806–1898)
Minister Webster, MA			Andover Theological Seminary 1834		Music teacher Hartford Female Seminary

Grandchildren:

Edward Tenney (1830–1914)	m. 1878	Lucene Haines (1859–1928)	**Catharine Beecher Kidder** (1839–1926)	Helen Kidder (1842–1929)	m. 1867	David Alden (1835–1911)
Lumber dealer Hazelton, IA			Music teacher			Bank cashier New Haven

Children of Edward Tenney and Lucene Haines:
- Lena 1879
- Charles 1882

Children of Helen Kidder and David Alden:
- Louis 1865
- Charles 1868
- Mary 1870
- John 1872
- Helen 1876

NOTES

Introduction

1. Kathryn Kish Sklar, *Catharine Beecher: A Study in Domesticity* (New York: W. W. Norton, 1973), 270.
2. Milton Rugoff, *The Beechers: An American Family in the 19th Century* (New York: Harper & Row, 1981), 314.

Chapter 1—Kate

1. Wikipedia, s.v. "Litchfield Law School," accessed September 5, 2023, https://en.wikipedia.org/wiki/Litchfield_Law_School.
2. Wikipedia, s.v. "Litchfield Female Academy," accessed September 5, 2023, https://en.wikipedia.org/wiki/Litchfield_Female_Academy. The school also allowed a handful of local boys to attend, including some of Kate's brothers.
3. Mark Boonshoft, "The Litchfield Network, Education, Social Capital and the Rise and Fall of a Political Dynasty, 1784–1833," *Journal of the American Republic* 34 (Winter 2014): 581. The career benefits of Litchfield matches were demonstrated by this research, which calculated that students of LLS who married those from LFA were 66 percent more likely to serve some significant role in government. This is an excellent article and is recommended for those who want to learn more about the Litchfield network.
4. Ebenezer Baldwin, *History of Yale College* (New Haven, CT: Benjamin and William Noyes, 1841). Nineteenth-century school terms were different from those in twenty-first-century America. Some analysis is necessary to understand the school terms and vacation breaks. The three terms at Yale are discussed on page 229, with commencement typically falling on the second Wednesday in September, followed by six weeks of vacation. It is believed that three terms were customary among colleges at the time. See also Litchfield Historical Society, "Litchfield Law School History," *Litchfield Ledger*, accessed October 3, 2023, https://ledger.litchfieldhistoricalsociety.org/ledger/studies/history_school. Technically, LLS did not offer degrees. The LLS program was a fourteen-month course of lectures that prepared one for taking the bar exam. See Litchfield Historical Society, "Litchfield Female Academy History," *Litchfield Ledger*, accessed October 3, 2023, https://ledger.litchfieldhistoricalsociety.org/ledger/studies/history_lfa. LFA offered diplomas to women who completed a

full course of studies. If there was no graduation for LLS, it must have been the granting of diplomas by LFA that was the cause of the Annual Commencement Ball in Kate's poem. See Emily Noyes Vanderpoel, *Chronicles of a Pioneer School from 1792 to 1833, Being the History of Miss Sarah Pierce and Her Litchfield School*, ed. Elizabeth Buel (Cambridge: Cambridge University Press, 1903), 160–176. The diary of Eliza Ogden has entries that show the dates of the end of the various school terms. Summer term ended in late October. That would have been a plausible date for the graduation ceremonies and the Annual Commencement Ball.

5   Wikipedia, s.v. "Cotillion," accessed June 26, 2023, https://en.wikipedia.org/wiki/Cotillion. What is described was the most common form of cotillion in America at the time. It was the forerunner of square dancing.

6   Lyman Beecher, *The Autobiography of Lyman Beecher*, ed. Barbara Cross, 2 vols. (Cambridge, MA: Harvard University Press/Belknap, 1961), 1173. (Hereafter cited as L. Beecher, *Autobiography*; all references are to Volume I unless otherwise noted.)

7   Catharine Beecher, "Bumble Bees Ball," A-102, folder 317, Beecher-Stowe Collection, Schlesinger Library, Radcliffe Institute, Harvard University. The description of the ball and the date are based on Kate's poem. Although it is her whimsical account of attending her first Annual Commencement Ball, the descriptive portions of her narrative are considered to be reasonably accurate. It is undated. The balls were held in the fall each year, and subsequent events in 1816 make it unlikely she would have attended then. At age fourteen, she would have been too young to attend with a beau, so it appears reasonable to assume that the date of the poem was 1815.

8   C. Beecher, "Bumble Bees Ball."

9   Boonshoft, "The Litchfield Network," 526, 594.

10 Karen Lystra, *Searching the Heart: Women, Men and Romantic Love in Nineteenth-Century America* (Oxford: Oxford University Press, 1989), 3–11. For a good explanation of Victorian romance and the transition, see Lystra's introduction.

11 L. Beecher, *Autobiography*, 1:165.

12 Emily Noyes Vanderpoel, *More Chronicles of a Pioneer School 1792–1833* (New York: Cadmus Book Shop, 1927), 94.

13 L. Beecher, *Autobiography*, 1:165.

14 Ibid., 166.

15 This description of Kate is based on the author's observations of a painting of her that is part of the collection at the Harriet Beecher Stowe Center in Hartford, Connecticut.

16 Catharine Beecher, *Educational Reminiscences and Suggestions* (New York: J. B. Ford and Company, 1874), 13.

17 C. Beecher, *Educational Reminiscences*, 15.

18 L. Beecher, *Autobiography*, 1:168. Roxana was an intellectual who enjoyed math puzzles and chemistry. The fact that she didn't train Kate in these sciences may have been to lower her educational expectations as a wife like herself. Roxana says with a sense of irony, "I expect to be obliged to be content (if I can) with the stock of knowledge I already possess."

19 L. Beecher, *Autobiography*, 1:36.

20 C. Beecher, *Educational Reminiscences*, 15.

21 L. Beecher, *Autobiography*, 1:94.
22 Catharine Beecher, "My Autobiography for the Entertainment of Family Friends," Katharine Day Collection, Harriet Beecher Stowe Center, Hartford, CT, p. 9.
23 L. Beecher, *Autobiography*, 1:173.
24 L. Beecher, *Autobiography*, 1:101.
25 Wikipedia, s.v. "Romanticism," accessed May 26, 2023, https://en.wikipedia.org/wiki/Romanticism#Literature.
26 L. Beecher, *Autobiography*, 1:166, 391. Lyman Beecher disapproved of "novels as trash" (391), but he approved of Scott's Romantic novel *Ivanhoe*. Kate would have been allowed to read novels brought by her uncle Samuel. She read *Angelina . . . L'Amie Inconnue* by the legendary Maria Edgeworth (166), which was far more degenerate than any works of Jane Austen.
27 Charles Hinnant, "Jane Austen's Wild Imagination: Romance and the Courtship Plot in the Six Canonical Novels," *Narrative* 14, no. 3 (2006): 294–310. See this essay for dates and a good description of Austen's novels and their universal courtship themes. The original publication of *Sense and Sensibility* (1811) and *Pride and Prejudice* (1813) in London would have clearly had them in Kate's hands before 1815.
28 Jane Austen, *Pride and Prejudice* (Westport, CT: Easton Press, 1977), 137.
29 Vanderpoel, *More Chronicles*, 124–125.
30 Litchfield Historical Society, "Louisa Wait," *Litchfield Ledger*, accessed May 24, 2023, https://ledger.litchfieldhistoricalsociety.org/ledger/students/6876.
31 Catharine Beecher, "Kate's First Music Book," A102, folder 319, Beecher-Stowe Collection, Schlesinger Library, Radcliffe Institute, Harvard University. Note that the index shows songs in alphabetical order, but they are numbered by page number, with the lowest numbers listed first. "Auld Lang Syne" is the first piece listed. L. Beecher, *Autobiography*, 1:396, describes Louisa as very fond of Scottish ballads.
32 Rugoff, *The Beechers*, 35.
33 Litchfield Historical Society, "James Gore King," *Litchfield Ledger*, accessed May 24, 2023, https://ledger.litchfieldhistoricalsociety.org/ledger/students/1455; Litchfield Historical Society, "Edward King," *Litchfield Ledger*, accessed May 24, 2023, https://ledger.litchfieldhistoricalsociety.org/ledger/students/1447.
34 Vanderpoel, *More Chronicles*, 147.
35 Litchfield Historical Society, "John Pierce Brace," *Litchfield Ledger*, accessed September 5, 2023, https://ledger.litchfieldhistoricalsociety.org/ledger/students/384.
36 Vanderpoel, *More Chronicles*, 147. Brace describes, "My flirtations continued, but they were frequently merged in with attachments."
37 L. Beecher, *Autobiography*, 1:219.
38 Wikipedia, s.v. "Tuberculosis," accessed August 31, 2022, https://en.wikipedia.org/wiki/Tuberculosis.
39 L. Beecher, *Autobiography*, 1:219. It is the author's interpretation that Roxana would have suspected consumption earlier.
40 L. Beecher, *Autobiography*, 1:217.
41 Ibid., 1:215–221.
42 Ibid., 1:224.
43 Ibid., 226–227.

44 Ibid., 236–238.
45 Sklar, *Catharine Beecher*, 24.
46 L. Beecher, *Autobiography*, 1:236–238.
47 Wikipedia, s.v. "1816 US Presidential Election," accessed September 5, 2023, https://en.wikipedia.org/wiki/1816_United_States_presidential_election. Rufus King won only 34 electoral votes to 183 for James Monroe. King won only Massachusetts, Connecticut, and Delaware. This was the end of the Federalist Party as a national contender in presidential elections.
48 Litchfield Historical Society, "Uriel Holmes, Jr.," *Litchfield Ledger*, accessed September 8, 2023, https://ledger.litchfieldhistoricalsociety.org/ledger/students/8006.
49 Catharine Beecher to Louisa Wait, 7 December 1824, Beecher-Stowe Collection, Schlesinger Library, Radcliffe Institute, Harvard University (hereafter cited as CB to [addressee], [date], Schlesinger). In 1817 Kate apparently didn't know about Louisa's engagement to Uriel Holmes. She expressed surprise in 1824 when she guessed it from Louisa's comments in a letter to Lucy: "One other thing, I have felt some curiosity to know since I read your letter to J & Lucy—you spoke of feeling about your expectations if U.H. had lived that I suppose there must have been some understanding between you and him. Was this known by his friends?" Kate's feelings may have been wounded by the fact that she was not told about it in 1817.
50 Charles Loring to Mary Pierce, 20 January 1817, folder 13, item 1, Loring Family Correspondence, Litchfield Historical Society, Litchfield, CT.
51 Vanderpoel, *More Chronicles*, 147.
52 L. Beecher, *Autobiography*, 1:238.

Chapter 2—Alexander

1 Alexander Fisher, 7 October 1815, Religious Diary, box 2, folder 28, Alexander Metcalf Fisher Papers, General Collection, Beinecke Rare Books and Manuscript Library, Yale University (hereafter cited as AF Religious Diary, [date]). Note: In this collection, box 2, folder 27 covers May–July 1815; box 2, folder 28 covers July 6–24, 1815; and box 2, folder 29 covers July 30, 1815–August 1, 1819.
2 Baldwin, *History of Yale College*. See Baldwin's appendix IV for an overview of the education system (225–233). See also Yale University Library, "Yale University Catalogue 1817–1824," accessed October 6, 2023, https://elischolar.library.yale.edu/yale_catalogue/3/. My assessment of the tenure of tutors is based on analysis of this time period. The longest tenure was five years. Of the seven relevant examples for which complete tenure data could be collected between 1819 and 1826, five tutors served four years, two served five years, and one served two years. See also "Original Papers in Relation to a Course of Liberal Education," *American Journal of Science and Arts* XV (1820): 297–324, https://archive.org/details/americanjournalo151829newh/page/296/mode/2up. This article provides a good explanation of how colleges operated in the early nineteenth century.
3 Denison Olmsted, "Reminiscences of Alexander Metcalf Fisher," *New Englander* IV (October 1843): 468.

NOTES 243

4 David Z. Hambrick, "What Makes a Prodigy?" *Scientific American*, September 22, 2015, https://www.scientificamerican.com/article/what-makes-a-prodigy1/. People often ask if prodigies are born or made, and the answer is, interestingly, *both*. Recent research indicates two inherited characteristics are common in prodigies. The first is that they are blessed with amazing working memories. Imagine being told a series of fifteen random numbers and then being able to repeat them immediately in the reverse order; your mind would have to work a bit like the random access memory (RAM) of a computer. The second characteristic is an intense commitment to a specific domain at a very young age, something that would have had to be facilitated by his parents. Wikipedia, s.v. "Child Prodigy," accessed July 15, 2024, https://en.wikipedia.org/wiki/Child_prodigy. Technically, Alexander did not meet today's definition of a child prodigy because there is no evidence that he "produced meaningful output in some domain at the level of an adult expert *before the age of ten*." But allowing for his humble rural circumstances, Alexander was definitely a math prodigy in the practical sense of the term.

5 Franklin Dexter, "Alexander Metcalf Fisher," in *Biographical Sketches of Yale College*, vol. 6 (New Haven, CT: Yale University Press, 1912), 567–570. Dexter notes, "His mother was a woman of uncommon mathematical talent."

6 Alexander Fisher, "A Practical Arithmetic in Manuscript," 2 vols., 1805–1806, Series II writings, box 8, folder 122–123, and "A Practical Arithmetic in Manuscript," 1807, Series II writings, box 17, Alexander Metcalf Fisher Papers, General Collection, Beinecke Rare Books and Manuscript Library, Yale University.

7 Alexander Fisher to Parents, 18 November 1816, box 1, folder 13, Alexander Metcalf Fisher Papers, General Collection, Beinecke Rare Books and Manuscript Library, Yale University (hereafter cited as AF to [addressee], [date], Fisher Correspondence). Note: Folio numbers run sequentially by year (folder 7, 1809/10; folder 8, 1811; folder 9, 1812; folder 10, 1813; folder 11, 1814; folder 12, 1815; folder 13, 1816; folder 14, 1817; folder 15, 1818; folder 16, 1819; folder 17, 1820; folder 18, 1821).

8 David McCullough, *The Greater Journey* (New York: Simon and Schuster, 2011). This book is the story of all the American intellectuals who made the journey to Paris to study at the great universities, which were far superior to anything in the United States. Notable scholars included Charles Sumner, the abolitionist senator from Massachusetts; Samuel F. B. Morse, the painter who became an inventor; and Elizabeth Blackwell, the first female doctor in America.

9 Dexter, "Alexander Fisher," *Biographical Sketches of Yale College*, 567–570; Lee Wilson, "Fisher Family Tree," Ancestry.com (login required). The tree includes details on the lives of Alexander's three siblings.

10 Dexter, "Alexander Fisher," *Biographical Sketches of Yale College*, 567–570.

11 AF to Caleb Fisher, 28 November 1815, Fisher Correspondence.

12 For a general understanding of the conversion process made popular by Philip Doddridge, see Geofrey F. Nuttall, *Philip Doddridge 1702–51* (London: Independent Press, 1951). For a better understanding of doctrines, see John Calvin, *Institutes of the Christian Religion*, trans. John Allen (Philadelphia: Philip H. Nicklin, 1816), 33–37. The best summarized discussion of these doctrines and alternatives can be found in Sidney Mead, *Nathaniel William*

Taylor, 1786–1856: A Connecticut Liberal (Chicago: University of Chicago Press, 1942).

13   AF Religious Diary, 7 July 1815.
14   AF to Parents, 23 March 1813, Fisher Correspondence.
15   Entry for 29 January 1809, RG4842, Franklin, MA, First Congregational Church Records, 1737–1877, Congregational Library & Archives, Boston, MA (hereafter cited as Franklin Church Records): "Caleb Fisher was admitted to full communion in this church" when he was forty (b. October 11, 1768). Entry for 30 January 1820, Franklin Church Records: "Sally Fisher and Rachel Bullard were admitted to full communion in this church" when she was thirty-eight (b. May 12, 1771).
16   Randall Balmer, *Mine Eyes Have Seen the Glory* (New York: Oxford University Press, 2014). See Balmer's chapter 5, where he references this problem of passing on faith to the next generation. He cites Chaim Potok, *The Chosen* (New York: Simon & Schuster, 1967), and calls the Beechers a textbook case of this problem.
17   AF to Caleb Fisher, 28 August 1815, Fisher Correspondence.
18   AF Religious Diary, 20 August 1815.
19   AF to Parents, 28 October 1815, Fisher Correspondence: "This 30$ I am willing to consider as borrowed at 6 percent till paid as well as the 65 I brot on." AF to Caleb Fisher, 28 August 1815, Fisher Correspondence: "I am anxious that something should now be done for the education of the other children." AF to Parents, 1 March 1816, Fisher Correspondence: "I feel anxious to do something, if possible towards the education of Willard, Eliza + Nancy. It is true that I could do but a little in three weeks; but I will engage to spend other employments, and to do what lies in my power for their advancement."
20   Alexander Metcalf Fisher, Alexander Metcalf Fisher Papers, box 2, folder 26, page 5, General Collection, Beinecke Rare Books and Manuscript Library. Personal notes, formerly identified as "Papers written during derangement" (hereafter cited as Fisher Personal Notes). Note: The pages in this document are not numbered. The author has numbered them from the first entry as an aid to finding specific references.
21   See the Mayo Clinic website for a brief description of bipolar symptoms. Mayo Clinic, "Bipolar Disorder," accessed August 27, 2022, https://www.mayoclinic.org/diseases-conditions/bipolar-disorder/symptoms-causes/syc-20355955.
22   Wilson, "Fisher Family Tree."
23   Norfolk County Registry of Deeds, "Records Database," http://www.norfolkresearch.org/ALIS/WW400R.HTM?WSIQTP=LR01D&WSKYCD=N. A search of the deed registry, Book 77-156,157, shows a transaction from Hezekiah Fisher to Caleb Fisher on January 7, 1795. See also E. O. Jameson, *The History of Medway Mass. 1713–1885* (Medway, MA: Town of Medway, 1885), 92.
24   Wilson, "Fisher Family Tree." The primary family relationship between Alexander and Eliza was through the Daniels family in Medway. Uncle Asa Daniels, the husband of Caleb's sister Eunice, was a third cousin of Eliza's mother, Betsey. Alexander was a fourth cousin of Eliza through a different branch of the Daniels family. And coincidentally, the Fisher's next-door neighbor was a Richardson and related to Eliza's mother, Betsey Richardson Wheeler. See also AF to Eliza Fisher, 19 December 1818, Fisher

Correspondence: "Do not be scared if you should see me coming down across from widow Richardson's on a pair of rackets, about four weeks hence." A review of an old map of Norfolk County, 1858, by H. F. Walling (see https://collections.leventhalmap.org/search/commonwealth:9s161933d) shows the close proximity of Caleb and Willard Fisher ("C&W Fisher" on the map) and S. W. Richardson. Note that Alexander's younger brother, Willard, eventually married Betsey Wheeler (Eliza's younger sister) on January 1, 1828.

25   AF to Caleb Fisher, 28 October 1815, Fisher Correspondence.

26   Dexter, "Denison Olmsted," *Biographical Sketches of Yale College*, 592–600. Selected quote: "The youngest child of Nathaniel Olmsted, a farmer in moderate circumstances, of East Hartford. At graduation he delivered a striking Oration on the Causes of Intellectual Greatness. Yale tutor 1815–1817. Elected Professor of Chemistry at University of North Carolina in 1817 and prepared under Professor Silliman at Yale before entering his duties. September of 1825 he was appointed to the chair of Mathematics and Natural Philosophy at Yale, vacant by reason of the death of Professor Matthew Dutton and continued at Yale for the rest of his career."

27   Yale University, "Yale University. University Catalogue, 1820," *Yale University Catalogue* 6, accessed August 27, 2022, https://elischolar.library.yale.edu/yale_catalogue/6.

28   Wikipedia, s.v. "Benjamin Silliman," accessed August 27, 2022, https://en.wikipedia.org/wiki/Benjamin_Silliman. Wikipedia notes, "Silliman was an early supporter of coeducation in the Ivy League. Although Yale wouldn't admit women as students until over 100 years later, he allowed young women into his lecture classes. His efforts convinced Frederick Barnard, later President of Columbia College, that women ought to be admitted as students." The following Wikipedia passage in the Benjamin Silliman entry is quoted from Frederick Barnard, "Higher Education of Women; Passages Extracted from the Annual Reports of the President of Columbia College, Presented to the Trustees in June, 1879, June, 1880, and June, 1881": "The elder Silliman, during the entire period of his distinguished career as a Professor of Chemistry, Geology and Mineralogy in Yale College, was accustomed every year to admit to his lecture-courses classes of young women from the schools of New Haven. In that institution the undersigned had an opportunity to observe, as a student, the effect of the practice, similar to that which he afterward created for himself in Alabama, as a teacher. The results in both instances, so far as they went, were good; and they went far enough to make it evident that if the presence of young women in college, instead of being occasional, should be constant, they would be better."

29   AF to Caleb Fisher, 1 June 1811, Fisher Correspondence. Kingsley and Alexander grew much closer after he returned to Yale, as evidenced by their activities. AF to Caleb Fisher, 28 August 1815, Fisher Correspondence: "Received a letter from Professor Kingsley of Yale College; from which I can calculate on being called there this fall."

30   Wikipedia, s.v. "*Cheaper by the Dozen* (1950 Film)," accessed August 26, 2021, https://en.wikipedia.org/wiki/Cheaper_by_the_Dozen_(1950_film).

31   Olmsted, "Reminiscences," 466.

32   AF to Parents, 28 October 1815, Fisher Correspondence. Alexander's maternal grandfather served as a fifer in the American Revolution. There is no evidence

of musical talent on the Fisher side of the family, so it is assumed his talent for music came from his mother.
33 Olmsted, "Reminiscences," 464.
34 Ibid.
35 Ibid., 462.
36 AF to Parents 21 January 1816, Fisher Correspondence.
37 Baldwin, *History of Yale College*. See Baldwin's appendix IV for an overview of the education system, including vacations (225–233).
38 AF to Parents, 18 November 1816, Fisher Correspondence.
39 AF to Parents, 16 May 1817, Fisher Correspondence.
40 Olmsted, "Reminiscences," 463.
41 It is mathematically impossible to tune a piano perfectly. The piano has only twelve keys per octave, and it requires more than twelve notes to create the precise harmony that results from specific ratios of analogue sound waves. In contrast, the violin and human voice have the ability to create minute variations in tone to deliver exact harmony in any key signature. As a result, when pianos perform with orchestras, the strings must make adjustments to match the piano pitch. For an entertaining YouTube video explanation, see https://www.sciencealert.com/watch-the-physics-of-music-and-why-it-s-impossible-to-tune-a-piano.
42 Alexander Fisher, "Essay on Musical Temperament," *American Journal of Science* 1 (1819): 9–35, 176–199. Well tempering of pianos in the nineteenth century sought to minimize these slight imperfections by tuning selected harmonic intervals, such as thirds or fifths, a bit sharp or flat. That allowed Bach and Beethoven piano pieces to be performed in their original keys and brought forth distinctive sounds as intended. But a piano tuned to make pieces composed in G major sound better could make those written in other key signatures sound worse. The trick with well tempering was to tune a piano so that it sounded good in more than one key signature, which was a very complicated task. Alexander's solution for well tempering a piano was to minimize the number and size of disharmonies for the chords and key signatures most commonly performed. It was an optimization approach based on scientific observations of 1,800 pieces of music and involved clever statistical calculations. Equal tempering of pianos, which is commonly used today, is an alternative solution to this problem. This approach sets all the frequency intervals the same (equal), which makes it easy to play a piece in any key signature but does not seek to minimize any of the small disharmonies. It's not perfect harmony but it is dangerously close. Our ears are accustomed to the equal tempering of pianos, and contemporary composers tend to avoid the notes that will sound wrong, but Bach and Beethoven pieces no longer retain the tonal richness as originally composed and performed. Concert violinists must make minor compromises in pitch to stay "in tune" with today's pianos when they perform together. There is no perfect answer, but Alexander's approach was a practical alternative.
43 AF Religious Diary, 26 July 1817.
44 Gary Lee Schoepflin, "Denison Olmsted (1791–1859), Scientist, Teacher, Christian: A Biographical Study of the Connection of Science with Religion in Antebellum America" (PhD thesis, Oregon State University, June 17, 1977). See pages 75–97 for an interesting discussion about the timing and politics of the

hiring of Olmsted at the University of North Carolina (UNC). Interesting but not key to the story, there was another Yale tutor in the mix for the UNC job, Elisha Mitchell. In the end, both Olmsted and Mitchell were hired by UNC.

45 Olmsted, "Reminiscences," 463.
46 AF Religious Diary, 15 February 1817: "I cannot say that I have ever positively disbelieved the existence of God, the truth of the scriptures and the reality of a future existence; but it is equally true that I have had no fixed belief in their truth . . . I confess that I seldom feel a decided inclination to make these subjects the things of my contemplation . . . this is unquestionably a <u>diseased</u> state of the intellect, as well as moral faculties."
47 AF Religious Diary, 4 May 1817.
48 AF to Caleb Fisher, 16 May 1817, Fisher Correspondence.
49 Olmsted, "Reminiscences," 466.
50 AF to Parents, 23 July 1817, Fisher Correspondence.
51 AF Religious Diary, 26 July 1817.
52 Biographical sketch of Dr. Eleazar Fitch, Yale Archives, accessed September 22, 2021, https://archives.yale.edu/repositories/4/resources/312. Eleazar graduated from Andover Theological Seminary in 1815, which overlapped with Alexander.
53 AF Religious Diary, September 1817.

Chapter 3—Dispatched

1 Lyman Beecher to Harriet Porter, 5 October 1817, Acquisitions, Harriet Beecher Stowe Center, Hartford, CT. (This series of letters between Lyman and Harriet hereafter cited as LB to HP or HP to LB, [date], Beecher Stowe Center).
2 L. Beecher, *Autobiography*, 1:257. For the story of Kate meeting Harriet at the Homes' house, see page 261.
3 Lee Wilson, "Beecher Family Tree," Ancestry.com (login required). Lyman was forty-two when he married Harriet Porter, who was twenty-seven. Kate Beecher was seventeen at the time of the wedding, and her friend Lucy Porter was twenty.
4 Emily Noyes Vanderpoel, *Chronicles of a Pioneer School from 1792 to 1833, Being a History of Miss Sarah Pierce and Her Litchfield School*, ed. Elizabeth Buel (Cambridge: Cambridge University Press, 1903), 171.
5 LB to HP, 9, 11, [15], 16, 21 September 1817 and 2, 5, 15 October 1817, Beecher Stowe Center; HP to LB, 11, 13, 18, 22, 25 September 1817 and 2, 6, 13 October 1817, Beecher Stowe Center. See HP to LB, 18 September 1817, Beecher Stowe Center, for the quote about God's mission. God presented Lyman to her: "You have appeared in my path and are entirely drawing me away . . . I trust you will lead me to life & blessedness, that you are offering me facilities in the way to Heaven" (HP to LB, 11 September 1817). Harriet declared herself "totally depraved" (HP to LB, 22 September 1817). She accepted the promise of obedience: "Tho it may be new to my time, not yet having promised obedience" (HP to LB, 18 September 1818).
6 LB to HP, 11 September 1817, Beecher Stowe Center.
7 Wilson, "Beecher Family Tree," entries for Lucy and Harriet Porter.

NOTES

8   LB to HP, 5 October 1817, Beecher Stowe Center.
9   L. Beecher, *Autobiography*, 1:264–265.
10 Ibid., 1:269.
11 Ibid.
12 Ibid., 1:270.
13 Catharine Beecher, "My Own Diary 1821," Miscellaneous materials, folder 317, Beecher-Stowe Collection, Schlesinger.
14 C. Beecher, *Educational Reminiscences*, 24.
15 L. Beecher, *Autobiography*, 1:271–273.
16 Lyman Beecher Stowe, *Saints, Sinners and Beechers* (Indianapolis: Bobbs-Merrill Co., 1934), 139.
17 L. Beecher, *Autobiography*, 1:288. This is in a letter Lyman wrote to William on February 6, 1819.
18 Litchfield Historical Society, "Elizabeth Burr Mason," *Litchfield Ledger*, accessed November 3, 2023, https://ledger.litchfieldhistoricalsociety.org/ledger/students/3655.
19 Wikipedia, s.v. "Diana," accessed November 3, 2023, https://en.wikipedia.org/wiki/Diana_(mythology); Wikipedia, s.v. "Momus," accessed November 3, 2023, https://en.wikipedia.org/wiki/Momus. Kate positioned herself as Diana, paired with John P as Momus.
20 Vanderpoel, *Chronicles*, 183–187.
21 Litchfield Historical Society, "Uriel Holmes," *Litchfield Ledger*, accessed November 3, 2023, https://ledger.litchfieldhistoricalsociety.org/ledger/students/1226; Litchfield Historical Society, "William Tracy Gould," *Litchfield Ledger*, accessed November 3, 2023, https://ledger.litchfieldhistoricalsociety.org/ledger/students/1050.
22 Vanderpoel, *More Chronicles*, 200. Kate gives up her attractive position at LFA to go to Boston. The job is given to Julia Anna Shepard. This is a powerful clue that Boston was intended to be a more permanent move.
23 Litchfield Historical Society, "John Pierce Brace"; John Brace to Catharine Beecher, 20 July 1819, Acquisitions, Harriet Beecher Stowe Center, Hartford, CT. On the suggestive reference to "sixpence" related to Henry VIII's lust for Anne Boleyn, see Oliver Tearle, "A Short Analysis of the 'Sing a Song of Sixpence' Nursery Rhyme," Interesting Literature, November 3, 2023, https://interestingliterature.com/2018/10/a-short-analysis-of-the-sing-a-song-of-sixpence-nursery-rhyme-origins-history/. For the series of John P. Brace affairs, see Vanderpoel, *More Chronicles*, 147.
24 Wilson, "Beecher Family Tree," Frederick Beecher entry. Harriet and Lyman were married on October 30, 1817, and Frederick was born September 11, 1818.
25 Wikipedia, s.v. "Federalist Party," accessed November 3, 2023, https://en.wikipedia.org/wiki/Federalist_Party.
26 Catharine Beecher to Samuel Foote, 13 April 1819, Acquisitions, Harriet Beecher Stowe Center, Hartford, CT (hereafter referred to as CB to [addressee], [date], Beecher Stowe Center).
27 Vanderpoel, *More Chronicles*, 147. It appears that Brace may have had a behavioral disorder similar to limerence, in which there is a strong, uncontrollable romantic attachment combined with a deep melancholy that

NOTES

the love is not equally returned. See Wikipedia, s.v. "Limerence," accessed November 3, 2023, https://en.wikipedia.org/wiki/Limerence.

28 CB to Louisa Wait, May 1819, Schlesinger. Kate's first letter home to Louisa describes Hobart without any context, thus the assumption that Louisa was already familiar with him. See also Sklar, *Catharine Beecher*, 23. Beecher's biographer describes Kate's visit to Boston with "Cousin Lucy" and does not make the connection that it is her friend Lucy Porter. This connection is critical to understanding the motives and what transpired. Kate was leaving her LFA teaching job (see chapter 3, note 22), which she would not have done if the trip to Boston was simply a vacation. Combined with all the information in Kate's letters to Louisa Wait in May and June 1817, it appears fairly certain that the purpose of the trip to Boston was a proposed courtship rather than a rite of passage.

29 CB to Samuel Foote, 13 April 1819, Beecher Stowe Center.

30 CB to Louisa Wait, 11 May 1819, Schlesinger.

31 CB to Louisa Wait, May 1819, Schlesinger.

32 CB to Louisa Wait, 11 May 1819, Schlesinger: "You see I have nothing to write about but self & I hope you will write with as much egotism as I have—Do be very particular for I think it is trifles that constitute the interest of a letter. You can't think how I long to hear from home & how much I think about my dear parents & the children & you & John & all my dear Litchfield friends . . . It is the remembrance of that home & my kind friends on 'the hill' that gives enjoyment to my pleasures here."

33 CB to Louisa Wait, May 1819, Schlesinger. The Litchfield friend who had not written was John P. Brace.

34 Wilson, "Beecher Family Tree," John Brace entry. John and Lucy were married in November 1819.

35 John P. Brace to Catharine Beecher, 20 July 1819. Acquisitions, Harriet Beecher Stowe Center, Hartford, CT.

36 See chapter 3, note 23.

37 *Stimpson's Boston Directory* (Boston: Charles Stimpson, Jr., 1834). This directory lists two dry goods stores under the name of Hobart on page 201. One is for Nathaniel Hobart & Co, but it lists J. L. Dutton as the proprietor, so he does not fit the profile. The other listing is for Albert Hobart & Co. at 21 Central Street, home 58 Mount Vernon. There are two other Hobarts listed at the same business address—Aaron boards at a coffee shop, and James rents a room at the store address, 21 Central. Aaron and James appear to be too young and not prosperous enough to have been courting Kate Beecher fifteen years earlier. From the 1855 Massachusetts census, accessed through Ancestry.com (login required), Albert Hobart was sixty-two, which would have made him twenty-six in 1819, the perfect age to court Kate Beecher. Based on the age of his oldest child, he would have been married around 1826, so it appears it took a while for him to find the right person. In the same directory on page 205, Henry Homes of Homes, Homer & Co. hardware is listed at 34 Union Street, with a home address of 2 Bowdoin Place. This is Isabella Homes's husband. His business address is only 0.3 miles from Hobart's business at 21 Central, so it is likely they knew one another. As a result, the logical candidate for Kate Beecher's suitor is Albert Hobart.

38 CB to Louisa Wait, 11 May 1819, Schlesinger.

39 Ibid.

40 Propriety was quite important in nineteenth-century social interactions. Women needed chaperones when in the presence of men, or they could sully their reputation. For an interesting overview of propriety, see Jane Austen's *Mansfield Park* (multiple editions available), which was originally published in 1814.
41 CB to Louisa Wait, 11 May 1819, Schlesinger.
42 CB to Louisa Wait, May 1819, Schlesinger.
43 Ibid.
44 Ibid.
45 Ibid.
46 William Shakespeare, *The Tragedies of William Shakespeare* (Norwalk, CT: Easton Press, 1980), 652. Quote from *Hamlet*: "A beast that wants discourse of reason, would have mourn'd longer—married with mine uncle, My father's brother; but no more like my father, Than I to Hercules."
47 CB to Louisa Wait, 4 June 1819, Schlesinger.
48 Lucy Porter to Louisa Wait, 4 June 1819, Beecher-Stowe Collection, Schlesinger Library, Radcliffe Institute, Harvard University.
49 CB to Lyman Beecher, 5 June 1821, Schlesinger. Kate reminded her father that lack of affection had doomed her relationship (with Albert Hobart) in Boston.

Chapter 4—Focused

1 Olmsted, "Reminiscences," 464–465.
2 AF to Caleb Fisher, 4 May 1813, Fisher Correspondence.
3 AF to Caleb Fisher, 3 January 1818, Fisher Correspondence.
4 Alexander Fisher, Lecture Scripts, boxes 3–6, Alexander Metcalf Fisher Papers, General Collection, Beinecke Rare Books and Manuscript Library (hereafter cited as AF, [Topic], [number], Lectures).
5 AF to Caleb Fisher, 30 July 1817, Fisher Correspondence.
6 AF to Parents, 11 November 1817, Fisher Correspondence.
7 AF Religious Diary, 25 July 1817.
8 AF Religious Diary, 11 November 1817.
9 AF Religious Diary, 12 July 1818, and 24 July 1818.
10 AF Religious Diary, 6 September 1818.
11 AF Religious Diary, 1 August 1819. Note: There is a blank page available after the August 1, 1819, entry in box 2, folder 29. The other two diaries—box 2, folder 27 and box 2, folder 28—are completely filled to the last line of the last page. This is a clue that Alexander ended his diaries at this point.
12 AF to Parents, 23 July 1817, Fisher Correspondence.
13 AF to Parents, 7 November 1817, Fisher Correspondence.
14 AF to Caleb Fisher, 3 January 1818, and AF to Sally Fisher, January 1818, Fisher Correspondence.
15 Dexter, "Denison Olmsted," *Biographical Sketches of Yale College*, 593. Olmsted was married on June 1, 1818, to Eliza Allyn of New London, CT.
16 AF to Caleb Fisher, 3 January 1818, Fisher Correspondence.
17 Vanderpoel, *More Chronicles*, 23. Vanderpoel shows list of attendance for Litchfield Female Academy in October 1818 that includes Eliza Wheeler from Medway, MA.

NOTES

18 Jameson, *The History of Medway Mass.*, 423.
19 AF to Parents, 10 September 1818, Fisher Correspondence.
20 Alexander Fisher, Travel Diary, Litchfield to New York, September 1818, box 2, folder 31, Alexander Metcalf Fisher Papers, General Collection, Beinecke Rare Books and Manuscript Library, Yale University (hereafter cited as AF, Travel Diary, [date], [location]).
21 L. Beecher Stowe, *Saints, Sinners and Beechers*, 80.
22 AF to Parents, 8 February 1819, Fisher Correspondence. Alexander cited his contributions to the new periodical *Christian Spectator*.
23 AF to Caleb Fisher, 8 August 1819, Fisher Correspondence.
24 Wikipedia, s.v. "Great Comet of 1819," accessed November 8, 2023, https://en.wikipedia.org/wiki/Great_Comet_of_1819.
25 AF to Caleb Fisher, 8 August 1819, Fisher Correspondence; see also Alexander Fisher, "Comet," *Christian Spectator* I, no. VII (1817): 376–377.
26 Ibid. See also Phi Beta Kappa, Connecticut Alpha, *Phi Beta Kappa Catalogue of Connecticut Alpha* (New Haven: Yale College, 1852), 4. Gardiner Spring delivered the oration in 1818, Alexander Fisher delivered it in 1820, and there was no oration in 1819.
27 Wilson, "Fisher Family Tree." Entries include dates of birth to calculate ages: Eliza Wheeler (twenty-two), born August 16, 1797; Alexander Fisher (twenty-five), born July 22, 1794; Sewall Harding (twenty-six), born March 20, 1793.

Chapter 5—Second Chances

1 L. Beecher, *Autobiography*, 1:387.
2 CB to Louisa Wait, 11 May 1819, Schlesinger. This letter describes fondness for the "hills of Litchfield." See also Catharine Beecher, "Volume of Poetry Presented to Lyman Beecher," Katharine S. Day Collection, Beecher Stowe Center, Hartford, CT. Her poem "Emerald Isle" depicts the beauty surrounding Litchfield that makes it a special place for her friend Mathilda (and her).
3 L. Beecher, *Autobiography*, 1:56–58. In Roxana's letter to Lyman on September 1, 1798, she describes a loving God and having experienced his goodness. L. Beecher Stowe, *Saints, Sinners and Beechers*, 31. Stowe describes an exchange between Roxana and Lyman where he asked if she was willing to be damned for God's honor and glory. She replied, "If to be damned meant anything it meant to be horribly wicked. The idea that for her to be wicked would contribute to the honor and glory of her Heavenly Father was unthinkable!" Lyman replied, "Oh, Roxana, what a fool I've been!" Kate saw the same goodness in God and his creation. She sounded remarkably like her mother.
4 Catharine Beecher, "The Evening Cloud," *Christian Spectator* II, no. II (February 1820): 81.
5 Horace Mann to Lydia Mann, 11 April 1822, Horace Mann Papers, Massachusetts Historical Society, Boston, MA.
6 Louisa Wait to Catharine Beecher, 13 May 1821, Acquisitions, Harriet Beecher Stowe Center, Hartford, CT. Note reference to becoming an "old maid," as some of her relations believed.
7 Catharine Beecher, "Music Book," Beecher Stowe Center, Hartford, CT.
8 AF to Parents, 7 November 1817, Fisher Correspondence.

9   AF Travel Diary, box 2, folder 30–33, see especially box 2, folder 33, page 44 (for the dinner party) and box 2, folder 33, pages 47–49 (for visit to US Mint). See also AF to Parents, 16 May 1817, 7 November 1817, 8 October 1818, and 4 May 1820, Fisher Correspondence, for general overview of trips to the home of his mother's parents.

10 Alexander Fisher, "A Newly Discovered Fragment of an Aerial Voyage by Captain Lemuel Gulliver," *Microscope* 2 (September 1820): 177–191.

11 AF to Caleb Fisher, 21 August 1820, Fisher Correspondence.

12 AF to Parents, 6 November 1820, Fisher Correspondence.

13 AF to Caleb Fisher, 10 January 1821, Fisher Correspondence.

14 AF to Parents, 6 November 1820, Fisher Correspondence. This letter describes the trip home after the fall break in Franklin. Wilson, "Fisher Family Tree," Eliza Wheeler entry, gives the date of the wedding to Sewall Harding as November 2, 1820.

15 C. Beecher, "The Evening Cloud." Note the context of the article. It appears between a Montreal travelogue and a biblical interpretation of Hebrew words.

16 AF Travel Diary, box 2, folder 33, page 15. This passage describes the Bible Convention in New York City and Dr. Beecher's address.

17 Mead, *Nathaniel William Taylor*, 154. Eleazar Fitch worked closely with Lyman Beecher, Nathaniel Taylor, and Chauncey Goodrich in New Haven on religious matters and were special friends. Eleazar collaborated with Lyman for the *Christian Spectator*. As such, he would have been privy to Lyman's personal life and knowledgeable about Kate.

18 Author's observations on character; ages from Wilson, "Beecher Family Tree" and Wilson, "Fisher Family Tree." On Federalist and Congregational membership general knowledge for Kate, see AF to Parents, 7 November 1817, Fisher Correspondence, for extensive expression of Alexander's Federalist views, difficulties with conversion, and romance, as previously noted.

19 L. Beecher Stowe, *Saints, Sinners and Beechers*, 81; L. Beecher, *Autobiography*, 1:328–329.

20 Ibid. Alexander most likely visited during his winter break in January 1821.

21 Ibid.

22 At that point, the family would have all been at home except William and Edward, who had moved out.

23 C. Beecher, "Volume of Poetry." Catharine's inscription: "The following was published in a periodical + was what first turned the thoughts of Prof. Fisher to me. How it foretold what followed!"

24 C. Beecher, "Music Book." Note that the calligraphy in the photograph, which was done by her brother William, has transposed the digits in the year 1821 as "8121." William was thought to be no scholar, but he may have simply been dyslexic. This would explain his difficulty with apprentice jobs as a clerk.

25 CB to Louisa Wait, 11 May 1819, Schlesinger. This letter talks about the importance of ego for Kate. CB to Louisa Wait, 25 March 1822, Schlesinger, talks about how much Alexander enjoyed listening to Kate play the piano. AF to Parents, July 1820, Fisher Correspondence, refers to Alexander's delight watching a young pianist's "fingers dance up & down the scale like lightning."

26 Olmsted, "Reminiscences," 464.

27 C. Beecher, "Music Book."

28 L. Beecher Stowe, *Saints, Sinners and Beechers*, 81.

NOTES 253

29 CB to Louisa Wait, 18 May 1821, Beecher Stowe Center.
30 As noted, propriety was quite important in nineteenth-century social interactions. Women needed chaperones, or they could sully their reputation. For an interesting look at propriety, read Jane Austen's *Mansfield Park* (multiple editions available), which was originally published in 1814.

Chapter 6—Courtship

1 Yale University, "Yale University. University Catalogue, 1820"; Wikipedia, s.v. "James Hillhouse," accessed November 13, 2023, https://en.wikipedia.org/wiki/James_Hillhouse.
2 Louisa Wait to Catharine Beecher, 9 May 1821, Acquisitions, Harriet Beecher Stowe Center, Hartford, CT.
3 Edward Beecher to Catharine Beecher, April 1821, Beecher-Stowe Collection, A-102, Schlesinger Library, Radcliffe Institute, Harvard University, Cambridge, MA (hereafter cited as EB to CB, [date], Schlesinger).
4 Isabel Mitchell, *Roads and Road-Making in Colonial Connecticut* (New Haven, CT: Yale University Press, 1933), 37, https://collections.ctdigitalarchive.org/islandora/object/30002%3A5349350#page/37/mode/1up. The route of Post Road can be seen here.
5 AF to Parents, 31 October 1821, Fisher Correspondence.
6 Wikipedia, s.v. "Yale University," accessed September 2, 2022, https://en.wikipedia.org/wiki/Yale_University.
7 CB to Louisa Wait, 31 May 1821, Schlesinger.
8 Lyman Beecher to Catharine Beecher, 20 October 1821, Beecher-Stowe Collection, Schlesinger Library, Radcliffe Institute, Harvard University (hereafter LB to CB, [date], Schlesinger). This letter refers to Alexander's issues with propriety and physical behavior.
9 Record of Marriages, 20 November 1793, Franklin Church Records. Alexander was born July 22, 1794, eight months after Caleb and Sally Fisher were married. It is estimated that 30 percent of all first births at the time were the result of premarital pregnancy. See Daniel Smith and Michael Hindus, "Premarital Pregnancy in America 1640–1971: An Overview and Interpretation," *Journal of Interdisciplinary History* 5, no. 4 (Spring 1975): 537.
10 LB to CB, 20 October 1821, Schlesinger. This letter refers to Kate's concerns about Alexander's odd physical behavior.
11 CB to Louisa Wait, 31 May 1821, Schlesinger.
12 Ibid.; see reference to Norwich ride.
13 Catharine Beecher, "My Own Diary 1821," Miscellaneous materials, folder 317, Beecher-Stowe Collection, Schlesinger Library, Radcliffe Institute, Harvard University, Cambridge, MA.
14 LB to CB, April 1821, Schlesinger.
15 CB to Mary Beecher, 13 May 1821, Schlesinger.
16 LB to CB, April 1821, Schlesinger.
17 L. Beecher Stowe, *Saints, Sinners and Beechers*, 35: "Lyman hated teaching as much as he hated farming."
18 CB to Mary Beecher, 13 May 1821, Schlesinger.
19 Ibid.

20. CB to Lyman Beecher, 5 June 1821, Schlesinger. Alexander would have written as soon as possible. The issue was that he wrote perhaps too frequently at first, as described in this letter from Kate to Lyman.
21. Louisa Wait to Catharine Beecher, 13 May 1821, Acquisitions, Harriet Beecher Stowe Center, Hartford, CT.
22. Ibid.
23. Lucy Brace to Catharine Beecher, 13 May 1821, Acquisitions, Harriet Beecher Stowe Center, Hartford, CT.
24. CB to Louisa Wait, 31 May 1821, Schlesinger.
25. C. Beecher, *Educational Reminiscences*, 15. Speaking of Lyman's passionate love for his children and the differences with Roxana: "I cannot remember that I ever saw her fondle and caress her little ones as my father did."
26. CB to Louisa Wait, 31 May 1821, Schlesinger.
27. Ibid.
28. Ibid.
29. Ibid.
30. CB to Lyman Beecher, 5 June 1821, Schlesinger.
31. Ibid. "You have seen how distrust of affection . . ."
32. CB to Louisa Wait, 28 June 1821, Schlesinger.
33. Ibid.
34. Lyman Beecher to William Beecher, 23 July 1821, in L. Beecher, *Autobiography*, 1:343.
35. LB to CB, 26 July 1821, Schlesinger.
36. Baldwin, *History of Yale College*, 157: "In the early spring of 1822, Professor Fisher at the request of the Corporation and Faculty, sailed on a voyage to Europe. His objects were, personal improvement, by an intercourse with the learned men of the old world, and the selection of books and apparatus for the use of the University." L. Beecher Stowe, *Saints, Sinners and Beechers*, 85. Stowe includes Alexander's letter to his parents about his salary while in Europe.
37. AF to Parents, 13 October 1821, Fisher Correspondence.
38. AF to Parents, 3 July 1820, Fisher Correspondence.
39. AF to Nancy Fisher, 6 August 1821, Fisher Correspondence.
40. CB to Louisa Wait, 25 March 1822, Schlesinger. Kate referred to meeting Eliza earlier in New London.
41. AF to Parents, 19 October 1821, Fisher Correspondence, refers to his visit home. LB to CB, 20 October 1821, Schlesinger, provides the reference to the visit with Kate.

Chapter 7—Trouble

1. LB to CB, 20 October 1821, Schlesinger. This letter refers to Kate's request for Lyman to meet with Alexander about her concerns.
2. See L. Beecher, *Autobiography*, 1:339, for comment on visit to Dr. Jackson.
3. LB to CB, 20 October 1821, Schlesinger.
4. Rugoff, *The Beechers*, 13.

NOTES

5   This idea was suggested by Elizabeth Burgess, former director of collections at the Harriet Beecher Stowe Center.
6   Esther Beecher to Catharine Beecher, 21 June 1821, in L. Beecher, *Autobiography*, 1:342. This is the reference to the original injury mentioned in Lyman's letter to Edward Beecher; see L. Beecher, *Autobiography*, 1:345.
7   L. Beecher, *Autobiography*, 1:343.
8   LB to CB, 20 October 1821, Schlesinger.
9   Ibid.
10   Ibid.
11   Ibid.
12   Ibid.
13   Ibid.
14   Ibid. A visual inspection of the envelope showed the postmark.
15   CB to Louisa Wait, 28 January 1822, Schlesinger.
16   LB to CB, 20 October 1821, Schlesinger. A visual inspection showed the date the letter was forwarded from New London to Litchfield.
17   Lyman Beecher to Edward Beecher, 6 November 1821, in L. Beecher, *Autobiography*, 1:345.
18   CB to Roxana Foote, 23 November 1821, Beecher Stowe Center.
19   L. Beecher, *Autobiography*, 1:346. In Lyman's letter to Edward dated December 6, he stated, "This is the first moment for several weeks I have felt as if I could sit down to write to you, for either the state of the family has been too distressing, or I have personally felt so bad as to preclude writing." If Lyman couldn't contact Edward, he didn't have the energy to dive into emotional discussions with Alexander.
20   AF to Caleb Fisher, 5 March 1821, Fisher Correspondence. Alexander reports that this was the last school year where he would have the duties of a tutor. It ended in September 1821, so Alexander would have only one job when school resumed in October.
21   AF to Parents, 13 October 1821, Fisher Correspondence.
22   Ibid.
23   AF to Nancy Fisher, 14 December 1821, Fisher Correspondence.
24   CB to Louisa Wait, 28 January 1822, Schlesinger.
25   Ibid.

Chapter 8—Romance

1   CB to Louisa Wait, 28 January 1822, Schlesinger. The date of their meeting was inferred from the timing noted in Kate's letter.
2   Wikipedia, s.v. "Horse Gait," accessed November 29, 2023, https://en.wikipedia.org/wiki/Horse_gait. Horses walk at about 4.3 mph and trot at about 8.1 mph. A combination of walking and trotting would have traversed the thirty-mile trail between Hartford and Litchfield in six to seven hours.
3   CB to Lyman Beecher, 5 June 1821, Schlesinger.
4   CB to Louisa Wait, 28 January 1822, Schlesinger.
5   Ibid.

6   L. Beecher, *Autobiography*, 1:342.
7   AF to Parents, July 1820, Fisher Correspondence. Alexander referred to how he watched the fingers of piano prodigies as they "danced" upon the keys.
8   William Shakespeare, CXXVIII Sonnet, in *Shake-speares Sonnets* (London, England: Thomas Thorpe, 1609). Note: No page numbers in the original version. "Do I envy those jacks that nimble leap, To kiss the tender inward of thy hand, Whilst my poor lips which should that harvest reap." John P. Brace was a Shakespeare aficionado who often quoted him. Note earlier example from *Hamlet* in chapter 3.
9   Moongiant.com, "Full Moon and New Moon for January 1822," accessed September 2, 2022, https://www.moongiant.com/moonphases/january/1822/.
10 Horace Mann to Lydia Mann, 11 April 1822, Horace Mann Papers, Massachusetts Historical Society, Boston, MA. In this letter to his sister, Mann gossiped that Alexander was "making love" to a Litchfield lady.
11 CB to Louisa Wait, 28 January 1822, Schlesinger.
12 CB to Louisa Wait, 25 March 1822, Schlesinger.
13 Ibid. Kate referred to Alexander sending his piano to Franklin for her to play during his absence. The reference to two boxes of specie was drawn from a later newspaper account of the salvage of the *Albion* carried in the *Connecticut Journal* on June 4, 1822.
14 Lyman Beecher to George Foote, 24 January 1822, in L. Beecher, *Autobiography*, 1:351.
15 CB to Louisa Wait, 25 March 1822, Schlesinger. This letter refers to exchanging weekly love letters.
16 AF to Parents, July 1820, Fisher Correspondence. This is the first of a series of letters from Alexander referring to the religious revival sweeping New Haven. See also letters dated 11 September 1820, 16 November 1820, 10 January 1821, and 5 March 1821. His increased belief in God is inferred from the quote in CB to Louisa Wait, 22 January 1823, Schlesinger.
17 CB to Louisa Wait, 22 January 1823, Schlesinger. This quote from Alexander's love letter is evidence that Kate and Alexander shared personal information that might qualify as the emerging sense of Victorian romance. See Lystra, *Searching the Heart*, 3–11. See Lystra's introduction for a good explanation of the Victorian notion of romance.
18 L. Beecher Stowe, *Saints, Sinners and Beechers*, 84.
19 CB to Louisa Wait, 25 March 1822, Schlesinger.
20 Ibid.
21 Ibid.
22 Ibid.
23 Alexander Metcalf Fisher Papers, box 9, folder 143, Beinecke Rare Book and Manuscript Library, Yale University. This was the poem that Kate composed for Alexander's departure.
24 Robert Burns, "Red, Red Rose," Poetry Foundation, accessed November 29, 2023, https://www.poetryfoundation.org/poems/43812/a-red-red-rose.
25 CB to Louisa Wait, 25 March 1822, Schlesinger. The date of Alexander's departure is inferred from Kate's comments in this letter.

NOTES

Chapter 9—Tempest

1. Moongiant.com, "Moon Phases April 1822," accessed July 19, 2024. https://www.moongiant.com/phase/4/1/1822.
2. Wikipedia, "Black Ball Line," accessed December 1, 2023, https://en.wikipedia.org/wiki/Black_Ball_Line. Note that Black Ball was originally founded as Wright, Thompson, Marshall and Thompson. This article provides the details about the *Albion* and its dock in New York.
3. National Oceanic and Atmospheric Administration, "Historical Tides and Currents," accessed November 20, 2023, https://www.tidesandcurrents.noaa.gov/noaatidepredictions.html?id=8518750&units=standard&bdate=18220401&edate=18220402&timezone=LST/LDT&clock=1. There was also a high tide at 4:42 p.m. on April 1, 1822. But sunset was less than two hours later at 6:23 p.m. It is assumed that the captain chose to sail with the morning tide rather than wait until late afternoon when daylight was fleeting.
4. Henry Laight, "Weather Diary: 1792–1826," MS 1672, New-York Historical Society, New York, NY. Laight kept his weather diaries for New York City for thirty-four years. Observations were made at 8:00 a.m., 3:00 p.m., and 10:00 p.m. daily. The entry for 10:00 p.m. on March 31, 1822, noted clear conditions with a south wind and a temperature of forty-three degrees. The observation for 8:00 a.m. on April 1, 1822, noted clear conditions with a west wind and a temperature of forty-eight degrees.
5. Wikipedia, s.v. "Sandy Hook Pilots," accessed December 1, 2023, https://www.tidesandcurrents.noaa.gov/noaatidepredictions.html?id=8518750&units=standard&bdate=18220401&edate=18220402&timezone=LST/LDT&clock=1.
6. L. Beecher Stowe, *Saints, Sinners and Beechers*, 84.
7. William Chauncey Fowler, *Essays: Historical, Literary, Educational* (Hartford: Case, Lockwood & Brainard Co., 1876).
8. L. Beecher Stowe, *Saints, Sinners and Beechers*, 85.
9. L. Beecher Stowe, *Saints, Sinners and Beechers*, 84. Assuming Alexander sent a final note to Kate, she would have kept it with his other correspondence, which she ultimately burned.
10. Wikipedia, "Black Ball Line." This article indicates the average time for passage in both directions.
11. Ibid.
12. Shannon Selin, "The Wreck of the Packet Ship *Albion*," accessed September 5, 2022, https://shannonselin.com/2017/04/wreck-packet-ship-albion/ (hereafter cited as "Wreck of the *Albion*").
13. Wikipedia, "Black Ball Line." The cost of a cabin fare was 35 guineas in 1822. A guinea was 5 percent more than a pound. That translates into $5,000 in 2020 dollars.
14. J. F. Layson, *Memorable Shipwrecks and Seafaring Adventures of the Nineteenth Century* (London: Tyne Publishing Company, 1884), 174.
15. William Everhart, Extract of Letter, box 9, folder 143, Alexander Metcalf Fisher Papers, Beinecke Rare Book and Manuscript Library, Yale University.
16. Wikipedia, s.v. "General Charles Lefebvre-Desnouettes," accessed September 5, 2022, https://en.wikipedia.org/wiki/Charles_Lefebvre-Desnouettes.
17. Selin, "Wreck of the *Albion*."

18. *Dictionary of Canadian Biography*, s.v. "Anne Powell," accessed September 5, 2022, http://www.biographi.ca/en/bio/powell_anne_6E.html; Wikitree, s.v. "Major William Gough," accessed September 5, 2022, https://www.wikitree.com/wiki/Gough-481.
19. Layson, *Memorable Shipwrecks*, 171.
20. CB to Louisa Wait, 25 March 1822, Schlesinger. Kate refers to plans to correspond with Eliza Fisher.
21. Horace Mann to Lydia Mann, 11 April 1822, Horace Mann Papers, Massachusetts Historical Society, Boston, MA.
22. L. Beecher, *Autobiography*, 1:353.
23. Ibid., 1:354.
24. Layson, *Memorable Shipwrecks*, 174. The belief of passengers that they would arrive safely the next day was the recollection of passenger Everhart.
25. Author's description of the likely cause of the *Albion*'s demise based on conversations with Richard Royce, professor of naval architecture at the Webb Institute. Layson, *Memorable Shipwrecks*, page 172, lists the six seamen and one cabin passenger lost. Some early newspaper accounts incorrectly stated that Captain Williams was lost overboard, but Everhart's account (see chapter 9, note 26) contradicts that and is believed to be correct.
26. William Everhart, "Everhart Account, the *Albion* Packet," *The Times*, September 7, 1822, accessed June 24, 2022, Newspapers.com (login required). This account refers to Alexander's head injury.
27. Layson, *Memorable Shipwrecks*, 173. This passage refers to Miss Powell at the pumps.
28. Everhart, "Everhart Account," refers to some of the crew refusing the captain's orders and drinking rum.
29. Layson, *Memorable Shipwrecks*, 176–177.
30. *Columbian Register*, "The Late Shipwreck, June 8, 1822, New Haven," accessed June 24, 2022, Newspapers.com (login required). Press accounts refer to finding the nude body of a beautiful French woman who is clearly Madame Garnier. The logical assumption is that she came on deck wrapped in her blanket. Once the ship struck the coast, it would have been impossible to disrobe.
31. Everhart, "Everhart Account," describes Alexander remaining in his cabin.
32. Layson, *Memorable Shipwrecks*, 175.
33. Ibid., 175. Eyewitness account by passenger Everhart.
34. Ibid., 173. Preceding paragraphs based on eyewitness account of First Mate Cammyer.
35. Ibid., 178. Eyewitness account by rescuer Mr. Purcell.
36. Ibid., 173. Eyewitness account by First Mate Cammyer with analysis of the number of passengers by author based on earlier descriptions.
37. Wikipedia, s.v. "List of Shipwrecks, April 1822," accessed September 5, 2022, https://en.wikipedia.org/wiki/List_of_shipwrecks_in_April_1822. Placement of wrecks on map by author.
38. Selin, "Wreck of the *Albion*."
39. Raymond White, *Their Bones Are Scattered: A History of the Old Head of Kinsale and Surrounding Area* (Kinsale, Ireland: Kilmore Enterprises, 2003), 164. The observations about the graveyard are based conversations with Raymond White during a visit by the author on June 5, 2024.

Chapter 10—Forlorn

1. General Blue, "Calendar for 1822," accessed December 4, 2023, https://www.generalblue.com/calendar/1822. This is a helpful reference that shows historical calendars so that one can see the day of the week. For example, May 25, 1822, was a Saturday.
2. Connecticut General Assembly, "Litchfield County Postmasters," accessed December 4, 2023, https://www.cga.ct.gov/hco/img/history/norton/LitchfieldPostmasters.pdf. Seymour served from 1802 to 1825. See also Litchfield Historical Society, "Moses Seymour Jr.," *Litchfield Ledger*, accessed December 4, 2023, https://ledger.litchfieldhistoricalsociety.org/ledger/students/2264.
3. Payne Kenyon Kilbourne, *Sketches and Chronicles of the Town of Litchfield* (Hartford, CT: Case, Lockwood and Company, 1859), 169–170. Stagecoaches ran daily except on Sundays.
4. L. Beecher, *Autobiography*, 1:355. Lyman's letter was dated May 30, 1822. That was a Thursday, and the letter presumably was delivered in Litchfield the next day on the daily stagecoach.
5. "Catherine E. Beecher Obituary," *New York Herald*, May 13, 1878. Note that the paper misspelled her name. Henry Ward Beecher was quoted as saying, "It was not intended that she should see the letter announcing the calamity, but she came upon it accidentally in the absence of the family, and when they returned, she was lying insensible on the floor." It is assumed that the portion about Kate reading the letter and collapsing unconscious on the floor was true, but the assertion that she was not intended to read a letter addressed to her may have been fabricated to protect Lyman. The letter was published in Lyman's *Autobiography*, which attempted to paint the best picture of him.
6. L. Beecher, *Autobiography*, 1:354–356.
7. Ibid.
8. Ibid.
9. Edward Beecher to Caleb Fisher, box 1, folder 1, Alexander Metcalf Fisher Papers, Beinecke Rare Book and Manuscript Library, Yale University. References to Edward's role as administrator are found in his letters to Kate on 27 October 1822, 13 November 1822, and 11 December 1822, Beecher Family Collection, Schlesinger Library, Radcliffe Institute, Harvard University. Edward specifically mentioned on the second page of the 11 December 1823 letter to Kate, "Mr. Fisher's private papers are all in father's hands except for the letters to him which Mr. Kingsley has." Lyman's custody of the diaries has been reported in other books, but Kingsley's possession of Alexander's personal correspondence has not been reported.
10. AF, Religious Diary, 3 vols., box 2, folder 27–29, Alexander Metcalf Fisher Papers, General Collection, Beinecke Rare Book and Manuscript Library, Yale University. As discussed earlier, these journals appear to end definitively in September of 1819.
11. AF to Parents, 23 March, 1813, Fisher Correspondence. From his senior year at Yale going forward, Alexander dutifully tried to achieve conversion to please his parents, but he found serious faults with the doctrines of his church: "I am unable to reconcile the opinions which prevail here [Yale] concerning the use of the means of grace with either reason or scripture."

12 Kate Beecher to Edward Beecher, 4 June 1822, in L. Beecher, *Autobiography*, 1:356.
13 Edward Beecher to Kate Beecher, in L. Beecher Stowe, *Saints, Sinners and Beechers*, 89.
14 L. Beecher Stowe, *Saints, Sinners and Beechers*, 91.
15 L. Beecher, *Autobiography*, 1:354–356.
16 "Very Late from England," *Connecticut Journal* (New Haven), June 4, 1822, Newspapers.com (login required).
17 "The Late Shipwreck," *Columbian Register* (New Haven), June 8, 1822, Newspapers.com (login required).
18 Alexander Fisher to Parents, in L. Beecher Stowe, *Saints, Sinners and Beechers*, 85.
19 "CPI Inflation Calculator," Officialdata.org, accessed September 6, 2022, https://www.officialdata.org/us/inflation/1822?amount=2000. The value today of $2,000 in 1822 is estimated to be $50,645.
20 CB to Roxana Foote, 23 November 1821, Beecher Stowe Center. In this letter to her grandmother, Kate wrote, "I have very much prospered this summer; and after paying all my expenses at New London and journey, I had a hundred dollars, all of my own earnings left."
21 Probate Bond for Estate of Alexander Fisher, signed June 25, 1822, by Caleb Fisher and James L. Kingsley, Connecticut Wills and Probate Records, accessed September 6, 2022, Ancestry.com (login required). See also chapter 10, note 9 about Edward's role.
22 James L. Kingsley, *An Eulogy on Alexander Metcalf Fisher* (New Haven, CT: Journal Office, 1822). Lyman Beecher Stowe wrote in *Saints, Sinners and Beechers* (93) that Edward wrote to Kate describing the eulogy, which implies that she did not attend but rather discovered that she was ignored later from Edward or by reading a printed copy.
23 "Fisher, Professor" [Eulogy], *Connecticut Courant*, July 9, 1822; "Review of an Eulogy of Professor Fisher," *Christian Spectator* 4, no. VIII (August 1822).
24 EB to CB, 11 December 1822, Schlesinger.
25 Annotated copy of Alexander Fisher, Eulogy, Litchfield Historical Society, Beecher Collection, Litchfield, CT. Author's interpretation about Kingsley's motivation based on stated objections to her inscription on the Fisher monument.
26 L. Beecher, *Autobiography*, 1:56–58.
27 L. Beecher Stowe, *Saints, Sinners and Beechers*, 31.
28 L. Beecher, *Autobiography*, 1:57–59, on conversion: On September 1, 1798, Roxana skeptically wrote to Lyman, "When I pray for a new heart and a right spirit, must I be willing to be denied, and rejoice that my prayer is not heard? Could any real Christian rejoice if God should take from him the mercy bestowed?" In the same September 1 letter, Roxana described her conversion: "On Sunday night I experienced emotions which I can find no language to describe. I seemed to be carried to heaven . . . I was almost in heaven, but sunk to earth again by fears that I should rejoice without cause; but when I prayed my fears seemed to remove." Lyman also described her conversion: "She experienced resignation, if anyone ever did. I never saw the like—so entire,

without reservation, or shadow of turning." There is no doubt that Roxana was a devout Christian. But Lyman was not going to marry her unless she was converted according to his doctrines. Her concept and description of her conversion don't appear to be precisely the same, but he decided to accept it. L. Beecher, *Autobiography*, 1:85, on an obedient wife: Lyman asserted that Roxana was an obedient wife. He once warned her that he had a quick temper, and she "entered into my character entirely"; that is, she was submissive to him. She may not have argued with him, but she knew how to manage her husband. A good example is Kate's story from East Hampton (L. Beecher, *Autobiography*, 1:102), recounting that Lyman would get bored and play the violin while Roxana was trying to run her school upstairs: "Mother would come into the room, quietly walk up to him—not a word said by either of them, only a funny twinkle of the eye—and would take the violin out of his hands, go upstairs and lay it on her table in the schoolroom." Roxana was a strong woman. She may have seemed obedient, but she was a smart, sophisticated woman who played the game. All it took to set him straight was a twinkle of her eye. L. Beecher, *Autobiography*, 1:134, on male versus female education: Roxana saw to it that her sons were educated for college, whereas Kate was trained for marriage. Roxana wrote Lyman that "the boys go to school with Mr. Parsons and Catharine continues her studies at home."
29 L. Beecher, *Autobiography*, 1:288, 357–360.
30 Edward Lawrence, *The Life of Rev. Joel Hawes*, 2nd ed. (Boston: 1881), 27, 37–40; AF to Parents, 1 March 1816, folder 13, Fisher Correspondence: "I received a letter by Mr. Kingbury from my roommate Ely, from Mr. Hawes and Mr. Baldwin." Joel Hawes grew up in Medway, next door to Franklin, and attended Brown, where he graduated second in his class before attending Andover.
31 L. Beecher, *Autobiography*, 1:360.
32 Ibid.
33 Ibid., 361.
34 EB to CB, 23 August 1822, Schlesinger.
35 Sklar, *Catharine Beecher*, 43.
36 CB to Louisa Wait, 28 September 1822, Schlesinger.

Chapter 11—Renewed

1 CB to Louisa Wait, 22 January 1823. Schlesinger.
2 Ibid. "This instrument, his portrait, his letters & books and the memorials of his early genius preserved by maternal love & above all the renewed testimonials of his tender care & affection for me." This passage in particular is a clue that Sally Fisher preserved Alexander's letters as a memorial in her decorated box. Note: Text italicized by author.
3 Ibid.
4 Wilson, "Fisher Family Tree." The details of Alexander's immediate family are provided in the family tree. The personality traits were derived from Alexander's letters to his family (Fisher Correspondence) over a period of thirteen years.

NOTES

5   Mead, *Nathaniel William Taylor*, 12–23. Mead's chapter 2 provides a concise overview of the doctrines of the New Divinity. Emmons was a leader of this movement.
6   L. Beecher Stowe, *Saints, Sinners and Beechers*, 94.
7   LB to CB, 27 October 1822, Schlesinger.
8   LB to CB, 5 November 1822, Schlesinger.
9   Alexander Fisher, small domed top trunk, box 11, and wallpaper from the Fisher homestead in Franklin, MA, box 10 (oversize), folder 153, Alexander Metcalf Fisher Papers, General Collection, Beinecke Rare Book and Manuscript Library, Yale University. The wallpaper sample is what covers the exterior of the box.
10 Edward Beecher to Lyman Beecher, 31 December 1822, Beecher-Stowe Collection, Schlesinger Library, Radcliffe Institute, Harvard University. See second page of letter: "I wish also that you would send me by the trunk (Miner's) Mr. Fisher's private papers. Mrs. Fisher wishes Catharine to read them to her before she goes." This is the critical piece of evidence that Kate read Alexander's letters and papers to Sally Fisher.
11 Author's observation based on reading Alexander's letters from 1809–1822.
12 C. Beecher, *Educational Reminiscences*, 28–30.
13 CB to Louisa Wait, 22 January 1823, Schlesinger.
14 Nancy Fisher Kidder obituary, box 9, folder 146, Alexander Metcalf Fisher Papers, General Collection, Beinecke Rare Books and Manuscript Library. Nancy Fisher followed Kate to attend and then teach music at Hartford Female Academy. She named her daughter Catharine Beecher Kidder. This daughter also became a music teacher. Based on this evidence, it is believed that Kate was likely a mentor for Nancy's career.
15 EB to CB, 13 November 1822, Schlesinger.
16 CB to Louisa Wait, 22 January 1823, Schlesinger.
17 EB to CB, 11 December 1822, Schlesinger. The final version varied slightly from what Edward translated here for Kate.
18 EB to CB, 13 January 1823.
19 Ibid.
20 This was transcribed by the author from the memorial in Franklin, Massachusetts.
21 Author's observations based on a personal visit to the Union Cemetery in Franklin, Massachusetts, on October 12, 2023. The epitaph and poetry are on the front of the monument, which faces the same direction as all the other Fisher monuments. The words were not legible until cleaned by the author using a safe biological cleaner, D/2, with permission of the cemetery authorities. The front epitaph was deciphered and the poetry verified by the author.
22 EB to CB, 13 December 1822, Schlesinger.
23 CB to Lyman Beecher, 1 January 1823, in L. Beecher, *Autobiography*, 1:369. See also AF, Religious Diary, 1 August 1819, for final entry.
24 Franklin Church Records, 30 January 1820: "Sally Fisher was admitted to full communion in this Church"; Wilson, "Fisher Family Tree." The family tree notes that Sally was born May 12, 1771.
25 AF to Parents, 23 March 1813, Fisher Correspondence.

26 Alexander Metcalf Fisher, Fisher Personal Notes, box 2, folder 26, page 5. See note 20, Chapter 2 for discussion of page numbers.
27 Ibid., 18. Alexander believed that he was using science as the representative of God.
28 Ibid., 27.
29 See the Mayo Clinic website for a brief description of bipolar symptoms. Mayo Clinic, "Bipolar Disorder," accessed August 27, 2022, https://www.mayoclinic.org/diseases-conditions/bipolar-disorder/symptoms-causes/syc-20355955.
30 EB to CB, 14 February 1823, Schlesinger. Note: This letter was improperly dated 1822. Edward is answering Willard's questions about Alexander's scientific manuscripts and references the density of air and the nature of electric fluids.
31 CB to Louisa Wait, 22 January 1823, Schlesinger.
32 Ibid.
33 Catharine Beecher to Lyman Beecher, 15 February 1823, in L. Beecher *Autobiography*, 1:376–377.
34 L. Beecher, *Autobiography*, 1:378–384. This is the last letter from Lyman to Kate where he pressed her for conversion. He apparently took her attitude as permanent and a sign from God that he had special plans for her.
35 Catharine Beecher to Lyman Beecher, 15 February 1823, in L. Beecher, *Autobiography*, 1:376–377.
36 LB to CB, 27 January 1823, Schlesinger.
37 Catharine Beecher to Lyman Beecher, 15 February 1823, in L. Beecher, *Autobiography*, 1:376–377.
38 LB to CB, 21 March 1823, Schlesinger.
39 Wikipedia, s.v. "Grief," accessed June 27, 2023, https://en.wikipedia.org/wiki/Grief. The two-track model for bereavement developed by Simon Shimshon Rubin is complicated. But simplified, it says two things are required to successfully exit: (1) determine a new purpose in life, and (2) settle the ongoing relationship with the deceased.
40 "Auld Lang Syne," Poets.org, accessed April 6, 2024, https://poets.org/poem/auld-lang-syne.

Chapter 12—Crusader

1 Hartford Female Seminary, *Reunion Hartford Female Seminary June 9, 1892* (Hartford, CT: Case Lockwood and Brainard, 1892), 18 (on the location); Rugoff, *The Beechers*, 53 (on the seven students).
2 CB to Louisa Wait, 1 June 1824, Schlesinger.
3 Sklar, *Catharine Beecher*, 59–60, 90 (on the size estimate).
4 C. Beecher, *Educational Reminiscences*, 34–43.
5 CB to Louisa Wait, 23 August 1824, Schlesinger.
6 CB to Louisa Wait, 30 September 1824, Schlesinger.
7 Sklar, *Catharine Beecher*, 60.
8 CB to Louisa Wait, 17 February 1825, Schlesinger.
9 CB to Louisa Wait, 8 November 1825, Schlesinger.
10 Litchfield Historical Society, "Louisa Wait."

NOTES

11. Catharine Beecher to Harriet Porter Beecher, [1817–1826], *Acquisitions*, Harriet Beecher Stowe Center, Hartford, CT (on Lyman's church); Rugoff, *The Beechers*, 55 (on Hawes's church).
12. Joan D. Hedrick, *Harriet Beecher Stowe: A Life* (Oxford: Oxford University Press, 1994), 39.
13. Sklar, *Catharine Beecher*, 68–71.
14. Hartford Female Seminary, *Reunion*, 6 (on number of students and halls); Hartford Female Seminary, Financial Records, MS 100697, box 2 (on the exact amount of the money raised from investors through a stock subscription). Kate invested $150.
15. Catharine Beecher to Harriet Porter Beecher, [1817–1826], *Acquisitions*, Harriet Beecher Stowe Center, Hartford, CT.
16. Nancy Fisher Kidder obituary, Alexander Metcalf Fisher Papers; Hedrick, *Harriet Beecher Stowe*, 55; Hartford Female Seminary, Annual Catalogue, 1828–1831, Connecticut Museum of Culture and History, Hartford, CT. The annual catalogues for 1828–1831 all listed (Nancy) Ann Fisher and Harriet Beecher as teachers.
17. Wilson, "Fisher Family Tree." There is an extension for the Wheeler family. Willard married Betsey Wheeler. Kate was probably unaware that Alexander had once fancied Betsey's older sister, Eliza Wheeler.
18. Wikipedia, s.v. "Denison Olmsted," accessed December 28, 2023, https://en.wikipedia.org/wiki/Denison_Olmsted.
19. Sklar, *Catharine Beecher*, 59–63; Hedrick, *Harriet Beecher Stowe*, 34–55; Rugoff, *The Beechers*, 51–56; Wikipedia, s.v. "Edward Beecher" accessed December 28, 2023, https://en.wikipedia.org/wiki/Edward_Beecher; Yale University, "Yale University. University Catalogue, 1820"; Wikipedia, s.v. "Henry Ward Beecher," accessed December 28, 2023, https://en.wikipedia.org/wiki/Henry_Ward_Beecher.
20. Sklar, *Catharine Beecher*, 90.
21. C. Beecher, *Educational Reminiscences*, 49.
22. Sklar, *Catharine Beecher*, 91.
23. L. Beecher Stowe, *Saints, Sinners and Beechers*, 115.
24. Rugoff, *The Beechers*, 59–60.
25. Ibid., 58. Rugoff is quoting a letter from Harriet to Elizabeth Phoenix.
26. Sklar, *Catharine Beecher*, 102. Sklar is quoting a February 8, 1830, letter from Kate to Mary Dutton.
27. Rugoff, *The Beechers*, 79.
28. Sklar, *Catharine Beecher*, 99.
29. Hartford Female Seminary, *Reunion*, 6–7; Hedrick, *Harriet Beecher Stowe*, 36.
30. Sklar, *Catharine Beecher*, 103.
31. Ibid., 107.
32. Wikipedia, s.v., "List of States by Historical Population," accessed September 6, 2022, https://en.wikipedia.org/wiki/List_of_U.S._states_and_territories_by_historical_population.
33. Wikipedia, s.v. "List of Largest US Cities of US States by Historical Population," accessed December 28, 2023, https://en.wikipedia.org/wiki/List_of_largest_cities_of_U.S._states_and_territories_by_historical_population. See also Wikipedia, s.v. "Hartford, CT, Demographics," accessed December 28, 2023, https://en.wikipedia.org/wiki/Hartford,_Connecticut#Demographics.

NOTES

34 Wikipedia, s.v. "History of Cincinnati, OH," accessed December 28, 2023, https://en.wikipedia.org/wiki/Cincinnati. See also Wikipedia, s.v. "Hartford, CT, Demographics."
35 Wikipedia, s.v. "St. Louis Demographics," accessed December 28, 2023, https://en.wikipedia.org/wiki/St._Louis#Demographics; Wikipedia, s.v. "Chicago Demographics," accessed December 28, 2023, https://en.wikipedia.org/wiki/Chicago#Demographics.
36 Wikipedia, "History of Cincinnati, OH."
37 Sklar, *Catharine Beecher*, 109–111.
38 C. Beecher, *Educational Reminiscences*, 84.
39 Sklar, *Catharine Beecher*, 6–7. The two young Black girls were named Drusilla (Zillah) and Rachel. Although the practice was legal, Zillah was bound to the Beechers at the age of five, shortly after Kate was born. The Beechers maintained that they treated the girls like family. But while the terms of these indentures are unknown, the actual terms of another Black girl in East Hampton at the time are assumed to be representative. The East Hampton Historical Society Digital Collection notes the indentured servitude of Rachel Beeman Cuff to Edward Mulford, East Hampton Township, New York, June 6, 1810. It states that Rachel, "aged seven years," with the consent of her parents, "hath of her own free will bound herself a servant of Edward Mulford." Her servitude until the age of eighteen was in return for "sufficient meat, drink washing, lodging and apparel and all other necessities suitable for such a servant . . . to teach her to read and at the expiration of her servitude to give unto . . . said servant all her common wearing apparel and one new suit of clothes throughout and eight dollars and seventy-five cents in cash."
40 Sklar, *Catharine Beecher*, 116. Sklar is quoting from Randolph Randall, *James Hall: Spokesman of the New West* (Columbus, OH: Ohio State University Press, 1964), 245.
41 Ibid., 114–118. The quote is from C. Beecher, *Educational Reminiscences*, 83.
42 Sklar, *Catharine Beecher*, 131.
43 Rugoff, *The Beechers*, 154–159.
44 Ibid., 162; Wilson, "Beecher Family Tree." According to the family tree, Harriet Porter Beecher died July 7, 1835.
45 Wilson, "Fisher Family Tree." According to the tree, Sarah Cushing Fisher died August 11, 1835.
46 Nancy Fisher Kidder obituary, Alexander Metcalf Fisher Papers.
47 Catharine Beecher, *An Essay on Slavery and Abolitionism with Reference to the Duty of American Females* (Philadelphia: Henry Perkins, 1837), 58–78.
48 Ibid., 56–68.
49 Ibid., 114.
50 Ibid., 128–129.
51 Sklar, *Catharine Beecher*, 132.
52 C. Beecher, *Essay on Slavery and Abolitionism*, 141.
53 Ibid., 107.
54 Sklar, Catharine Beecher, 132–137.
55 Catharine Beecher and Harriet Beecher Stowe, *The American Woman's Home* (New York: J. B. Ford & Co., 1869), 97 (unbolted flour), 53–57 (proper ventilation).

56 Catharine Beecher, *Treatise on Domestic Economy for the Use of Young Ladies at Home and School* (Boston: T. H. Webb & Company, 1843), 82 (spine picture), 88 (organ picture), 262 (house floor plan).
57 Rugoff, *The Beechers*, 183.
58 Sarah Levitt, *From Catharine Beecher to Martha Stewart* (Chapel Hill: University of North Carolina Press, 2002). For a quick overview, read the introduction. For more on Kate's impact on home economics, see Charlotte Biester, "Catharine Beecher, Founder of Home Economics," *Journal of the American Dietetic Association* 28, no. 2 (1952): 136–139.
59 Rugoff, *The Beechers*, 203.
60 Sklar, *Catharine Beecher*, 146–148.
61 Ibid., 168.
62 Wikipedia, s.v. "Calvin Stowe," accessed September 6, 2022, https://en.wikipedia.org/wiki/Calvin_Ellis_Stowe.
63 Wikipedia, s.v. "Horace Mann," accessed December 29, 2023, https://en.wikipedia.org/wiki/Horace_Mann.
64 Sklar, *Catharine Beecher*, 176–183.
65 Rugoff, *The Beechers*, 188–189.
66 Sklar, *Catharine Beecher*, 187–190. She attended First Church in Hartford, whose minister was Joel Hawes. Alexander's friend and Kate's one-time supporter eventually became her foe.
67 Wikipedia, s.v. "Delia Bacon," accessed December 30, 2023, https://en.wikipedia.org/wiki/Delia_Bacon.
68 Sklar, *Catharine Beecher*, 190–192.
69 Rugoff, *The Beechers*, 169 (Edward), 276–277 (Henry), 317–318 (Harriet), 168–170 (Lyman).
70 Ibid., 193.
71 Litchfield Historical Society, "John P. Brace"; Litchfield Historical Society, "Lucy Porter Brace," *Litchfield Ledger*, https://ledger.litchfieldhistoricalsociety.org/ledger/students/385; Litchfield Historical Society, "Charles Greely Loring," *Litchfield Ledger*, https://ledger.litchfieldhistoricalsociety.org/ledger/students/1597; Hartford Female Seminary, *Reunion*, 7. Brace served as principal for thirteen years, longer than any other individual. He was succeeded by Helen Swift in December 1845.
72 Sklar, *Catharine Beecher*, 202 and 224.
73 Catharine Beecher, *Woman's Profession as Mother and Educator with Views in Opposition to Woman's Suffrage* (Philadelphia: George Maclean, 1872). See Catharine Beecher, "An Address on Female Suffrage" [delivered December 1870], https://teachingamericanhistory.org/document/an-address-on-female-suffrage/ (hereafter cited as Boston Address).
74 Rugoff, *The Beechers*, 307.
75 Wikipedia, s.v. "Lawrence University," accessed September 6, 2022, https://en.wikipedia.org/wiki/Lawrence_University.
76 Debby Applegate, *The Most Famous Man in America* (New York: Crown Publishing Group, 2006), 13.
77 Ibid., 241–251.
78 Ibid., 281–282.
79 Hedrick, *Harriet Beecher Stowe*, 221–223.

80. Ibid., 274–278.
81. Ibid., 287–289.
82. L. Beecher Stowe, *Saints, Sinners and Beechers*, 100. Beecher Stowe expressed his belief that "in fact, The Minister's Wooing is merely a fictionalized account with a happy ending of Catharine's romance and tragedy. The minister, Doctor Hopkins, is Doctor Emmons; the sailor lover, James Marvyn, is Professor Fisher; and the mother, Mrs. Marvyn, is Mrs. Fisher."
83. Rugoff, *The Beechers*, 302.
84. Ibid., 294.
85. Ibid., 404.
86. Wikipedia, s.v. "Catharine Beecher," accessed December 29, 2023, https://en.wikipedia.org/wiki/Catharine_Beecher.
87. Hedrick, *Harriet Beecher Stowe*, 302.
88. Catharine Beecher, *Religious Training of Children in the School, the Family and the Church* (New York: Harper & Brothers, 1864), 223: "The rule of common sense for deciding when a word is figurative or literal is this: Every word is literal except when that meaning contradicts the known nature of things or the expressed opinions of the writer, in which case it is figurative."
89. Ibid., 137–139 (for common sense and facts), 213 (for own interpretation of the Bible), and 216 (for best good).
90. Ibid., 175–176 and 186. The author created this memorable summary sentence.
91. Beecher and Beecher Stowe, *The American Woman's Home*.

Chapter 13—Legacy

1. L. Beecher Stowe, *Saints, Sinners and Beechers*, 134–135.
2. C. Beecher, Boston Address, 41.
3. Minute Book of the Board, Hartford Female Seminary Records, 1827–1890, MS 16802, Connecticut Museum of Culture and History, 117–118. This record describes Kate's brief return as principal from August 1870 to February 1871. She was replaced in March 1871 by Miss Mary Beecher.
4. Author's analysis of population figures from US Census of 1870.
5. Wikipedia, s.v. "Hartford, CT," accessed December 30, 2023, https://en.wikipedia.org/wiki/Hartford,_Connecticut. The term "Silicone Valley of its day" for Hartford was coined by the author.
6. Sklar, *Catharine Beecher*, 265–266; Beecher Stowe Collection, A-102, folder 317, Schlesinger.
7. L. Beecher Stowe, *Saints, Sinners and Beechers*, 134–135.
8. Applegate, *The Most Famous Man in America*, 412–455.
9. C. Beecher, *Educational Reminiscences*, 208.
10. C. Beecher, Boston Address, 5.
11. C. Beecher, *Educational Reminiscences*, 201.
12. Ibid., 51.
13. Ibid., 28–30.
14. Wikipedia, s.v. "Lawrence University," accessed May 18, 2024, https://en.wikipedia.org/wiki/Lawrence_University.
15. Wikipedia, s.v. "Sarah Pierce," accessed May 18, 2024, https://en.wikipedia.org/wiki/Sarah_Pierce.

NOTES

16. Wikipedia, s.v. "Emma Willard," accessed May 18, 2024, https://en.wikipedia.org/wiki/Emma_Willard.
17. Wikipedia, s.v. "Zilpah Grant Banister," accessed May 18, 2024, https://en.wikipedia.org/wiki/Zilpah_P._Grant_Banister.
18. Wikipedia, s.v. "Mary Lyon," accessed May 18, 2024, https://en.wikipedia.org/wiki/Mary_Lyon.
19. Wikipedia, s.v. "Harriet Beecher Stowe," accessed May 18, 2024, https://en.wikipedia.org/wiki/Harriet_Beecher_Stowe; Wikipedia, s.v. "Hartford Female Seminary," accessed December 30, 2023, https://en.wikipedia.org/wiki/Hartford_Female_Seminary. The list of students was taken from the Hartford Female Seminary entry.
20. Wikipedia, s.v. "Fanny Fern," accessed May 18, 2024, https://en.wikipedia.org/wiki/Fanny_Fern.
21. Wikipedia, s.v. "Sarah Walker Davis," May 18, 2024, https://en.wikipedia.org/wiki/Sarah_Woodruff_Walker.
22. Wikipedia, s.v. "Mary Hawes Van Lennep," accessed May 18, 2024, https://en.wikipedia.org/wiki/Mary_E._Van_Lennep.
23. Wikipedia, s.v. "Rose Terry Cooke," accessed May 18, 2024, https://en.wikipedia.org/wiki/Rose_Terry_Cooke.
24. Wikipedia, s.v. "Virginia Thrall Smith," accessed May 18, 2024, https://en.wikipedia.org/wiki/Virginia_Thrall_Smith.
25. Wikipedia, s.v. "Annie Trumbull Slosson," accessed May 18, 2024, https://en.wikipedia.org/wiki/Annie_Trumbull_Slosson.
26. Wikipedia, s.v. "Kate Foote Coe," accessed May 18, 2024, https://en.wikipedia.org/wiki/Kate_Foote_Coe.
27. C. Beecher, *Religious Training*, 176.
28. L. Beecher Stowe, *Saints Sinners and Beechers*, 121, provides a good example where Kate summarily fired the servants working at the home of her niece because they weren't doing things in the kitchen the way she preferred. When he found out, her niece's husband ordered her to leave the next day. Two years later when she saw him on the street, rather than avoiding him, she offered to show him a new purchase of books. Totally disarmed, he invited her to come stay with them. At 129–130 is the famous story of her visit to Cornell where she asked the president if she could take a course they were offering. He told her that no courses were open to women. She replied, "Oh, that is quite all right . . . in fact I prefer to take it with men." He was so disarmed that he allowed her to take the course.
29. L. Beecher, *Autobiography*, 1:17.
30. L. Beecher Stowe, *Saints, Sinners and Beechers*, 354.
31. Ibid., 369.
32. "Catherine Beecher Dying," *New York Times*, May 11, 1878, p. 5. Note: The *Times* misspelled Catharine's name as *Catherine* throughout the article.
33. "Funeral of Catherine Beecher," *New York Times*, May 15, 1878, p. 5. Note: The *Times* misspelled Catharine's name as *Catherine* throughout the article.

Epilogue

1. Antoine de Saint-Exupéry, *Le Petit Prince* (New York: Harcourt, Brace & World, Inc., 1943), 76. Translation by the author (Lee Wilson).
2. Wikitree, s.v. "Lyman Beecher Stowe," accessed September 7, 2022, https://www.wikitree.com/wiki/Stowe-336.
3. Royal Astronomical Society of Canada, "Willard James Fisher," *Meteor News*, accessed September 7, 2022, https://adsabs.harvard.edu/full/1934JRASC..28..377M.
4. L. Beecher Stowe, *Saints, Sinners and Beechers*, 135. This is Willard Fisher's eyewitness account of Kate burning Alexander's letters that was retold by Stowe.
5. Wilson, "Fisher Family Tree." According to the family tree, Willard J. Fisher was born in September 1867, the son of George Fisher, roughly dating the story to September 1872 to September 1873, based on Willard's account to Stowe that he was a boy of five at the time. Note that Sewall had three children, none of whom were named Willard.
6. L. Beecher Stowe, *Saints, Sinners and Beechers*, 135.
7. Sklar, *Catharine Beecher*, 271.
8. Norfolk County Registry of Deeds, "Records Database," http://www.norfolkresearch.org/ALIS/WW400R.HTM?WSIQTP=LR01D&WSKYCD=N. Based on author analysis of deed transactions. To understand the ownership of the Fisher family farm, one must trace a series of sales. The farm was ultimately sold to Emerson Bullard in October 1866. Notable transactions include the following:
    - Deed Book 126-268—Caleb Fisher to Willard Fisher, 10 acres, January 19, 1838
    - Deed Book 185-449,450—Caleb Fisher to Willard Fisher, 123 acres, March 22, 1843
    - Deed Book 317-312—Willard Fisher to Sewall Fisher, one-half of land, May 9, 1863
    - Deed Book 340-297,298—Clara Fisher to Sewall/George Fisher, one-half land, March 23, 1866
    - Deed Book 378-441—Sewall/George to Bullard, 70 acres, October 12, 1866—reserves use of house until April 1, 1867
    - Deed Book 348-518,519—Sewall/George to Whiting, 27 acres, October 31, 1866
    - Deed Book 378-441,442—Sewall Fisher (of Framingham) to Bullard, April 23, 1869
9. Wilson, "Fisher Family Tree." Sewall and George Fisher were sons of Willard and were the only two living on the family farm according to the 1860 census records appended to this tree. The 1870 census describes Sewall as a florist, living in Framingham, Massachusetts, and George as living in Albany, New York. George ultimately became a minister.

10 L. Beecher Stowe, *Saints, Sinners and Beechers*, 135.
11 Sklar, *Catharine Beecher*, 271; Rugoff, *The Beechers*, 314.
12 Trunk, box 11 (art), Alexander Metcalf Fisher Papers, General Collection, Beinecke Rare Book and Manuscript Library, Yale University. Late-eighteenth-century or nineteenth-century dome-top wood trunk covered in decorative paper. Dimensions: 23 (height) by 44 (width) by 26 (depth) cm. Previously contained manuscripts donated as part of the collection in 1921.

BIBLIOGRAPHY

Manuscript Collections by Location

Beinecke Rare Book and Manuscript Library, Yale University
    Alexander Metcalf Fisher Papers, https://hdl.handle.net/10079/fa/beinecke.fisheram.
Connecticut Historical Society, Hartford, CT
    Hartford Female Seminary Papers.
Harriet Beecher Stowe Center, Hartford, CT
    Acquisitions.
    Foote Collection.
    Katharine S. Day Collection.
Litchfield Historical Society, Litchfield, CT
    Archives Collection.
    Artifact Collection.
    Loring Family Papers.
Massachusetts Historical Society, Boston, MA
    Horace Mann Papers.
New-York Historical Society, New York, NY
    Henry Laight Weather Diary, 1792–1826.
Schlesinger Library, Radcliffe Institute, Harvard University
    Beecher-Stowe Collection, https://guides.library.harvard.edu/schlesinger/beecher-stowe-family.

Unpublished Works

Garrison, Taylor. "What's Love Got to Do With It: Courtship in Antebellum America." PhD diss., Muhlenberg College, May 2020.
Schoepflin, Gary Lee. "Denison Olmsted (1791–1859), Scientist, Teacher, Christian: A Biographical Study of the Connection of Science with Religion in Antebellum America." PhD diss., Oregon State University, June 17, 1977.

Published Works

Adrain, R. "Question 9, or Prize Question." *American Monthly Magazine and Critical Review* 1, no. 7 (September 1817): 400.

BIBLIOGRAPHY

Applegate, Debby. *The Most Famous Man in America*. New York: Crown Publishing Group, 2006.

Baldwin, Ebenezer. *History of Yale College*. New Haven: Benjamin and Noyes, 1841.

Balmer, Randall. *Mine Eyes Have Seen the Glory*. New York: Oxford University Press, 2014.

Beecher, Catharine. *The Biographical Remains of Rev. George Beecher*. New York: Leavitt, Trow and Co., 1844.

Beecher, Catharine. *Common Sense Applied to Religion, or the Bible and the People*. New York: Harper & Bros., 1857.

Beecher, Catharine. *Educational Reminiscences and Suggestions*. New York: J. B. Ford and Company, 1874.

Beecher, Catharine. *Essay on Slavery and Abolitionism with Regard to the Duty of American Females*. Philadelphia: Henry Perkis, 1837.

Beecher, Catharine. "The Evening Cloud." *Christian Spectator* 1, no. 2 (February 1820).

Beecher, Catharine. *Miss Beecher's Domestic Receipt Book*. 5th ed. New York: Harper & Brothers, 1871.

Beecher, Catharine. *Religious Training of Children in the School, the Family and the Church*. New York: Harper & Brothers, 1864.

Beecher, Catharine. *Treatise on Domestic Economy for the Use of Young Ladies at Home and School*. Boston: T. H. Webb & Company, 1843.

Beecher, Catharine. *Truth Stranger Than Fiction; A Narrative of Recent Transactions Involving Inquiries in Regard to the Principles of Honor, Truth and Justice which Obtain in a Distinguished American University*. New York: Printed for the author, 1850.

Beecher, Catharine. *Woman's Profession as Mother and Educator with Views in Opposition to Woman's Suffrage*. Philadelphia: George Maclean, 1872.

Beecher, Catharine, and Harriet Beecher Stowe. *The American Woman's Home or Principles of Domestic Science*. New York: J. B. Ford & Co., 1869.

Beecher, Edward. *Conflict for the Ages*. Boston: Crosby & Nichols, 1852.

Beecher, Lyman. *The Autobiography of Lyman Beecher*. Ed. Barbara Cross. 2 vols. Cambridge: Harvard University Press/Belknap Press, 1961.

Biester, Charlotte. "Catharine Beecher, Founder of Home Economics." *Journal of the American Dietetic Association* 28, no. 2 (1952): 136–139.

Biester, Charlotte. "Catharine Beecher's Views on Home Economics." *History of Education Journal* 3, no. 3 (1952): 88–91.

Blake, Mortimer. *History of the Town of Franklin, Mass*. Franklin, MA: Committee of the Town, 1879.

Boonshoft, Mark. "The Litchfield Network, Education, Social Capital and the Rise and Fall of a Political Dynasty, 1784–1833." *Journal of the American Republic* 34, no. 4 (Winter 2014): 561–595.

Burstyn, Joan. "Catharine Beecher and the Education of American Women." *New England Quarterly* 47, no. 3 (1974): 386–403.

Calvin, John. *Institutes of the Christian Religion*. Translated by John Allen. Philadelphia: Philip Nicklin, 1816.

Campbell, Leon. "Willard James Fisher, 1867–1934." *Popular Astronomy* 43 (1935): 475–477.

Collins, William, Perry Cicero, and John Tillson. *Past and Present of the City of Quincy and Adams County, Illinois*. Chicago: S. J. Clarke Publishing Co., 1905.

Day, Jeremiah. "Original Papers in Relation to a Course of Liberal Education." *Journal of Science and Art* XV (January 1829): 297–325.

Dexter, Franklin. *Biographical Sketches of Yale College Vol. 6*. New Haven, CT: Yale University Press, 1912.

Doddridge, Philip. *The Rise and Progress of Religion in the Soul Illustrated in the Course of Serious and Practical Addresses Suited to Persons of Every Character and Circumstance with a Devout Meditation, or Prayer Subjoined to Each Chapter*. New York: American Tract Society, 1847.

Edwards, Park. *Memoir of Nathanael Emmons*. Boston: Congregational Church Board of Publication, 1861.

Fisher, Alexander Metcalf. "Essay on Musical Temperament." *American Journal of Science and Arts* 1 (1818).

Fisher, Alexander Metcalf. "Mathematical Lucubrations." *American Monthly Magazine and Critical Review* 2, no. 4 (February 1818).

Fisher, Alexander Metcalf. "A Newly Discovered Fragment of an Aerial Voyage by Captain Lemuel Gulliver." *Microscope* 2 (September 1820).

Fisher, Alexander Metcalf. "Review of Dr. Brown's Essay on the Existences of a Supreme Creator." *Christian Spectator* 1, no. 8 (August 1819); 1, no. 11 (November 1819).

Foster, Charles. "The Genesis of Harriet Beecher Stowe's 'The Minister's Wooing.'" *New England Quarterly* 21, no. 4 (December 1948).

Fowler, William Chauncey. *Essays: Historical, Literary, Educational*. Hartford: The Case, Lockwood & Brainard Co., 1876.

Fowler, William Chauncey. "Origin of the Theological Department of Yale College." *College Courant* 13, no. 11 (September 1873).

Gilbert, Josiah H. *Dictionary of Burning Words of Brilliant Writers*. New York: Wilbur Ketcham, 1895.

Griswold, Mary Hoadley. *Yester-Years of Guilford*. Guilford, CT: Shore Line Times Publishing Company, 1938.

Hambrick, David Z. "What Makes a Prodigy?" *Scientific American*, September 22, 2015. https://www.scientificamerican.com/article/what-makes-a-prodigy1/.

Hartford Female Seminary. *Catalogue of the Officers, Teachers, Pupils*. Hartford, CT: Hartford Female Seminary, 1828–30.

Hartford Female Seminary. *Hartford Female Seminary Records, 1827–1890, MS 16802*. Hartford, CT: Connecticut Historical Society.

Hartford Female Seminary. *Reunion Hartford Female Seminary, 1892*. Hartford, CT: Case, Lockwood & Brainard, 1892.

Hedrick, Joan D. *Harriet Beecher Stowe: A Life*. Oxford: Oxford University Press, 1994.

Hinnant, Charles. "Jane Austen's 'Wild Imagination': Romance and the Courtship Plot in the Six Canonical Novels." *Narrative* 14, no. 3 (October 2006): 294–310.

Jameson, E. O. *The History of Medway Mass. 1713–1885*. Medway, MA: Town of Medway, 1885.

Keller, Charles. *The Second Great Awakening in Connecticut*. New Haven, CT: Yale University Press, 1942.

Kilbourne, Payne Keynon. *Sketches and Chronicles of the Town of Litchfield*. Hartford, CT: Case, Lockwood and Company, 1859.

Kingsley, James. "Eulogy of Alexander Metcalf Fisher." New Haven, CT: Published by request—printed at the Journal Office, 1822.

Lawrence, Edward. *The Life of Rev. Joel Hawes*. 2nd ed. Boston: Intitutio Theologica, 1881.
Layson, John F. *Memorable Shipwrecks and Seafaring Adventures of the Nineteenth Century*. London: Tyne Publishing Company, 1884.
Levitt, Sarah. *From Catharine Beecher to Martha Stewart*. Chapel Hill: University of North Carolina, 2002.
Lystra, Karen. *Searching the Heart: Women, Men and Romantic Love in Nineteenth-Century America*. Oxford: Oxford University Press, 1989.
Mansfield, E. D. *Personal Memories: Social, Political and Literary with Sketches of Many Noted People, 1803–1843*. Cincinnati: Robert Clarke & Co., 1879.
Mead, Sidney. *Nathaniel William Taylor, 1786–1856: A Connecticut Liberal*. Chicago: University of Chicago Press, 1942.
Millard, Abel. "Nathanael Emmons," *American Journal of Theology* 6, no. 1 (January 1902): 17–34.
Mitchell, Isabel. *Roads and Road-Making in Colonial Connecticut*. New Haven, CT: Yale University Press, 1933.
"Obituary: Alexander Metcalf Fisher." *Christian Spectator* 4, no. 8 (August 1822): 414–421.
Olmsted, Denison. "Reminiscences of Alexander Metcalf Fisher." *New Englander* 4 (October 1843): 457–469.
Park, Edwards A. *Memoirs of Nathanael Emmons; With Sketches of His Friends and Pupils*. Boston: Congregational Board of Publication, 1861.
Parramore, Thomas. *The Ancient Maritime Village of Murfreesborough: 1787–1825*. Murfreesboro, NC: Johnson Publishing Company, 1969.
Purcell, Richard. *Connecticut in Transition: 1775–1818*. Washington, DC: American Historical Association, 1918.
"Review of an Eulogy on Professor Fisher." *Christian Spectator* 4, no. 8 (August 1822).
Rugoff, Milton. *The Beechers: An American Family in the 19th Century*. New York: Harper & Row, 1981.
Shakespeare, William. *Shake-speares Sonnets*. London: Thomas Thorpe, 1609.
Shakespeare, William. *The Tragedies of William Shakespeare*. Norwalk, CT: Easton Press, 1980.
Sklar, Kathryn Kish. *Catharine Beecher: A Study in Domesticity*. New York: W. W. Norton, 1973.
Smith, Daniel, and Michael Hindus. "Premarital Pregnancy in America 1640–1971: An Overview and Interpretation." *Journal of Interdisciplinary History* 5, no. 4 (Spring 1975): 537–570.
Stevens, Agnes. *How Men Propose: The Fateful Question and Its Answer*. London: T. Fisher Unwin, 1890.
Stowe, Lyman Beecher. *Saints, Sinners and Beechers*. Indianapolis: Bobbs-Merrill Co., 1934.
Vanderpoel, Emily Noyes. *Chronicles of a Pioneer School from 1792 to 1833, Being the History of Miss Sarah Pierce and Her Litchfield School*. Edited by Elizabeth Buel. Cambridge: Cambridge University Press, 1903.
Vanderpoel, Emily Noyes. *More Chronicles of a Pioneer School 1792–1833*. New York: Cadmus Book Shop, 1927.
Wells, Robert. *Uncle Sam's Family: Issues in and Perspectives on American Demographic History*. Albany: State University of New York Press, 1985.
White, Barbara. *The Beecher Sisters*. New Haven, CT: Yale University Press, 2003.

White, Raymond. *Their Bones Are Scattered: A History of the Old Head of Kinsale and Surrounding Area*. Kinsale, Ireland: Kilmore Enterprises, 2003.

Online Materials

Connecticut General Assembly. "Litchfield County Postmasters." Accessed December 4, 2023. https://www.cga.ct.gov/hco/img/history/norton/LitchfieldPostmasters.pdf.

General Blue. "Calendar for 1822." Accessed December 4, 2023. https://www.generalblue.com/calendar/1822.

Hefner, Bob. "The History of East Hampton." East Hampton Historical Society. Accessed August 23, 2022. https://easthamptonvillage.gov/documents/history-of-the-village-of-east-hampton/.

Litchfield Historical Society. *Litchfield Ledger* [Database of students of the Litchfield Law School and the Litchfield Female Academy]. https://ledger.litchfieldhistoricalsociety.org/ledger/.

Macauly. "Gradual Emancipation." City University of New York. Accessed August 23, 2022. https://macaulay.cuny.edu/seminars/henken08/articles/g/r/a/Gradual_Emancipation_ec2a.html.

Mayo Clinic. "Bipolar Disorder." Accessed August 27, 2022. https://www.mayoclinic.org/diseases-conditions/bipolar-disorder/symptoms-causes/syc-20355955.

Moongiant.com. "Full Moon and New Moon for January 1822." Accessed September 2, 2022. https://www.moongiant.com/moonphases/january/1822/.

National Oceanic and Atmospheric Administration. "Historical Tides and Currents." Accessed November 20, 2023, https://www.tidesandcurrents.noaa.gov/noaatidepredictions.html?id=8518750&units=standard&bdate=18220401&edate=18220402&timezone=LST/LDT&clock=1.

Norfolk County Registry of Deeds. "Records Database." http://www.norfolkresearch.org/ALIS/WW400R.HTM?WSIQTP=SY00.

Selin, Shannon. "The Wreck of the Packet Ship *Albion*." Accessed September 5, 2022. https://shannonselin.com/2017/04/wreck-packet-ship-albion/.

Statista. "Childhood Mortality Rates, 1800–2020." Accessed April 7, 2024. https://www.statista.com/statistics/1041693/united-states-all-time-child-mortality-rate/.

Wilson, Lee. "Beecher Family Tree." Ancestry.com (login required).

Wilson, Lee. "Fisher Family Tree." Ancestry.com (login required).

Yale University. "Yale University. University Catalogue, 1820." *Yale University Catalogue* 6. Accessed August 27, 2022. https://elischolar.library.yale.edu/yale_catalogue/6.

INDEX

References to AF stand for Alexander Fisher; CB for Catharine (Kate) Beecher; and LB for Lyman Beecher.

A

abolitionism, 187, 189, 191–92, 201, 214
Albion (ship)
    about, 120–22
    Caleb Fisher's concern about, 119
    passengers on, 122–24
    wreck of the, 126–37, 145–46, 258n25
    wreck of the, survivors, 134, 135
Alexander, Archibald, 185
American Lyceum speech (teachers needed in the west), 189–90
American Woman's Home, The (CB and Stowe), 205
American Women's Education Association, 200
Andover Theological Seminary, 29
Annual Commencement Ball, 3–7, 240n4, 240n7
Anthony, Susan B., 203
An Appeal to the People in Behalf of Their Rights as Authorized Interpreters of the Bible (CB), 204
arms industry, 207
Austen, Jane, 12–13

B

Bacon, Delia, 197–99
Banister, Zilpah Grant, 182, 212, 213, 214
battles, CB on behalf of
    Hobart, 52
    Wait, 176–77
    LB, 189–90
    Bacon, 197–99

    Henry, (brother) 208–9
battles, CB with male establishment
    AF papers, 143, 164
    AF monument, 160–64
    Cincinnati teachers endowment, 190
    HFS endowment, 182
    HFS finances, 206–7
    Kingsley eulogy, 148
    Milwaukee Female Seminary building, 200
    National Board of Popular Education control, 196–97
Beecher, Catharine (Kate)
    AF, courtship with, 76–91, 254n20
    AF's gravestone, controversy over, 160–64
    AF's introduction to, 69–75
    and AF's salvation, 143–44, 165–66
    AF's visit to resurrect relationship with, 101–3
    The American Woman's Home, collaboration on, 205, 218
    battles with male establishment (*see* battles, CB with male establishment)
    battles to defend the honor of friends and family (*see* battles, CB on behalf of)
    bereavement of, 139–54, 170–71, 259n5, 263n39
    death of, 219–20
    as education crusader, (*see under* women's education)
    engagement and marriage of friends of, 20–21, 44–47, 242n49

278   INDEX

Beecher, Catharine (Kate) (*continued*)
   engagement to AF, 104–14
   and father's second marriage, 41–44
   at the Fisher family house after AF's death, 155–58
   genealogy of, 234
   images of, xii, 9, 198, 212
      impasse in courtship, 92–100
      legacy of, 211–19
      letter from AF before departing for Europe, 120
      life of, while AF was aboard the *Albion*, 124–25
      love letters, retrieval and burning of, 221–27
      management of sister Harriet's household, 201
      mother's illness and death, 16–19
      music book of, 66, 73, 231, 252n24
      personality of, 268n28
      as philosopher author, 191–200, 203–5
      publication of *Treatise on Domestic Economy*, 193–95
      religion, rekindling of interest in, 204
      religion, on spiritual awakening, 64–65
      religious conversion (*see* conversion, religious)
      return to Litchfield, from Boston, 63–64
   as romantic, 11–13, 14, 16, 21, 45–47, 48–49, 50–53, 64, 72–74, 85–87, 102–4, 109–10, 112–13
      Sally Fisher's bond with, 155, 156, 159–60, 167, 170–71, 262n10
      social life of, as LFA student, 3–16
      trip to Boston, with Lucy Porter, 47–53
      work on LB's autobiography, 203–4
Beecher, Charles (brother), xii, 16, 93, 97, 203, 234
Beecher, Edward (brother)
   AF's death, letter from CB to, 143–44
   AF's familiarity with, 69
   AF's gravestone, controversy over, 160–62
   AF's personal papers, disposition of, 164, 262n10
   career, as educator in Hartford, 180
   career, as Illinois College president, 183
   emotional distress of LB, letter from LB to, 255n19
   and the engagement of CB and AF, 108
   genealogy of, 234
   graduation of, CB's refusal to attend, 153
   Harriet (stepmother) on, 44
   images of xii, 134
   LB's concerns about, 93
   musical interests of, 14
   as pallbearer for CB, 220
   religious conversion, CB's debates with, (*see under* conversion, religious)
   religious conversion of (*see under* conversion, religious)
   walk with AF and CB, 77
Beecher, Esther (Aunt Esther), 19, 21, 44, 97, 180, 233
Beecher, George (brother), 180, 181, 195, 234
Beecher, Harriet Porter (stepmother)
   CB's postengagement relationship with, 125
   death of, 190
   genealogy of, 234
   loss of first child, 93
   Lucy Porter, as live-in helpmate for, 46
   Lucy Porter, matchmaking motives, 42–43, 47–48
   marriage to LB, 41–44, 247n5
   pregnancy, 107–8
Beecher, Harriet (sister). *See* Stowe, Harriet Beecher
Beecher, Henry Ward (brother)
   in Boston, 181
   eulogy of CB, 219–20
   fame of, 201
   genealogy of, 234
   in Hartford, 180
   images of, xii, 201, 208
   at Plymouth Church in Brooklyn, 199
   and Roxana Beecher's death, 18
   in sex scandal, 208, 209
   as witness to grief of CB and LB, 144

INDEX

Beecher, Isabella. *See* Hooker, Isabella Beecher
Beecher, Lydia Jackson (LB's third wife), 190, 234
Beecher, Lyman (father)
    AF on, 69
    AF's death, to CB, 139–42, 259n5
    AF's personal papers, disposition of, 142–43
    after AF's death, first meeting with CB, 144
    alienation of, from Cincinnati society, 189
    Autobiography, 203–4
    Black indentured servants, employment of, 189, 265n39
    career choice, letter from CB, 170
    and CB's courtship, 70, 74–75, 76–77, 86–87, 88–89, 92–96
    CB's relationship with, after George Beecher's death, 195–96
    and CB's religious status, 65, 149, 151–53, 158, 168, 263n34
    conversion, Edward Beecher, 125–26
    Eleazar Fitch, as colleague of, 69, 252n17
    on engagement of CB and AF, 108–9
    genealogy of, 233, 234
    heresy charges against, 190
    images of xii, 10, 143, 201
    mental health of, 92–93, 97, 255n19
    move of, to Boston, 181
    personality of, 10, 66
    physical affection of, 10, 84, 254n25
    the potential of the West, letter to CB, 183
    prominence of, 6, 7
    religious debates, with Roxana Beecher, 149–50, 260n28
    second marriage of, 41–43
    third marriage of, 190
Beecher, Mary (Grandma Beecher), 19, 21, 44, 233
Beecher, Mary (sister), xii, 19, 80, 81, 180, 234
Beecher, Miss Mary (Kate's replacement at HFS 1871), 207, 267n3
Beecher, Roxana Foote (mother)
    CB's Episcopal identification with, 204
    genealogy of, 233, 234
    image of, 10
    intellect of, 10–11, 150, 169, 240n18
    lack of physical affection from, 254n25
    personality of, 10–11
    religious conversion (*see under* conversion, religious)
    sickness and death of, 16–18
Beecher, Thomas (brother), xii, 219, 220, 234
Beecher, William (brother), xii, 14, 44, 73, 93, 234, 252n24
Beinecke Library, 223
The Biographical Remains of Rev. George Beecher (CB), 195
Black indentured servants, 189, 265n39
Bonfils, Monsieur, 89, 108
Boston
    Beecher family members' relocation to, 180–81
    CB's address in, 210
    CB's summer in, 47–53, 248n22
    CB's visit to, after AF's death, 153
    LB's consultation with Dr. Jackson in, 93
    LB's engagement in, 41–42
    return of Edward Beecher to, 199
Bowdoin College, 199
Brace, Charles Loring, 200
Brace, John P.
    on CB, as student, 8
    to CB, in Boston, 49–50
    and CB's engagement to AF, 106
    CB's narrative poem, as subject in, 44
    CB's relationship with, 45
    CB's writing, influence on, 52
    engagement of, to Lucy Porter, 46–47
    first engagement of, 20–21
    Hartford Female Seminary, as head of, 184–85, 266n71
    Hartford Female Seminary, resignation from, 199–200
    image of, 45
    mental health of, 47, 248n27
    as potential love match for CB, 15–16
    as Rose Terry Cooke's teacher, 216

INDEX

Brace, Lucy Porter. *See* Porter, Lucy
Brooklyn, Plymouth Church, 199, 219
Brunswick, Maine, 199
Burlington, Iowa, 199
"The Bumble Bees Ball" (poem), 6, 240n7
Burns, Robert, 12, 14, 72, 113–14, 171
Burr, Betsy, 44
Byron, Lord, 72

C

Cammyer, Henry, 121, 129, 134, 135, 145
Chase, Stephen, 134
Christian Spectator, 59, 65, 69, 148
Cincinnati, Ohio, 185–90, 196–97
Cincinnati Law School, 186
Coe, Kate Foote, 215, 216
Colt, Samuel, manufacturing, 207
Columbian Register, 145
coming out, 3
Common Sense Applied to Religion (CB), 204
Confiance, HMS, 135, 136
The Conflict of Ages (Edward Beecher), 204
Congregational Church, doctrine, 29–31, 141, 149, 151
Connecticut Children's Aid Society, 216
consumption (disease), 12, 16–17, 100, 153, 176–78
conversion, religious
    and AF's death, 141–44, 157
    AF's struggle with, 29–31, 38, 57, 165–67, 259n11
    CB's correspondence with AF about, 109–10
    CB's debates with Edward Beecher over, 149, 151, 168
    CB's debates with father and brother over, 149–53, 168
    CB ends debate with LB, 168, 263n34
    CB's struggle with, 64, 79–80, 109, 111–12, 143–44, 151–52
    Congregational Church doctrine on, 29–30
    of Caleb Fisher, 30–31, 244n15
    of Edward Beecher, 125–26
    of Harriet Porter Beecher, 42
    LB's concern for CB's conversion, 44, 63–65, 85, 109, 141–42, 151, 155, 158, 165
    LB on sons' status regarding, 44
    Roxana Beecher's debates with husband about, 149–50, 251n3
    Roxana Beecher's struggles with, 64, 150, 260n28
    of Sally Fisher, 31, 67, 244n15
Cooke, Rose Terry, 215, 216
courtship
    of CB and AF, 74–91, 254n20
    impasse in CB's courtship with AF, 92–100
    as purpose for CB's trip to Boston, 50–53
    and romance, timelines of, 90, 99, 111
    See also engagement of CB to AF
courtship novels, 12–13
courtship practices in 1815, 7–8
Criterion (ship), 145

D

Davis, David, 214
Davis, Sarah Walker, 214, 215
Day, Jeremiah, 37, 40, 119, 146
Desnouettes, Charles Lefebvre-, 123, 135
Dillwyn, Lydia, 149
domesticity, doctrine of, 192–95, 217–18
Downer College, 200
Drake, Daniel, 189, 190
Dutton, Mary, 188, 190
Dwight, Sereno, 42
Dwight, Timothy, 37, 39–40
Dwight, William, 137
dyslexia, 73, 252n24

E

education of women. *See* women's education
Educational Reminiscences and Suggestions (CB), 209–11, 219
The Elements of Mental and Moral Philosophy (CB), 185
Elmira, New York, 219, 220
Emerson, Joseph, 213
Emmons, Nathanael, 28–29, 30, 157, 262n5
engagement of CB to AF, 104–14
Episcopal Church,

revival of, 68,
  CB's joining of the, 204
  CB joins Trinity Episcopal, 207–08
"Essay on Musical Temperament" (AF),
  36–37, 59, 246n42
An Essay on Slavery and Abolitionism
  (CB), 192
"The Evening Cloud" (CB), 64–65
Everhart, William, 122, 130, 134, 135

F

feminist thought. *See* women's rights
Fern Leaves (Willis), 214
First Congregational Church (Hartford),
  178
First Congregational Church (Litchfield),
  6
Fisher, Alexander
  on the *Albion*, 118–19, 122, 124, 127,
    131
  CB's eulogy, mention of in, 220
  in CB's memoir, 211
  celebrity status of, 66–67
  courtship and marriage, thoughts of,
    57–59
  courtship with CB, 76–91, 254n20
  death of, 137, 157
  death of, aftermath, 138–53
  Eliza Wheeler as potential match for,
    32–33, 59–60
  engagement to CB, 104–14
  "Essay on Musical Temperament" by,
    36–37, 246n42
  eulogy of, by James Kingsley, 260n22
  genealogy of, 235, 236
  gravestone controversy, 160–64
  Great Comet of 1819, interest in,
    59–60
  image of, 25
  impasse in courtship, 92–100
  introduction to CB, 69–75
  letters from, before departure for
    Europe, 119–20
  Litchfield, visit to resurrect
    relationship with CB, 101–4
  love letters, 221–27
  mental health of, 31–32, 166–67
  personality, 25–26
  personal papers of, 164, 262n10
  professional life, as the priority for,
    54–57
  religious concerns of, 29–31, 38, 56,
    57, 165–67, 247n46
  resolve to repay parents for
    education costs, 244n19
  travel to France, plans of, 27–28, 89,
    97–98, 108, 254n36
  Yale professorship, choice of, 39–40
  Yale, as tutor at, 23–25, 34–39,
    242n2, 255n20
  written lectures of, 167
Fisher, Caleb
  after AF's death, CB's stay with,
    155–56
  AF's gravestone, collaboration with
    Yale on, 160, 162–63
  and AF's papers, 142, 143, 167, 191
  aspirations for AF, 28
  concern for AF's travel on the *Albion*,
    119
  engagement news, reaction to, 110
  and estate of AF, 146–48
  genealogy of, 235, 237
  religious conversion of (*see*
    conversion, religious)
Fisher, Eliza, 89–91, 125, 156–57, 180,
  235, 237
Fisher, George, 223, 226, 236
Fisher, Nancy "Ann"
  AF's frustration with, 99
  after AF's death, CB's visit to, 157
  on Eliza, letter to from AF, 90
  genealogy of, 235, 237
  Hartford Female Seminary, as music
    teacher, 180
  musical talent of, 160
  naming of daughter for CB, 191, 237,
    262n14
Fisher, Sally
  AF's personal papers, sharing of, 164,
    262n10
  and AF's religious journey, 165–66
  Alexander's keepsakes, box kept by,
    223–24
  CB's bond with, 155, 156, 159
  in CB's memoir, 211
  death of, 190–91
  and death of AF, 146–47

Fisher, Sally (*continued*)
　engagement news, reaction to, 110
　genealogy of, 235, 237
　love letters, CB's entrusting of, 170–71
　mathematical ability of, 26, 169
　religious conversion (*see* conversion, religious)
Fisher, Sewall, 223, 225–26, 236, 269n5, 269n8, 269n9
Fisher, Willard, 156, 180, 235, 236
Fisher, Willard J., 222–23, 236, 269n3
Fisher family
　after AF's death, CB's stay with, 155–58
　family farm, history of ownership, 269n8
　music in the household of, 160
Fitch, Eleazar
　and AF's introduction to CB, 70–72
　as colleague of LB, 40, 69, 252n17
　engagement of, 57–58
　trip to France, 97–98
Foote, George, 108, 233
Foote, Mary (aunt), 11–12, 17, 218, 233
Foote, Roxana Ward (grandmother), 97, 233
Foote, Samuel (uncle), 12, 46, 47, 185, 187, 190, 233
France
　as academics' destination, 27–28, 243n8
　AF's plans to travel to, 89, 108, 254n36
　AF's possible early departure for, 97–98
Franklin, Massachusetts
　AF's return to, before leaving for France, 110
　CB's stay with Fisher family in, 155–58
　Fisher farm in, 32
　religious roots in, 28–29

G

Garnier, Madame, 123, 130, 145–46, 258n30
Garrison, William Lloyd, 191–92
Gleason, Mr., 219, 220

Goddard, Almira, 48
Goddard, John, 48
Gough, William, 123, 131, 137
Gould, William, 45, 87, 176–77
Grant, Zilpah. *See* Banister, Zilpah Grant
gravestone controversy, 160–64
Great Comet of 1819, 59–60
Greeley, Horace, 199
Grimké, Angelina, 183–84, 191, 193

H

Hall, James, 189
Hanover Street Church, 181
Harding, Sewall, 60, 68
Hartford
　arms industry in, 207
　manufacturing in, 207
Hartford, Connecticut, 180, 186, 206–7
Hartford City Mission, 216
Hartford Female Seminary (HFS)
　Angelina Grimké's visit to, 183–84
　CB's return to, in 1870, 206–7
　endowment campaign for, 181–82
　establishment of, 175–76, 213
　funding of, 178–79, 181–82
　John P. Brace as head of, 184–85, 266n71
　John P. Brace's resignation from, 199–200
　moral education vs. religious education at, 181, 182
　spiritual leadership at, 178
Hawes, Joel, 151, 169, 178, 180, 199, 261n30
Hillhouse, James, 77
Hillhouse, Mary, 96
Hobart, Albert, 50–53, 84, 249n28, 249n37
Holmes, Uriel, Jr., 20, 44, 242n49
Homes, Henry and Isabella, 42, 48, 153
Hooker, Isabella Beecher, xii, 108, 208, 209, 234
Horr, Elijah, 220

I

Illinois College, 183
indentured servants, 189, 265n39
Ipswich Female Seminary, 182, 213, 214

INDEX

J

Jackson, Dr., 93
Judd, Reverend, 79, 80

K

Kidder, Catharine Beecher, 191, 237, 262n14
Kidder, Nancy Fisher. *See* Fisher, Nancy "Ann"
King, Edward, 14–15, 186
King, James, 14–15
King, Rufus, 14, 46, 242n47
Kingsley, James
    AF's friendship with, 34
    and AF's papers, 108, 142, 143, 167, 259n9
    CB's conflicts with, 153, 160, 162, 164
    eulogy of AF, 148–49, 260n22
    image of, 143
    letters from AF, before departure for Europe, 120

L

Lane Theological Seminary, 183, 185, 189, 196, 199
Langdon, Olivia, 219
Lawrence University, 200, 213
limerence, 47, 248n27
Lincoln, Abraham, 214
Litchfield, Connecticut
    AF's return to, before leaving for France, 110–14
    AF's visit to, in January 1822, 102–7
    Annual Commencement Ball in, 3–6
    LB's position in, 6–7
    Louisa Wait's permanent departure from, 99–100
    network of influence in, 6–7, 14–15, 239n3
Litchfield Female Academy (LFA)
    and the Annual Commencement Ball, 4–5
    CB's scholarship award at, 8
    CB's teaching position at, 45, 248n22
    CB's withdrawal from, 19
    Eliza Wheeler at, 58
    founding of, 213
    John P. Brace as teacher at, 15–16
    and the Litchfield network, 7, 58
    Louisa Wait's position at, 13, 87
    Lucy Porter at, 14–15
Litchfield Law School (LLS), 4, 6–7, 66, 105, 125, 186
Lyon, Mary, 212, 213–14

M

MacWhorter, Alexander, 197–99
Mann, Horace, 66, 125, 196, 197
Mark, Jacob, 145
Martha (ship), 145
Mason, Stephen, 44
mathematics, 26–27, 159
memoirs of CB, 209–11
mental health issues
    of AF, 31–32, 166–67
    of CB, 182, 197
    of George Beecher, 195
    of John P. Brace, 47, 248n27
    of LB, 92–93, 95, 97, 255n19
Microscope literary magazine, 67
Milwaukee College, 213
Milwaukee-Downer College, 200, 213
Milwaukee Female Seminary, 200
Milwaukee Normal Institute and High School, 200, 213
The Minister's Wooing (Stowe), 202, 267n82
Miss Beecher's Domestic Receipt Book (CB), 195
moral education and philosophy, 181, 182, 183, 185, 193, 217
Mount Holyoke Female Seminary, 213, 214
music
    AF's interest in, 35, 36–37, 58, 246n42
    CB's teaching of, 66
    in the Fisher household, 160
    Louisa Wait's teaching of, 14
    as a shared interest of CB and AF, 73–74, 105–6, 114

N

National Board of Popular Education, 196–97
New Haven, Connecticut
    LB in, after AF's death, 142

New Haven, Connecticut (*continued*)
    LB's meeting with AF in, 93–95
    religious revival in, 67–68
    visit of AF's sister to, 89–90
    See also Yale College
New London, Connecticut, 79–83, 90, 95
Nook Farm neighborhood, 207
Northwest Territory, 183
Norwich, horseback riding excursion, 83

O

Olmsted, Alexander Fisher, 180
Olmsted, Denison
    AF's friendship with, 33–34
    on AF's interest in music, 37
    after AF's death, CB's contact with, 180
    image of, 33
    marriage of, 58
    professional positions of, 245n26
    as University of North Carolina professor, 39
    Yale professorship, as candidate for, 37–38

P

Park Church (Elmira), 220
Park Street Church (Boston), 41–42, 181
physical affection
    AF's lack of, 78–79, 84, 91, 93–94
    of LB, 10, 84, 254n25
Pierce, Sarah, 4, 8, 87, 105, 138, 212, 213
Plymouth Church, Brooklyn. *See* Brooklyn, Plymouth Church
Poetry written by CB
    on AF's departure for France, 112–13
    on AF's gravestone, 161
    after AF's death 167–68
    on Annual Commencement Ball, 5–6
    commemoration of the wedding of CB's friend, 44
    on death of CB's mother, 18
    "The Evening Cloud," 64–65
    get well poem for CB's teacher, 232
Poetry as a shared interest of CB and AF, 72
Porter, Julia, 153
Porter, Lucy
    on Beecher sons, letter from sister Harriet, 44
    death of, 200
    engagement of, 46–47
    joint letter to CB from Louisa Wait and, 82–83
    at Litchfield Female Academy, 14–15
    matchmaking efforts of, 42–43, 50–51
    return of, to Massachusetts, 20
    trip to Boston, with CB, 47–53
Powell, Anne, 123–24, 128, 133, 137
premarital pregnancy, 78–79, 253n9
Princeton, professorship offer for AF, 98
propriety, rules of
    AF's adherence to, 78–79, 91, 94, 95, 102
    and CB's limited social interaction in New London, 81
    and CB's meeting with Albert Hobart, 50–51, 250n40
    for women's travel, 75, 253n30
public education for women, 206–7
Purcell, John, 135, 145

Q

Quincy, Illinois, 199

R

"A Red, Red Rose" (Burns), 113–14
Reeve, Tapping, 6, 105
religion and spirituality
    of AF, 56, 67–68, 247n46
    of CB, 64–65, 79–80, 204, 217
    religious conversion (*see* conversion, religious)
    revival activity at Hartford Female Seminary, 178, 179
    revival, religious, 67–68, 178, 179
Religious Training of Children in the School, the Family, and the Church (CB), 204, 267n88
Robinson, John, 124

S

Saints, Sinners and Beechers (Stowe), 221, 222
Salem Church (Boston), 199
Saugus, Emerson, 170
Scott, Sir Walter, 12, 74

INDEX

Second Presbyterian Church
    (Cincinnati), 185, 199
Seymour, Moses, Jr., 139
Silliman, Benjamin, 34, 59, 245n28
Slade, William, 196–97
slavery, abolition of. *See* abolitionism
Slosson, Annie Trumbull, 215, 216
Smith, Virginia Thrall, 215, 216
social life
    in Cincinnati, 185–86, 188, 189, 190
    in Hartford, 207–8
    lack of, in Franklin, 158
    lack of, in New London, 81
sociocultural issues
    in Cincinnati, 187–88, 189
    courtship practices, transition in, 7
Stanton, Elizabeth Cady, 203
Stowe, Calvin, 196, 197, 199, 202
Stowe, Harriet Beecher (sister)
    accomplishments of, 214
    The American Woman's Home,
        collaboration on, 205, 218
    in Brunswick, Maine, 199
    CB to, from Cincinnati, 186
    death of son Henry, 202
    fame of, 201
    genealogy of, 234
    at Hartford Female Seminary, as
        student, 180
    at Hartford Female Seminary, as
        teacher, 181–82
    marriage of, 196
    images of xii, 201, 215
    Nook Farm, residence in, 207
    women's education, on CB's crusade
        for, 182–83
Stowe, Henry Beecher, 202
Stowe, Lyman Beecher, 70, 221–22
suffrage movement, 193, 203, 209, 210
Swift, Helen, 266n71
Swift, Jonathan, 36, 67

T

Taylor, Nathaniel, 198–99, 252n17
teacher recruitment and training, 189–
    90, 196–97, 199
Tilton, Elizabeth, 208–209
Treatise on Domestic Economy (CB),
    193–95

Troy Female Seminary, 213
*The True Remedy for the Wrongs of
    Woman* (CB), 203
Truth Stranger Than Fiction (CB), 199
tuberculosis. *See* consumption (disease)
Twain, Mark, 207, 219

U

Uncle Tom's Cabin (Stowe), 201, 214
University of North Carolina, 38, 39,
    247n44

V

Van Lennep, Mary Hawes, 214, 215, 216
Van Rensselaer, Cortlandt and
    Catharine, 196

W

Wadsworth, Daniel, 178–79
Wait, Louisa
    on AF's death, letter from CB to, 153
    arrival of, in Litchfield, 13–14
    on arrival of sister, letter from CB
        to, 108
    on being engaged, letter from CB to,
        107
    CB's final letter to, 177–78
    and CB's public courtship
        termination, 96
    CB's sharing of love letter from AF,
        109–10
    CB to, from Boston, 48–49, 50, 51–
        52, 249n28, 249n32
    on concerns about courting AF, letter
        from CB to, 85–86
    engagement of, 20, 242n49
    fiancé's desertion of, 176–77
    joint letter to CB from Lucy Porter
        and, 82
    Litchfield, permanent departure
        from, 99–100
    on plans during AF's absence in
        France, letter from CB to, 111
    request for CB to share poetry with,
        167–68
    second engagement of, 44–45
    on stay with Fisher family, letter from
        CB to, 156
    South Carolina, potential move to, 87

Ward, Andrew, 11, 233
Ware, Henry, 185
water cures, 197, 199, 219
Western Female Institute, 188, 190
Wheaton Female Seminary, 214
Wheeler, Eliza
  AF's family connections with, 33, 244n24
  marriage of, 68
  as potential match for AF, 32–33, 58–59, 60
  Willard Fisher's marriage to sister of, 180
Willard, Emma Hart, 212, 213
Williams, John, 121, 127, 128, 129, 132, 258n25
Willis, Sarah Payson "Fanny Fern," 214, 215
Wilson, Joshua, 190
women's education
  AF's support for, 89–90
  Benjamin Silliman's support for, 90, 245n28
  CB as a crusader, American Women's Education Association, 200
  CB as a crusader at HFS, 175–85
  CB as a crusader for, 182–83
  CB as a crusader, Milwaukee Female Seminary, 200
  CB as a crusader, National Board of Popular Education, 196–97
  CB as a crusader, *Treatise on Domestic Economy*, 193–95
  CB as a crusader, Western Female Institute, 188–90
  CB's decision to pursue career in, 170
  CB's stated purpose for, 192–93
  pioneers in, 211–16
women's rights
  abolitionism and, 191–92
  CB's philosophy, 192–93
  suffrage movement, 203, 209, 210
Woodhull, Victoria, 208, 209
Wooster, Elizabeth, 58
Wright, Thompson, Marshall & Thompson, 120–21

Y

Yale College
  AF's gravestone, controversy over, 160–64
  AF's papers at, 167, 222
  AF's professorship at, 39–40, 54–57, 98
  AF as student at, 28
  AF's trip to France, sponsorship of, 89
  AF as tutor at, 23–25, 34–39, 97, 242n2, 255n20
  CB's connections to AF through, 69–70
  Denison Olmsted as professor at, 180
  Edward Beecher's graduation from, 153
  Edward Beecher as tutor at, 181
  memorial service for AF at, 148–49

ABOUT THE AUTHOR

R. LEE WILSON is a passionate historian, scholar, and former CEO. He is a retired Booz Allen partner, Harvard MBA, and Phi Beta Kappa graduate of DePauw University. He was an executive vice president at Chase and Equitable Life before he finished his career as CEO of First Capital. He lives with his wife, Deb, on Sanibel Island in Florida and spends his summers in Greenwich, Connecticut, where they raised their three children. *Women's Crusader* is his first biography.